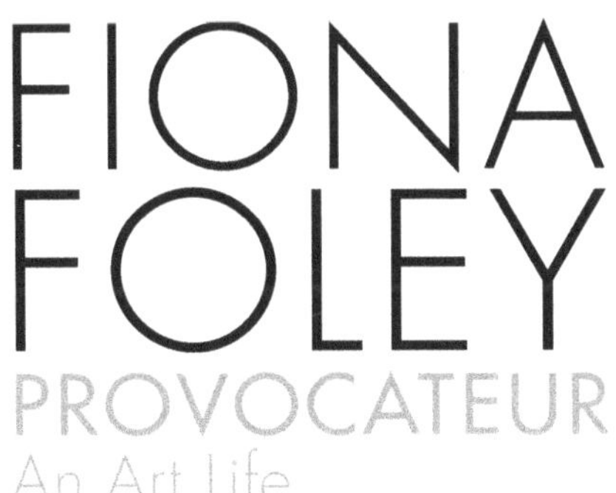

FIONA FOLEY

PROVOCATEUR

An Art Life

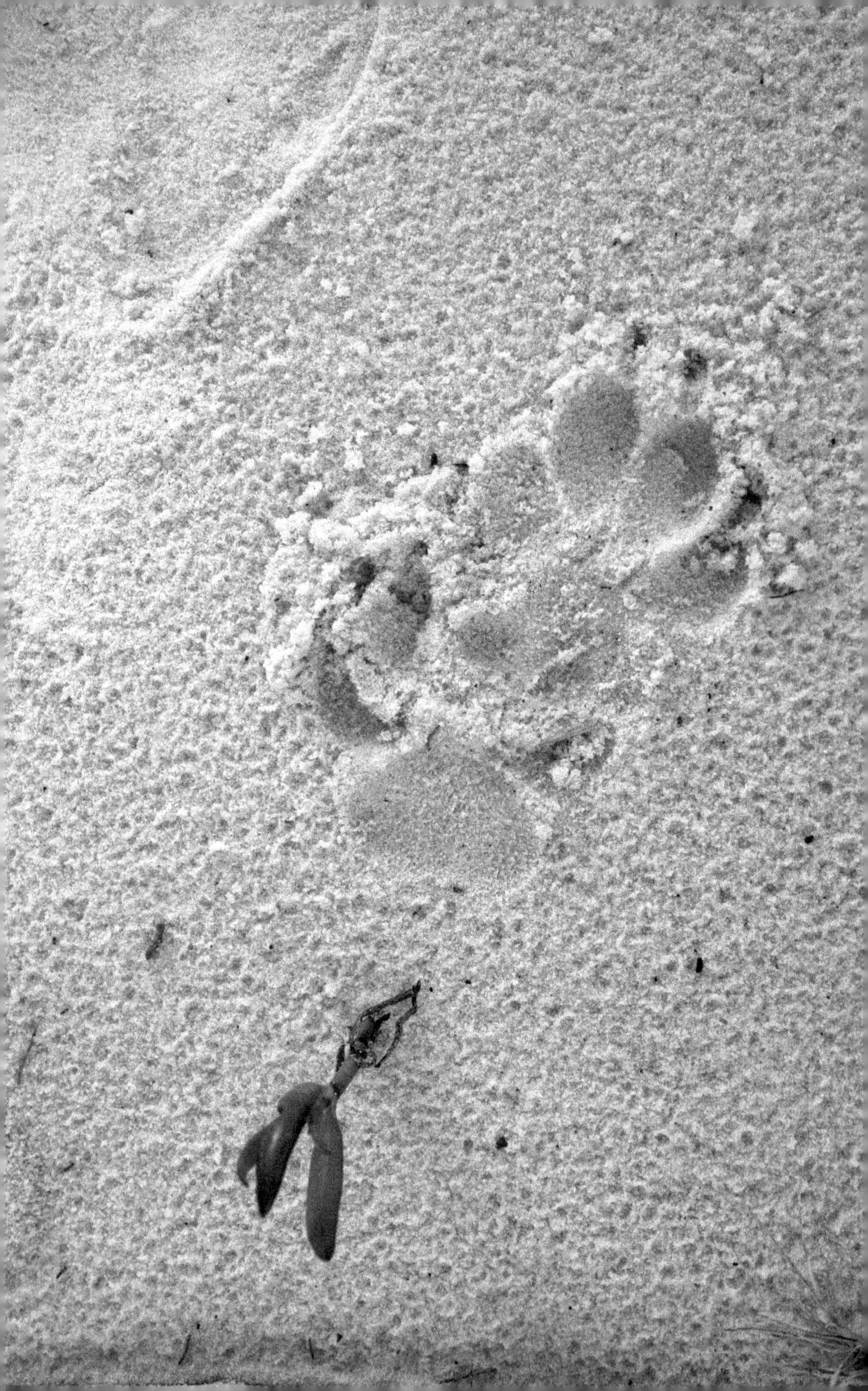

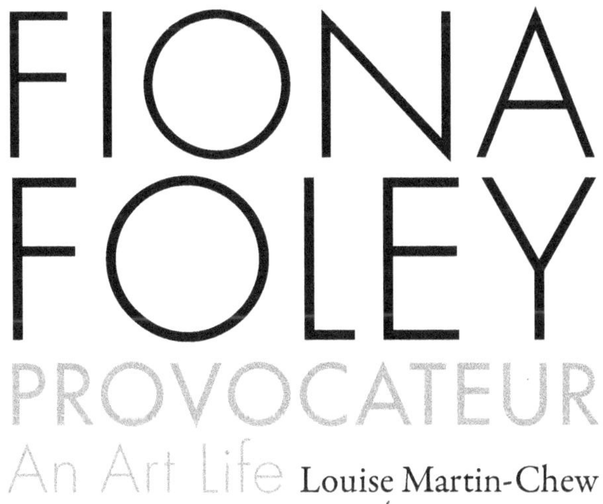

FIONA FOLEY

PROVOCATEUR

An Art Life

Louise Martin-Chew

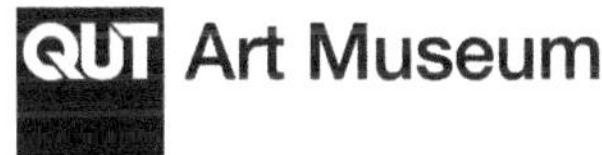

QUT Art Museum

This project has been assisted by the Australian Government through the Australia Council, its arts funding and advisory body.

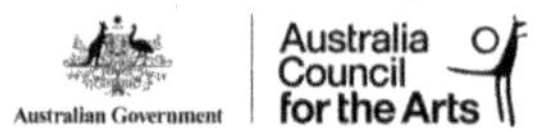

Published by QUT Art Museum,
QUT Gardens Point, 2 George Street, Brisbane Qld 4000
This edition published in 2021 in association with the exhibition
Fiona Foley: Veiled Paradise
19 June to 29 August 2021
ISBN 978-0-86856-003-8

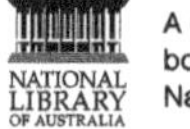

A catalogue record for this book is available from the National Library of Australia

Cover design by Sandy Cull
Edited by Bronwyn Mahoney
Text design by Sandy Cull
Typeset in 12/18 pt Garamond Premier Pro by Post Pre-press, Brisbane
Printed and bound by ColourChiefs, Brisbane
Cover image (detail) Fiona Foley, *The Oyster Fishermen #10*, 2011, inkjet print on Hahnemühle paper, edition 15, 60 × 80 cm. Courtesy the artist and Andrew Baker Art Dealer.

I acknowledge the Traditional Custodians of this Country,
and their descendants who continue to maintain connections—past,
present and future.

I acknowledge Fiona Foley and her Badtjala people who fought
so hard to retain their Country.
And I acknowledge the Quandamooka people,
on whose lands I live and work.

Contents

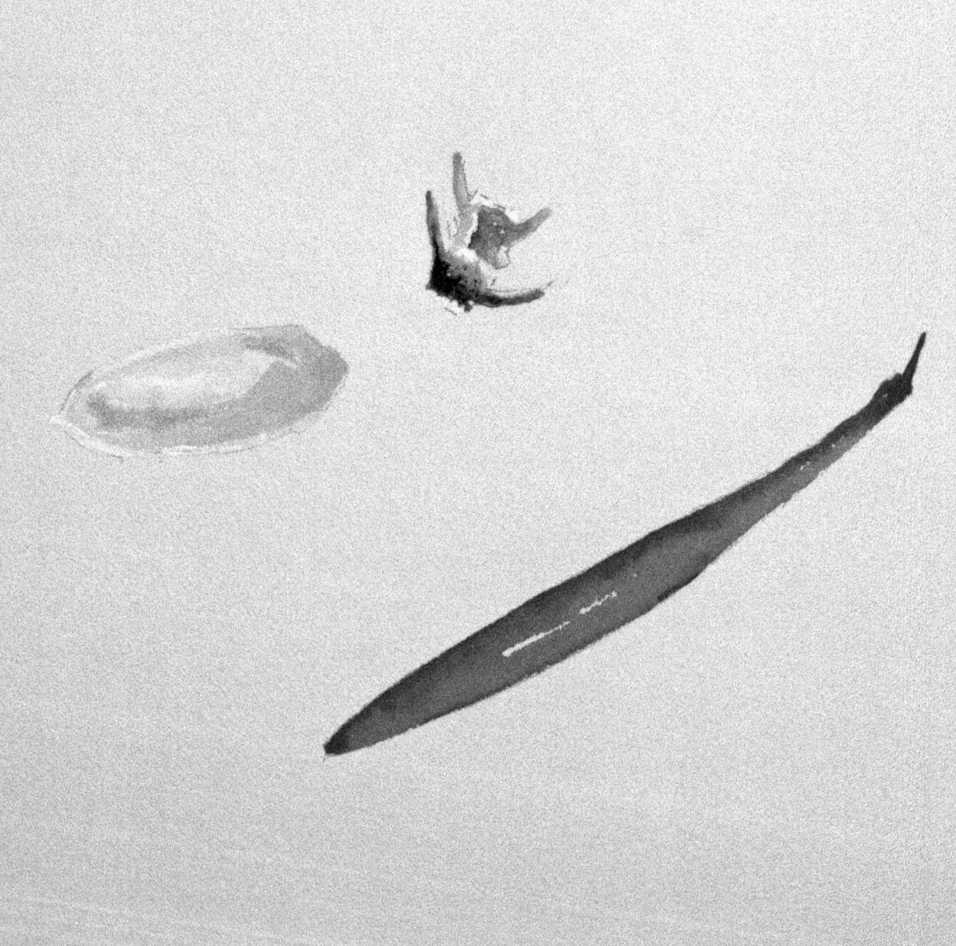

In researching and writing a biography of Australian Aboriginal artist Fiona Foley, discussions about the value of biography in evaluating art were critical. While biographical factors may be ordinary currency in contemporary critical practice, with art critics often employing biographical approaches in their writing,[1] their value is by no means uncontested. Art critics may resist the assumption that personal narrative adds meaning to the artwork, suggesting that the power of criticism lies in the connections critics may make "between one work of art and another, between the context of the work and the ideas it might embody. Focusing on connections underscores the constructive role of the critic."[2]

Yet others celebrate the connections between art history and biography, and support exploring the impact of the artist's life on the art. The relationship between an artist and their life has been the subject of speculation since Giorgio Vasari (1511–1574) wrote *Lives of the Most Excellent Painters, Sculptors, and Architects*, published in 1550 and 1568.[3] Assumptions relating to a real or perceived connection between artistic production and the producer have been linked, extended and applied under a variety of theoretical and political guises. As a result, debates surrounding art biography are driven by a strong sense of individual and scholarly agendas, together with varying ontological and epistemological approaches. The dimensions of this argument have been passionately disputed over the centuries.

What emerges with clarity in the debate about the importance of the artist's life with regard to interpretations of their art is the inability of a "one size fits all" approach to satisfy art's complexities. At the same time, the popularity of biography, the elucidation of the artist's work through the often seductive lens of the life (like the literary biography), indicates how mooted and actual connections have proven irresistible to writers (and readers) over the centuries. Art historian Colin Eisler writes scathingly about contemporary art critics turning aside from the life of the artist. He claims that "if an artist's work is worthy of scrutiny, the more we know about the artist the better".[4] He deems all detail about an artist's life—how and where they work, their views about the art of their colleagues and influencers, the prices of artworks and the purposes for which an artist uses the money they earn—valid and relevant for examination, describing the "flight from the personal, responsible for the drab shape of art-historical literature".[5] He argues that "all the world loves a *Life*, greatest romances not lovers' but those between the self and its fulfillment".[6]

I believe that a biography of Australian Aboriginal artist Fiona Foley offers important insights into her decades of artmaking and her oeuvre as a whole. This biography records the important issues that she conveys, not only in her artwork but as a spokesperson, curator, academic and leader. To understand the courage with which she

x

undertakes these roles requires an engagement with her life. However, the particular conditions of Foley's life also compel improvisation within the biographical genre. These include my approach to Foley as a living subject, the friendship I have with her personally, and the negotiation of an ethical model within which I, as a non-Aboriginal person, may engage with Foley as an Aboriginal subject.

Political and ethical concerns are inevitable when a non-Aboriginal writer becomes the biographer of an Aboriginal artist. Within the historical frame, biography as a genre has been significant for its insertion of "the history of Indigenous Australians into the national dialogue".[7] Historian Tom Griffiths writes about the responsibilities that ride on the shoulders of those who construct history, and the way in which focus may change regarding a past which is "alive and shifting".[8] Within that dialogue, clearly of most significance are the voices of Aboriginal and Torres Strait Islander people; agency in telling their own stories is paramount. These narratives have emerged as part of a broader and renewed understanding of Australian history in recent decades and represent a shift in historical understanding. Mark McKenna notes that "there was no history of Australia that was non-Indigenous".[9]

In this context, history and life narrative have particular application to the lives of Aboriginal artists. Their art and writing may be seen as integral to the broader historical change wrought within the debate about the theft of land and Australia's unceded sovereignty. For most Aboriginal and Torres Strait Islander artists, their own lives are relevant to their artistry, with subject matter drawn from the change and trauma that European invasion wrought on their sovereignty, which may ricochet through their work. In a recently published biography of Tracker Tilmouth, Alexis Wright notes "that it takes the voices of many to tell the stories of country, the story lines ... Each should speak for themselves, and for the whole to form the consensus, or complete story."[10]

I have looked to creative non-fiction to provide models for negotiating my own presence when discussing the impact of Foley's immediate family and Badtjala people on her work as an artist, and her sense of herself as "provocateur", driven to address historical silences around Australia's largely unacknowledged Frontier Wars. Accordingly, the biography includes features characterised as "bespoke",[11] its narrative tailored to frame the biography quite specifically. Many biographies exhibit bespoke elements, finding shape through particularities of their subjects, context of the source material, or responding to the requirements of publisher and/or audience.

In this biography of Foley, the introduction of specifically bespoke elements to a more traditional (cradle-to-the-grave) biographical approach include the development of material according to theme rather than chronology, and a reading of the artwork within the context of her life, with the text structured to reflect the personal, political and historical moments that have driven Foley's artwork since 2001.[12] I also pay attention to the sensitive issue of voice, making overt my views, position and presence with respect to and independent of Fiona Foley. I acknowledge that perceptions of artworks discussed are my own, albeit often informed by discussions with Foley.

In this context, I argue that for Aboriginal artists, their lives and ancestry are crucial to an understanding of the work they make and its often passionately political delivery. Judy Atkinson describes the ongoing impacts of colonial violence as transgenerational trauma, with effects that are "both individual and collective ... passed through the adult and child survivors to their children and grandchildren ... Today, the trauma remains in the hearts, minds and souls of Aboriginal families whose ancestors survived these times."[13] As a result, biography as a genre provides important context for Foley's work (and that of others of her generation). The breadth of function in contemporary biography, its audience appeal, and the flexibility inherent in its form have also compelled its use in presenting my research on Foley. Finally, I acknowledge that this biography represents a historical moment and set of circumstances as coalescing agents; as Wright notes, there are other voices to come—in response, by history, by new circumstances and by the decades to follow of Fiona's life and work. This is an evolving narrative.

//

Author's Note Notes

1   Some recent examples include Ingrid Perez on Robert MacPherson and the influence of his Catholic youth on his method, "The Painter's Reach", in *Robert MacPherson: The Painter's Reach*, ed. Queensland Art Gallery and Gallery of Modern Art (Brisbane: Queensland Art Gallery and Gallery of Modern Art, 2015), 39; Robert Leonard on Vernon Ah Kee and the importance of his Aboriginal identity in the definition of his practice, "Vernon Ah Kee: Your Call", Robert Leonard Contemporary-Art Writer And Curator, 2009, http://robertleonard.org/vernon-ah-kee-your-call/.

2   Susan Best, "Fogies, Insiders and Press Release Summarisers: Art Criticism in Australia", *The Conversation*, 7 November 2016.

3   Charles G. Salas, "Introduction: The Essential Myth", in *The Life and the Work: Art and Biography*, ed. Charles G. Salas (Los Angeles: The Getty Research Institute, 2007), 8.

4   Colin Eisler, "'Every Artist Paints Himself', Art History as Biography and Autobiography", *Social Research* 54, 1 (1987): 83.

5 Ibid., 88.

6 Ibid., 73.

7 Sidonie Smith and Julia Watson, *Reading Autobiography: A Guide for Interpreting Life Narratives*, vol. 2 (Minneapolis: University of Minnesota Press, 2010), 11.

8 Tom Griffiths, *The Art of Time Travel: Historians and Their Craft* (Carlton, Victoria: Black, 2016), 9.

9 Mark McKenna, quoted in Griffiths, *The Art of Time Travel*, epilogue.

10 Alexis Wright, *Tracker* (Sydney: Giramondo Publishing, 2017), 15.

11 The term "bespoke biography" was coined by biographical specialist Gillian Whitlock during initial discussions about this project in 2015.

12 Foley's first monograph, *Fiona Foley: Solitaire* by Benjamin Genocchio and Djon Mundine, was published by Piper Press, Sydney in 2001.

13 Cited in Karen Lillian Martin, *Please Knock Before You Enter: Aboriginal Regulation of Outsiders and the Implications for Researchers* (Teneriffe: Post Pressed, 2008), 76.

Today, power is not exercised by the military, it is exercised by narrative. There are gigantic fake narratives everywhere. So any person who engages simply, humbly, in a small-scale way, to give an alternative narrative, it doesn't matter whether as an artist or anything else … I want to be one of those people.

Francesco Clemente[1]

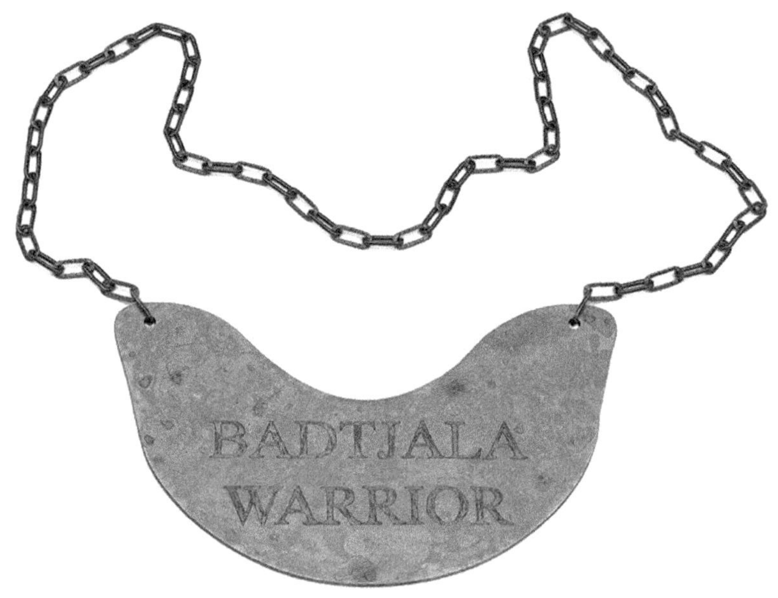

Badtjala Warrior II, 2017

BADTJALA WARRIOR

Setting off through the forest toward Lake Wabby, amid the coastal vegetation that characterises the eastern side of the island, Fiona stops abruptly to show me the celery bush. The leaf in her hand has a fresh, watery aroma. She passes me a Midjimberry to try, its muted sweetness touching my palate as gently as the subtlety of its pale colour and mauve spots. We begin the climb up a stairway in the direction of the sand blow that marks the side of the lake. The air warms as she says conversationally, "Hello Old People, this is Louise. Keep us safe on our visit to the lake: thanks for safe passage."[2]

The open coastal K'gari bush whispers with the movement of leaves; occasional bird calls break into soft harmonies. K'gari is the original name for the island on the Queensland coast known broadly as Fraser Island (since Eliza Fraser was shipwrecked here in 1830). The Badtjala people, its long-term inhabitants, call the island K'gari, and ask us all to use this name too.

Fiona and I ascend timber stairs up a steep slope, arriving at a vast expanse of sand blow under an open sky. It resonates with reflected heat and we squint at the striped poles that mark an otherwise indistinguishable expanse of sand. Following their path across the sand, feet sinking with each step, we pass two young men coming back out from the lake. At the top of a dune, the sand slopes steeply to slide under an extraordinary deep green body of water. Lake Wabby is one of the deepest lakes on the island, with sand encroaching on its width each year. Around its edges are grey-green reeds, and the atmosphere is still, watching. As we descend the vertiginous sand slope, sinking to our shins with every step, a fresh water turtle pops its head up to look, direct and curious. A second later it's gone, a tiny ripple in its wake.

We wade in and float around in the middle of the lake. I lie on my back and look up at the sky, puffs of cloud suspended in the clarity of blue. There is no wind and the silence is absolute; we are alone in this place. After a while we stand near the shore, our thoughts hidden, like the opacity of the green water. Tiny fish nibble at the skin on our ankles, while large catfish circle our legs lazily. As our feet sink slowly even further into the lake's sand, Fiona says, "I feel a sense of loss in this place. The island is always changing, but here, the sand will eventually cover this lake. One day it won't be here." We sit down, into the slope, staring into the stillness and the impenetrable vegetation on the other side of the water. Only after we rouse ourselves, gather our belongings and set off to walk back out, do we meet others on their way in. Group after group passes us, a busload of tourists. They chatter, their music blares from small stereos carried with backpacks, and the atmosphere shifts.

"How lucky to have the place to ourselves! Thank you, Old People."

BADTJALA WARRIOR, SEPTEMBER 2003

An inauspicious beginning: the Queensland College of Art (QCA) coffee-shop courtyard, pigeon-infested, grimy with city dust, scavenging ibis, chip fat hanging heavy in the humid air, and nerves. I was there to meet Aboriginal artist Fiona Foley and expected a personality to match her art: politically driven, tough, uncompromising. I knew her from photographs, in particular an early portrait from the *Native Blood* series (1994) that focuses on her youthful face. In the image, spirals of dark hair fall around her shoulders, while woven string encrusted with ochre and beeswax loops between her bare breasts. She looks down, away from the viewer, wearing accoutrements that assert her birthright as an Aboriginal woman. It is a mix of the shy and the proud yet, as she walks toward me that day, live and grinning, she is unchoreographed, and not as tall as I had imagined.

She pulls a plastic chair out from the table before noticing a large deposit of bird crap on the seat. "That'd be right!" she says, dry. I hand her a serviette from the dispenser on the table; she scrapes the mess off the seat and sits. I relax; she is real and direct. Before the coffee arrives she tells me that she needs a new voice, a writer to profile her artwork. *Fiona Foley: Solitaire*, her first monograph, published in 2001, was written by Benjamin Genocchio, whose gaze has shifted with a move to the United States.

At the table next to ours a group of art school students talk, their voices competing, loud. Smudge and the Falling Joys are mentioned—current indie favourites. There is a common uniform: dreadlocks, piercings, and colourful, mismatched garments. As we move towards the gallery, every eye turns. I wonder if they recognise her, or if it is the oddity of our pairing that interests them. Fiona's long, dark hair is frizzy with the wind, her small, curvy body wrapped in a bright red dress. I am taller, heavily pregnant with twin babies, belly impossibly distended: a ship in full sail. My hair, cropped close, is as white and controlled as Fiona's is dark and wild. Since then I have heard her tell the story of our first meeting. She tells how she met a very large woman that day, and "then, the next time, she wasn't!" A pause, and then a deep laugh, all the way from her own belly.

In the Queensland College of Art gallery an acrid smell rises from the work installed on the floor. *Massacre Site* is a rectangular, ten-metre section of gleaming black charcoal. Five white pyramids of ash are situated at regular intervals: an expression of light and shadow, black and white and, where they meet, a nuanced grey. The exhibition we are seeing, *Red Ochre Me*, is unflinchingly political, with an unusual mental toughness. Early in the new millennium, art that made Australia's violent histories so explicit was still rare—and Fiona was outing the racist, hateful words used to describe Aboriginal women, the physical and sexual abuse integral to the colonisation of Australia. In the darkened gallery space there are images of male buttocks titled *Anal Tantric Sex* and small vials of *Sacred Cunt Juice*. These artefacts expose fraudulent "tours", marketed under the auspices of late twentieth-century New Age sexual tourism, that trade on a fictionalised Aboriginal spirituality. Foley's artwork scorns these transparently pretentious and contemporary efforts to use Aboriginal belief systems—perpetuating the sexual exploitation that began with colonisation.

Fiona looks up, from the ash to me, a flash of the intensity palpable in the work in her face. "So, can you write something, a review?" she asks. She stands at the narrow end of the long section of ash. The printed blanket behind her reads "Aboriginal", one of seven that comprise her *Stud Gins* wall work. From where I stand, her silhouette runs down the long side of the ash, rectilineal, dress vibrant against the grey blanket, hair fanning around her face. Her weight is shared equally on both her feet; she is grounded, of the earth. I shift my weight from one leg to the other and feel a lurch in my belly. Was it the movement of my unborn babies? Or a change in my internal compass?

"Well, it depends, on where you'd like it placed." I ask, "Do you have a preference—a magazine? I could try *The Australian*?"

In many ways that was the moment this biographical project was conceived, the first step in a professional alliance that has also become a friendship. As the years have passed, and with them many words, formed as feature articles, reviews, catalogue essays and book chapters, Fiona has continued to intrigue me. Art writing is my stock in trade, yet agreeing to write for an artist is not a given. With Fiona I felt no instinct to hedge. The power of her work alone led me to meet her when it was an effort to move my heavily pregnant body. The directness with which she asked the question also told me, in an instant, that her art was driven as much by her belief in its message as by an artist's ego. The interplay between her life and her art, and the inexorable courage with which she has wielded her politics is uncompromising. Yet almost everyone I have related this story to has asked me why Fiona made such a direct approach. She told me:

I realised early in my career that you have to have people engaged in your work. And part of that is writing and press coverage. *Red Ochre Me* was an important show. I couldn't let the work languish. If no one reviews the work, it is like the

death of a show. I needed someone to write. I must have seen
your writing in *The Australian* and in other places.

At home after that first meeting, I free my heavy body from its
cotton dress and breathe in the cloying smell of the *Massacre Site* ash
that clings to its fibres. Despite my cramped internal organs there is
something new, a sting of excitement; the invitation to write about
Fiona's work an intriguing possibility. I like her, her large presence and
wholehearted laugh, but what I found most compelling, in a way in
which I could not really articulate then, was her drive. Her artwork,
public speaking and curating activities target the silence surrounding
the near destruction of her Badtjala people, and aim to build on the
fractured past of Australia's Aboriginal peoples. Was her earthy grasp on
the world, so different to my lightly rooted status in this place, a result
of her ancestral and familial connection? Her art offered a personal
entrée to this story, one I could not know without her guidance.

In 2013, after recording an interview with Fiona for the Queensland
State Library's *Portrait of the Artist* series, I asked her, tentatively, if she
would like to share more of her family story, her past and its present,
its reflection of the changing political landscapes of our times, toward
a written portrait of her work and life. She looked at me with interest.
It is not the case for every artist, but in Fiona's oeuvre there is an
embrace of her life, connections to her family story and her community.
Her work argues for better outcomes for Aboriginal people. And her
efforts, along with those of artists who have gone before, and others of
her generation, have brought increasing mainstream awareness to the
displacement of Aboriginal and Torres Strait Islanders.

As an art writer I look for the reasons that artists make what they do. Looking for these connections drives the way in which I approach writing about an artwork or an exhibition. The writing itself takes me into the core of the work as I try to unpick its meaning, structure and appearance, and resonance for the viewer—but perhaps first and foremost, for myself. In locating my own connection to the work, I try to build a bridge through the writing for others, one which does not dictate in a heavy-handed way, but offers threads for those who are willing to pick them up. My narrative is but one path amongst many possibilities. Who I am does not seem over-important within the lens of my understanding and the work of art. Yet, in the Aboriginal world, people often ask early in an acquaintanceship, "Where are you from?" This question is at the heart of the connections, to each other and to place. And it defines key aspects of a life journey—marriages, family relationships and future alliances.

A finely detailed bark painting in the Holmes à Court Aboriginal art collection by Jack Wunuwun (Murrungun/Djinang people), titled *Banumbirr Manikay—(Morning Star Song Cycle)* (1988), tells a creation story, a song cycle of the ancestral narrative of the artist's people. It is musical, arranged over a striped rarrk background. In the centre are waterholes that gave birth to the spirits, surrounded by a constellation of birds, butterflies and dragonflies that segue, one into the other. In the bottom left, a section defined by a darker brown background divides into two, each half showing four rows of four dark faces. From each head, two white eyes look back at the viewer, piercing, vivid in contrast with dark noses and mouths. This is a map for a community, with the dotted lines making explicit the connections between each individual, and a plan, framing who they may marry, the role each will take in this place.

As an Aboriginal woman, at the heart of Fiona's art is her place in the world, driven by "custodial responsibility".[3] She is from a strong Aboriginal family, with ancestral connections to Badtjala country (K'gari and Hervey Bay) and community. Her Badtjala ancestors watched Captain Cook's *Endeavour* sail by in 1770, an event recorded in song. Fiona's clan resisted white incursion into their country in the 1800s. By the 1900s they were working in the forestry and fishing industries. Her great aunt and uncle published the first book of Badtjala stories, *The Legends of Moonie Jarl* in 1964, the year of Fiona's birth. She grew up in a home speaking Badtjala, with a proud Aboriginal mother who published a Badtjala–English dictionary.[4] On her father's side there is Irish heritage. These relatives had heard nothing from her grandfather since he had arrived in Australia in his twenties. In 1984 Fiona became the first in her immediate family to return to Ireland, discovering a large extended family there. Her brother Rowan tells me this, with pride in Fiona's achievements and her fierce independence.[5]

Connection to place is not part of my family narrative. In my generation, the one previous and all those before that, there is transience. Convicts on both sides of my maternal ancestry meant that in my grandmother's childhood home discussion of grandparents was closed down, hard and tight. She remembered, "Father would never speak of his family". Convict heritage was hushed up, a source of shame, a skeletal spectre in the cupboard. It is partly impermanence, but also a competitive culture, that means that non-Aboriginal Australians tend to be defined as individuals, with family and ancestry inconsequential behind us.

Circumstances in my immediate family saw many moves within Australia; I attended nine primary schools. I cannot know if the reason for my habitual uncertainty lies in the transplantation of my settler and convict antecedents into unfamiliar territory four generations ago—it certainly echoes in my life. Kim Mahood's wanderings in her memoir *Position Doubtful* relates the making of maps of the Tanami Desert, which bring the Aboriginal view of this place together with the European grid, using longitude and latitude but also geomorphology, cartography and her own emotional investment. Mahood invokes new work in neuroscience that offers "hard evidence for what people have always known—that place, memory and emotion are inextricably linked".[6]

A photograph by Fiona hangs above the desk in my office where I write. *Signpost II* (2005) is an image of Lake McKenzie beach on K'gari under a portentously darkening sky. The bush framing the beach is dark, uninhabited, existing as it has done for millennia. Yet the place it represents is anything but static. Movement is constant: the coastal air, the animals in the undergrowth and those that live underground. These animals and their habitat thrive without being seen or acknowledged. Marked out on the sand in the foreground of the beach, using clothing sourced from local op shops, are the words "white trash". The vernacular classism of these words, and the suggestion that white equals rubbish, or that rubbish is constructed from whiteness, points to a divide between black and white, nature and culture and, perhaps, Fiona and me.

The review for the exhibition *Red Ochre Me* that Fiona and I met to discuss in 2003 was never written. The premature birth of my two babies in October that year overtook me. Yet, since late 2004 my writing has shadowed exhibitions of Fiona's work, her public sculpture and her public statements. This narrative engages with Fiona's life story as well as her art, a different style of biography that illuminates her journey with imagery. It is also underpinned by what Fiona and I cannot really know about each other's lives. I will never know what it is to be an Aboriginal Australian; she has not experienced life as a white woman. It is a divide, invisible but significant, a scrim that this biography seeks to draw back. It does not offer comfort; I am destined to remain on my side, and she on hers, no matter how we negotiate this territory.

Fiona has welcomed me into her life and shared her journey with generosity. Her public advocacy and her passion for justice for Aboriginal Australia are expanded with her art and ripple into the mainstream. Fiona has influenced all of those on her life journey, the people that have gone before and those who will come after. She tends the fire she inherited from her mother, father and all of her ancestors. Her family of Wondunna leaders, her voice and aesthetic power are part of a cultural continuum that relentlessly innovates, evolves and multiplies. In 2018 she wrote, "I am the spear point—*Nguthuru-Nur*—of my community and people see me as representative of them".[7]

That moment at QCA coffee shop was a starting point for my relationship with Fiona, but *Red Ochre Me* also marked a pivotal point in her career. Some years later she told me, "There was a before that and an after". The exhibition's explicit and scathing edge marked Fiona as a provocateur. Already known for her courage, the toughness of this work gave voice to her outrage about the violence visited on Aboriginal women for generations. Its anger, imagery and language confronted historical silences head on. Her fierce reputation since then has only escalated. When others resile from saying what may need to be said, it seems, inevitably, to be Fiona who steps up. In support of a nomination for the Australia Council Red Ochre Award in 2018, Djon Mundine claimed: "Lucy Lippard said that being a feminist-activist is not just being able to speak for yourself but to assist those without a voice to speak. I can think of no better candidate."[8]

//

Introduction Notes

1   Miriam Cosic, "Francesco Clemente's Encampment at Carriageworks", *The Saturday Paper*, 30 July–5 August 2016, 18–19.

2   Unless otherwise noted, all quotes from Fiona Foley from interviews undertaken by the author 2004–2020.

3   Olu Oguibe, "Medium and Memory in the Art of Fiona Foley", *Third Text* 9, 33 (1995): 51.

4   Badtjala is also spelt Butchulla. Fiona's preference is for the former.

5   During the course of this project, interviews were conducted with Fiona's brothers Rowan Foley and Shawn Wondunna-Foley and her father Barry Foley.

6   Kim Mahood, *Position Doubtful: Mapping Landscapes and Memories* (Melbourne: Scribe, 2016), 297.

7   Fiona Foley, "The Spectacle of Aboriginal Frontier War Memorial Research", *ArtsHub Australia*, 6 July 2018, n.p.

8   Djon Mundine, email to the author, 27 September 2018.

ONE

COUNTRY

"There's only one way to do this." Fiona takes a breath and dives straight under the surface of the water. Next minute, we are both weightless, gasping with cold. My body tingles in the lake's brisk embrace.

Shortly before we had walked barefoot on the paths behind the beach at Lake McKenzie, into a cool breeze. In the middle of the island, the perched, intensely blue lake is surrounded by the brightest white sand, fringed with native wattles, low-growing trees and densely green bush that recedes into infinity. The white sand, blinking with silica, is marked by dingo tracks, and yellow flowers on the tea trees exude a honeyed aroma.

The traditional owners and custodians of the island, the Badtjala people, call the island K'gari and their history with this place is ancient. K'gari is Fiona's country, a place she has spent weeks at a time, almost every year of her life. She is connected to this land by generations and by story—both from her own experience and the creation narratives that connect to the lives of her ancestors. Fiona is descended from a handful of surviving Badtjala people.

Some 120 kilometres long, K'gari is the world's largest sand island. It curves in and around the mainland, protecting the Wide Bay Burnett coastline. For contemporary visitors, their experience is about nature. This place is renowned for its pristine environment—abundant fish, unique rainforest and ancient vegetation, and beautiful lakes. With Fiona as my guide, culture also becomes a presence. The Aboriginal history of the island was acknowledged through Native Title determination in 2014, while recently the adoption of Aboriginal names (including K'gari for the island itself) by the Queensland government make this history overt.

Last time I visited the jewel-like Lake McKenzie, some twenty years ago, it was on a bus from the Kingfisher Bay Resort, accompanied by a dozen other tourists. Approaching the lake, the guide described the qualities of the silica sand which changes the water's pH. This lake, unique on the island, does not support aquatic life, algae or even weed growth at its edge. Clambering down from the high set four-wheel drive that had carried us, lumbering over the rough terrain, the intensity of the blue that is Lake McKenzie seared my retina. I headed off, away from my fellow travellers, bare feet reddening in the hot December sand. Behind me the guide exhorts, "Back here in half an hour!" I stood, knee deep in the water, engulfed by the scent of nearby flowering shrubs. A dragonfly hovered above the lake's surface. Native grasses extended into the clear water as though cautiously testing its qualities.

My other memories of K'gari from this trip, with my brother and sister, our partners and parents, are long beach views on the eastern and rugged side of the island. This was where Eliza Fraser became the first white woman to land, after a shipwreck in 1836. K'gari, known ever since as Fraser Island, was named for her and she is known for her experiences over fifty-two days with the island's Badtjala people.[1] This short sojourn changed the fate of K'gari and the Badtjala people who took Fraser in. The colonial version of these events, narrated by Fraser in terms that increased in drama as her distance from them grew, cast the Aboriginal people as cruel and savage. She described the Aboriginal women applying grease and charcoal to her body, complaining of their roughness, yet their care ensured her survival. After she left the island, her subsequent accounts of this time and place were as unsympathetic as the gritty coastal wind that whips the beach sand, blasting it into my face.

On my 1997 trip, after the Lake McKenzie stop, the bus took us through K'gari's Central Station. We walked the shallows of Eli Creek, looked into the *Maheno* wreck and at the coloured sands on cliffs that overhang the beach. The island has a rugged quality. The view out to sea, up and down the endless beach, is wild, untamed. The rough seas that proved destructive to the *Stirling Castle* in 1836 were also the end of SS *Maheno* and twenty-two other ships on this coastline between 1856 and 1935.

Travelling to K'gari with Fiona in May 2017 is an experience at odds with my previous visit. Our journey from Hervey Bay across the sea to the resort at Kingfisher, where Fiona and her brother Rowan own a villa, is punctuated by her commentary, of place, experience and Wondunna narratives. The place is similar—not the same, given sands that are shifting, inexorably, east to west with the movement of the sea. But Fiona's access offers another world of experience. Through her eyes

I see details, but I'm aware too that what she can show me—where to dig for wongs (or pippies) on the beach, and nature's signals that the bream are running—are only those things at the periphery of her vision.

The toughness of the conditions on the surf side of the island are balanced with the protective softness of the calm western side. There are greens, greys and yellows that colour the eucalyptus and native vegetation, with the hard follicles of banksia underfoot. At the resort, buildings are shrouded amongst abundant gardens of native vegetation, with Pandanus palms strident in their spikiness. Birdlife is loud, and the vegetation twitches with constant movement. Sand tracks wend their way across the island. You do not get far without a four-wheel drive yet, even at best, mechanical movement is slow across sand roads that are like irregular corrugated iron: the mode of travel as much vertical as horizontal.

Fiona moves through her country, open and unguarded. Her hands linger on the flowers, reading the signals they offer to the birds and the insects. They, in turn, come close, a mutual familiarity moving between them. As Fiona's friend Djon Mundine has written: "To know your country means to watch each small, warm movement, to see movement when there seems no movement, to recognise the residual shadow of each being present and passing."[2] Such is her affinity with this place.

Fiona painted *Thoorgine Country 1* in 1991. This painting of K'gari is small, only 26 × 36.5 cm, and hangs opposite my bed. In the 1990s Fiona made more paintings than in recent years. It is a medium that took her artistic skills into an intimacy with her places, K'gari and Badtjala country on the mainland. Other paintings from this time image the black cockatoo, a branch support and a feather, rendered in the hues of K'gari's coloured sands, with a burnt yellow background. These works are distinctive for their mono- or duo-tone backgrounds—a feather in black and red, drawn in pastel on paper, with a simple horizon line, moon and dingo-paw prints in white—all with an intense blue background. *Thoorgine Country I* echoes the island's natural shape. The mainland is curved, like a half moon, bigger than the island but elegantly truncated onto the vastness of its black background. Pointing at the centre of the island is a shape that looks like a small feathered arrow; it represents a ceremonial ground at its white tip, with trees at the "feathered" end. Four shields across the canvas are decorated with Badtjala designs: a counterpoint to the map. The white dot (ceremonial ground) lifts the visual tension to a level that twangs against the brightness of the symbols on the shields.

/

The mainland places shown in this painting are also Badtjala country, which extends from K'gari to the mainland: from Double Island Point and Tin Can Bay south of the island's tip, inland to Bauple Mountain and north to and Burrum Heads.[3] Yet all of the figurative elements in the painting are dwarfed proportionally by the blackness that surrounds them. It is as though the psyche, the unknown, is much larger and more powerful than the little I can know. I am reminded of the lines from *Hamlet*: "There are more things in heaven and earth, Horatio / than are dreamt of in your philosophy."

Yet K'gari's mysteries are familiar to Fiona. She recalls the eerie, yet comforting sense that the Old People were present every time that she was on the island as a girl:

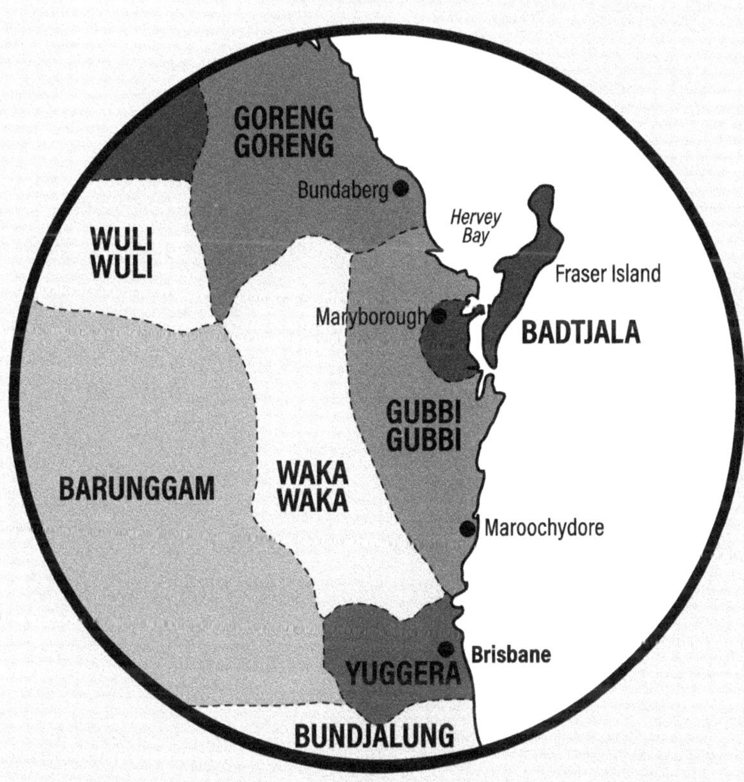

Based on the AIATSIS map of Indigenous Australia
(detail showing Badtjala and neighbouring nations),
https://aiatsis.gov.au/explore/articles/aiatsis-map-indigenous-australia

Everyone feels it. Years ago, Rowan brought two elderly couples from the Uluru community here, and they sang everything. They would sing to the trees before they cut them down for artefacts. And they had vivid dreams about the Old People. There is a sense of them watching. I can feel them every time I am in the bush, camping on the back beach. After Dad bought a four-wheel drive when we were kids, we would spend a month's holiday on K'gari, camping and exploring. You could see naked sand blows from the beach and we would cut our way back through the vegetation and go walking up there. Once, on one part of the island, at dusk, Mum saw an Aboriginal man with a red beard. He was painted-up. We all found stone artefacts: Mum would find the most, my sister found a beautiful green stone and I picked up a little tiny one. Those times are really special. It was a link to the past, to our forebears. We believe that the Old People showed us the artefacts. If you found an object, you were meant to have it—and things happened that are very hard to explain.

The most significant find came later:

When I was a teenager, we went up to Indian Head. Mum and Dad were going fishing but I was drawn to a sand blow with a grassy knob on the top. I asked if I could walk over to it. Mum said, "Yeah, but take your brothers and sister". So we were standing at the top of it and my sister Mellissa said, "Look! Down there: some shells." We ran down, but

what we found was actually a skeleton, of an Aboriginal
person. I picked up the skull and carried it back to the
car—I thought that Mum and Dad may not believe me
without it. We named the skull Eli, after the creek over there,
and kept him with us for a couple of years. Mum tried to
have the skull carbon-dated, but the Anthropology Museum
at Queensland University was not interested. We kept Eli for
two years back in Sydney, but eventually we re-buried him,
back at Indian Head.

Foley's early pastel drawings capture these enigmatic experiences.
Ephemeral Landscape (1990) is divided horizontally with a black
base and a red/orange sky. The moon sits high in the sky, tiny, with
other-worldly shadows cast across its strange reddish colour. Floating
driftwood hovers in the air, and behind them a dingo prowls the horizon
line. A figure vanishes over the edge on the left of the image, with only
feet remaining visible. Yet their footprints line the edge of the black
ground. This scene is located by a postcard-sized image of the beach
on K'gari, with sand dunes and blue sky. It renders visible the presences
that Fiona has always sensed on the island.

HERVEY BAY 2015

On a road trip north with my family in January 2015, we detour
through the coastal town of Hervey Bay. It feels like an older Australia:
even in the prestigious commercial zone on the waterfront, shops and
restaurants are worn rather than chic, the merchandise more remainder
outlet than mainstream. At dusk, nature is overwhelming. Awakening

bats darken the sky and screeching parrots jar my eardrums. From the jetty, which stretches a kilometre out to sea, large fish, even small sharks, are landing on the boardwalk. My children join the group, curiously looking into buckets, wincing as fishermen slice the head from a shark. The glossy surface of the water is disrupted by the jumping of smaller fish. The unknowingness of what lies below matches my mood. The next day I am meeting Fiona's father, Barry Foley. Interviews are a bit like fishing; you can never be sure what you'll catch. His testimony is crucial, particularly in the absence of Fiona's mother.

The next day I follow Barry's directions south of town, to Booral. The area is an old subdivision, with large eucalypts and remnant native vegetation. As I step through the thick grass toward the house and emerge from behind the trees, a small dog, white and fluffy, races toward me and hurls herself at my legs. A woman appears at the top of the back stairs. "Bar*ry!*" she yells into the house, before coming down the stairs to greet me.

Cleo is Barry's second wife. She and I wander around the verdant, productive garden, with Suzie the dog pressing a wet sticky nose to the backs of my bare legs. A vine, sprouting large pumpkins, winds through the vegetable garden area behind the shed. Rosemary and basil flourish in garden beds interspersed with rambling flowers. The grass is springy underfoot.

Barry steps carefully down the stairs. His large hand reaches out to encompass mine while the other one holds tight to the railing. His skin is papery, veins prominent and dehydrated-looking, like the seeds that lie desiccated under the large trees. We walk across the uneven grass to my car. As he directs me into town, he talks about Hervey Bay. His breathing is laboured. We drive into the shopping-centre carpark, making our way to a small cafe, bright with fluorescent lights, opposite Woolworths. It has an unappealing array—dim sims, chips, battered chicken in the bain-marie, and free doughnuts with the coffee. The smell of the chip fat is heavy in the air. Barry sits down and settles, opening an aged plastic bag. As our hot drinks arrive he opens a manila folder; smooths out the photographs and other documents with hands that span the width of their foolscap size.

He extracts pictures of Fiona with her mother Shirley at an opening at Roslyn Oxley9 Gallery, Sydney in the 1980s. Fiona is young and radiant, leaning over from behind Shirley, who is seated, hair striped with white, smiling. The few colour photographs from Fiona's childhood are faded, with that particular yellow tinge that proclaims 1970s processing. They show a family trip to K'gari, Shirley and their four children standing beside an old short-wheelbase Land Rover, looking up the endless surf beach. Then there are documents: copies of certificates, the awards Fiona has won, exhibition invitations. It is a proud father's dossier. How did they start this family? A white man married to an Aboriginal woman, a situation prohibited by legislation without special permission until 1959, a partnership unusual even in the 1960s. The noise of passing shoppers becomes distracting. "Is there somewhere quieter we can talk?" I ask. We make our way across the carpark to a large back room inside the Hervey Bay RSL.

Barry met Shirley Wondunna in Perth, at a film night hosted by the wharfies. Fiona has told me that the details of this meeting always depended on who told the story. They took a shine to one another. Shirley was travelling with a friend, moving from job to job, town to town, having an adventure that saw her cross Australia from a starting point in Hervey Bay.

Barry was born in Sydney in 1935, one of nine children in a large Irish Catholic family. His father had left the family farm in Ireland before the First World War to come to Australia and did not look back. From him Barry inherited a "no nonsense" independent spirit. He became a tiler, completing his trade qualification in Sydney during the 1950s. Fiona's brother Rowan said that Barry "never suffered fools gladly and had a strong sense of himself. He was a deep thinker and would often ponder matters for weeks on end from a very early age."[4] By all accounts, Barry and Shirley's romance progressed quickly. They married in Perth in 1963, then set off to drive to the Ord River, where a litany of "road trip" disasters befell them. Barry told me:

> The caravan broke down. We had to leave it at the station at Halls Creek on the way through. Then the car gearing jammed—in second gear. I had to leave Shirley by the side of the road, in the middle of nowhere, and hitch to the nearest town to get a tow, find someone to come back and help us. Finally, I had to ask Shirley for a hand out for some fuel because everything we had calculated, all the fuel and everything, blew out.

This is unlikely to have fazed Shirley. She was the youngest of four children and never knew her father, professional fisherman Horace Wondunna, who died tragically soon after her first birthday. On the eve of making the final payment on his fishing trawler, part of the Urangan fleet, he was lost at sea. His family were told he was the victim of an accident. A statue of Saint Peter, "In Memory of the Men Lost at Sea" at Urangan Harbour in Hervey Bay was erected in 2013. Horace Wondunna (1939), aged thirty-one, is first on the list.

Barry and Shirley's partnership was marked by their independence, yet at its heart was support for each other. Fiona remembers that "he embraced my mother's culture. He spoke her language and fully backed her Badtjala projects." According to Rowan, Barry "never looked for the approval from other people, he was self-assured and never compared himself to others. This independent spirit led to the marriage with Shirley Wondunna in 1963 ... a strong, spiritual Badtjala woman."[5] Yet the racism they suffered was real. At Barry's workplace, his relationship with an Aboriginal woman was known—and ignored. Barry told me:

> When we moved up here [to Hervey Bay] from Brisbane,
> I worked out of the Maryborough depot. The foreman said,
> "Listen—are you married?" and I said, "Yeah I am, yeah". And
> he said, "Well I can put you onto a widow, you know, a widow
> in my street". That was their outlook. And they never met my
> wife, never knew her.

As a white man married to an Aboriginal woman, Barry endured exclusion and disregard. "It was the racism of the day", he said. Ultimately, with their four children, they tried to escape. Moving, from Beenleigh to Hervey Bay to, Mount Isa, Sydney, Hervey Bay, then Sydney again and back to Hervey Bay. However, during Fiona's childhood, wherever they were living, every year, the family returned to holiday at Hervey Bay and K'gari, where they would camp, fish and explore, maintaining the bond with the island's shifting sands. Barry told me,

> It was hard to get to because the vehicles they used didn't have any springs in them much and it was hard going. So, we used to have a camp there, then, when we moved away, we used to still come back. That was a big thing for me. I used to start getting tinned peaches and stuff like that and boxes of this and boxes of that you know six months before we were going over, so yeah, so we had all our food. But [the children] had, when I look back on it and compare it to my younger life, they had a fantastic time because we used to go over for a month. Yeah it was pretty good then.

In the early days, Shirley's mother Alma would accompany them. Later on, Shirley's brother, Fiona's Uncle Horrie came with them and Badtjala traditional stories unfolded with their explorations.

In Sydney, Shirley's highly competent work was recognised with her promotion to supervisor at the PMG (Post-Master General's Department, now Australia Post). Yet her family had a profile in Queensland's Wide Bay region. In 1989, after they moved back to Hervey Bay, she was instrumental in securing land for the Badtjala people on K'gari from the National Party government, well before Native Title was enshrined in law. This became the site for the Thoorgine

Educational and Culture Centre Aboriginal Corporation. While this land remains in Aboriginal hands, it has been lost to the Wondunna clan, and is a source of much regret and family recriminations. A lost opportunity. Fiona writes,

> Throughout all of my life she was a tireless advocate for Badtjala culture ... My strength comes from her, an exceptional teacher with staunch morals, a jovial soul who loved life, a visionary who took an argument on and weaved a path around political obstacles and never settled for anything less for her nation. Yet where is her legacy in the visual landscape either at K'gari or Hervey Bay? For a lifetime of work to better the Badtjala people, Shirley Foley has been actively and passively written out of history.[6]

Shirley instilled in each of her four children pride in their origins. For Fiona this is palpable, in the sense that her life and work are entwined, with justice for her family, her community and her people at centre stage. She was key to an eighteen-year process for their group to be recognised as the traditional owners of K'gari in 2014. Fiona says that she learnt determination from her mother, and other lessons from her father: "I am a product of the support and love and intelligence of them both."

Shirley Foley was, without question, a powerful influence on each of her children. As the eldest, Fiona observed her mother's example closely. Shawn, as eldest son and, according to Fiona, Shirley's favourite, was also close to the vision. Shawn believes that Shirley's drive emerged from her early life: "My Mum didn't grow up in a mission, but in broader suburbia." This developed her positivity and aspiration, as did the precedent set by her familial role models. "She was not subject to depression and limited thinking. Dad as well: he was first-generation Irish Australian. Our strong, dark-skinned Aboriginal mother and father made for an inspiring and powerful household. The aspiration bar wasn't set low."[7] Rowan said, "Mum had bravery, personality and vision. She was just that sort of person. She wanted to get a job done and secure that land. Dad always said that if Mum was white, she would have been the Chief Executive Officer of an ASX 200 company. She had a strategic brain."[8]

Fiona's path to becoming an artist was preceded by an early visual awareness. Whenever they spent time in the bush, Fiona would collect leaves. "She loved to pick leaves that had a bump in them. Any leaf she picked had to have that little bump." When I ask Barry about Fiona's career as an artist, what she has managed to achieve, he thought hard before he said, "Her career is so immense that I just can't get my head around it really you know".

I have finished working through my questions. "Is there anything else that you think is important?" I ask him. Barry is not really able to explain how he completely sidestepped the racism so pervasive in his generation. For him, I begin to understand, what is simply is.

K'GARI

As an adult Fiona has visited K'gari regularly and made artwork while on the island. A series of sensitive watercolours of local flora and fauna emerged while staying in the villa during May 2011. On that trip, she made daily forays, bringing back feathers, cuttlefish and fish bones.

Her father's words echo in the tactile objects she took home to her villa at Kingfisher Bay: a mangrove root with a strangely truncated curve, a shell with white ridges standing proud of its surface, green seed pods with brown indented spots—so like those "bumpy leaves" Barry remembered. The lyrical watercolour paintings Fiona created during that trip are formed with a transparent wash that evokes the fragility and colours of the original natural objects. Her art dealer Andrew Baker had given her a pad of paper he had left over in the gallery. "I said, 'Take this and see what you can do'. When she came back, we were both shocked by what she had come up with—a series of watercolours so beautiful, so competent, so intimate. I think she had moments of joy in revisiting territory similar to that she had examined early on in her career."[9] In these works, it is white space that evokes the unknown. These drawings are sparer, their medium subtle, and quite different to the blocked colour drawings in pastel of K'gari from the late 1980s and early 1990s. While these are images of country, they capture nature with a light, confident, intuitive touch, testimony to the ground she has covered since.

These were exhibited as *Flotsam and Jetsam* (2011). Simple watercolours of a green mangrove root and two brown, speckled leaves, alone on the white page; a single feather, silver grey and white which arcs over the sheet; five mangrove roots in variable brown and green, arranged on the page like cicatrice; and brown spotted leaves with their variation in colour and tiny holes lovingly recorded. An irregular cream and beige cuttlefish takes me to the infinity of salt spray off the surf side beach, driving on K'gari with Fiona in 2017.

In these watercolours Fiona illustrates her attention to objects which document her familiarity in this place, the endless natural objects of her country. Fiona creates new stories inspired by the past and her present, to imprint Badtjala country as her own, owning it as it, equally, owns her.

One Notes

1 Larissa Behrendt, *Finding Eliza: Power and Colonial Storytetlling* (Brisbane: UQP, 2016), 30.

2 Djon Mundine, "Seeing Black: Degrees of Invisibility", *RealTime* 94 (2009): 52.

3 Wilf Reeves and Olga Miller, *The Legends of Moonie Jarl*, 50th Anniversary edition (Ultimo: The Indigenous Literacy Foundation, [1964] 2014), 3.

4 Rowan Foley, "Eulogy for Barry Foley", 2017. Unpublished.

5 Ibid.

6 Fiona Foley, *Biting the Clouds: A Badtjala Perspective on the Aboriginals Protection and Restriction of the Sale of Opium Act, 1897* (Brisbane: UQP, 2020), 112.

7 Shawn Wondunna-Foley, interview by the author, 12 May 2017.

8 Rowan Foley, interview by the author, 3 January 2019.

9 Andrew Baker, interview by the author, 19 August 2016.

TWO

STRANGERS ON K'GARI

Over the millennia, strangers made rare yet regular incursions to the Badtjala way of life on K'gari. A Portuguese chart from 1536 is marked with a land mass believed to be K'gari. Pumice and lead, dated about 1500, were found buried near Hook Point, and is likely Portuguese in origin. Other strangers to arrive and interact with the Badtjala people included the Dutch. Seventeenth-century clay pipes used for trading were found in an Aboriginal midden. British Captain James Cook sailed by in 1770, followed by Lieutenant Matthew Flinders in 1797, and again in 1802. Flinders left new place names to mark his voyage. Only in 1822 did William Edwardson find that K'gari was an island, separated from the mainland by a body of water he named the Great Sandy Strait. The Badtjala people had of course known this for all time.

Yet Cook's appearance in May 1770, observed by Badtjala people, heralded the beginnings of significant and inexorable change; an irrevocable disruption to their traditional ways of life. After the first sighting of Captain Cook's *Endeavour*, Badtjala followed the ship along the beach, curious. A large group assembled to observe its progress from the vantage point at the top of the island, a place called Takky Wooroo. This rare record of Aboriginal people looking back at Cook was preserved. An Irishman named Ned Armitage transcribed the words of the Badtjala song in 1923:

> These strangers, where are they going? Where are they trying to steer? They must be in that place Thoorvour, it is true. See the smoke coming from the sea. These men must be burying themselves like sand crabs. They disappeared like the smoke.[1]

In the context of an article on the history of Australian music, Graeme Skinner writes,

> With the help of unidentified Indigenous informants, [Armitage] transliterated and translated two songs in the Badtjala language, identified its reference to a dangerous shoal near Indian Head, and advanced this interpretation:
> "This short song clearly refers of Captain Cook, who passed the high, rocky bluff so close that he saw there, and mentioned in his log 'a number of Indians'. The blacks saw him and his men on the deck and noted the man at the wheel ... They thought he was going to hit the Thoorvoor shoal. His disappearance over the horizon they compared to the sand crabs and the smoke and clouds."[2]

I wonder whether this song was created the same evening, and imagine a group of seven Badtjala warriors, who had been amongst the group who gathered to witness Cook's passing, as they sat by the fire. The coals glowed red and the stars rose in a clear sky as the first songman's voice was joined by others, one by one, at first tentative and then, as the rhythms and words were established, resonant. Its sounds, the waver of uncertainty and the unknown became a wondering, repeated in a chorus which echoed out over the sand blow, into the she-oak, and penetrated the psyche of the sleeping birds, animals and the sands of time themselves. They were singing to those around them, to the women and the children, but also to their ancestors, and their unborn children. Winds of change were stirring.[3]

This song became part of the Badtjala corroboree. Its record of Badtjala looking at the incoming Europeans who in turn see them, reminds me of the sense of the "uncanny" that Ken Gelder and Jane Jacobs, drawing on Freud's theory of the *unheimlich*, describe. They define the uncanny as an experience which "may occur when one's home is rendered, somehow and in some sense, unfamiliar; one has the experience, in other words, of being in place and 'out of place' simultaneously".[4] It is discomfiting to consider my own European ancestors as similar to Cook's group who arrived and, overlooking what they saw and experienced of Aboriginal occupancy and connection, declared the continent *terra nullius* in order to seize it for the British crown. The sheer rarity of the Badtjala account that saw Cook's party integrated into the natural environment, "burying themselves like sand crabs" also offers an insight into the holistic nature of country. For Aboriginal people, country is both nurturer and nurtured. The gentle fascination and acceptance that this song expresses is an insight into an "uncanny" world view so different from my own.[5]

Eliza Fraser was not the first person to find herself out of place on K'gari, forced to seek sanctuary with the Badtjala people. Convicts on the run from the Moreton Bay penal settlement sought cover there between 1828 and 1842, finding Aboriginal life more palatable than the rigour of penal servitude. Yet when Fraser told of her experience for a few short weeks in 1836 she drew attention from all over the world, her experiences fuelling the myths and fantasies that swirled around the sexual involvement of white women and black men (and vice versa).

Captain James Fraser's ship *Stirling Castle* was wrecked on Swain Reefs in May 1836, a week after leaving Sydney en route to Singapore. His wife Eliza was part of a group that spent eight weeks at sea in two lifeboats before washing up on K'gari's beach, sunburnt, in need of food and water, and fearful. In the days that followed, Captain Fraser died, three of the crew returned to sea (arriving in Moreton Bay in August), and Eliza was absorbed into the Badtjala group. The story of the white Scotswoman living amongst the Aboriginal locals on K'gari has dominated this place ever since, with destructive consequences. Those who have used her narrative in their own creative work include the artists instrumental in constructing and probing the myths surrounding European presence in Australia, notably the painter Sidney Nolan and novelist Patrick White. The spark it has given to the imagination of Australian artists and writers ever since is disproportionate to her experience: Eliza Fraser spent five weeks on the island before the surviving crew initiated her rescue.

In a documentary made for SBS, Fiona says, "Eliza Fraser stole our humanity. She came but for a few weeks, but after that the Badtjala people became invisible. The island bears her name. In 2014 our Native Title was recognised. We can't build on it, we can't make our own decisions. We need you to let Eliza's words go, wash away out over the horizon. And call this place by its real name K'gari, paradise."[6]

Badtjala Elder Olga Miller's oral histories suggest that her female ancestors treated Fraser's severe sunburn after her shipwreck with compassion, and ensured she was protected. The time-honed skills of the Badtjala people ensured Eliza Fraser's survival; other white people rescued by K'gari's custodians reported caring treatment. Any cruelty toward Fraser is likely to have been a result of the type of misunderstanding described above, or her own attitudes, which— certainly following her return to England—were exploitative. Back in the United Kingdom (courtesy of fund-raising efforts in Sydney and donated clothing), Fraser sought more money, both in Liverpool where she landed and then in London. During these initiatives, her recent marriage to the captain of the boat that carried her back to England, Alexander Greene, is not mentioned; presumably to strengthen her case: she presented herself as a widow without resources.[7]

Larissa Behrendt suggests that Fraser's stories of maltreatment and inherent danger served the dominant narrative of the time. She writes that in "the Eliza Fraser narratives, the superiority of whites is asserted. In his descriptions of the Aboriginal people, John Curtis refers to their animalistic traits and their lowly status on the evolutionary ladder."[8] Bruce Pascoe also notes this sense of superiority in the first colonists, directed by a belief in the British Empire and "ideas of race and destiny". He writes, "The first British visitors sailed to Australia contemplating what they were to about to find, and innate superiority was the prism through which their new world was seen."[9]

Fraser's tales impacted negatively on relationships between whites in the area and the Badtjala. After 1842 the government opened what now comprises Queensland for white settlement. Fraser's exaggerated stories increased the fear of Aboriginals among the growing white community in the area and contributed to one of the many massacres of the Badtjala groups who had assisted in her survival. Behrendt writes:

> Eliza's captivity narrative helped to shape what was "known" about Aboriginal people and their culture ... Perhaps because these accounts contained so many generally accepted negative stereotypes of Aboriginal people—they were cannibals, they were cruel, they were lecherous, they were savage—readers simply saw her story as reinforcing what they already knew.[10]

By 1880 the Aboriginal population in this area had been reduced to a quarter of its 1867 levels.[11]

Fiona's ancestors were at the "front line" of European contact. The impact of Fraser's story on her country is a subject she has addressed since early in her career. She writes:

> In 1836 Eliza Fraser was marooned for five weeks on K'gari and her saga has been allowed to continue for throughout two centuries ... the absence of dialogue with the Badtjala

people has irrevocably damaged and put this people to rest.
I often wonder when she will be put to rest.[12]

Early in her career, Fiona recast the Eliza Fraser story from her perspective as a Badtjala woman, joining the narrative of her ancestors to overwrite Fraser's tales of her treatment at their hands. These small paintings see Eliza's bonneted face floating, odd and exotic, out of place over broad ochre plains, or under a moonlit sky. Fiona turned the Australian visual narrative (and Eliza Fraser's own) on its head, with its historic depiction of the landscape as exotic and potentially malignant. In *Eliza Heads for Trouble I* (1990), the canvas is divided into foreground and sky. Eliza's face lies upside down in the bottom corner, as though washed up on the beach. On the midnight-blue horizon stand five barely visible figures as the moon shines down above them all. The Aboriginal figures blend seamlessly into country, while Fraser's head is foreign, exotic, out of place and discomfited. Other paintings from this series feature rat traps, fixed on pastel surfaces, poised near Fraser's bonneted head, or positioned under the paintings. The whisper of air that could trigger their damaging release is a metaphor, conjuring the destructive impact of Fraser's short-lived sojourn on K'gari.

In 2017 the Queensland Art Gallery changed the way in which its Australian collection was displayed. It is the first Australian gallery to integrate Aboriginal and Torres Strait Islander art within the historical Australian painting, sculpture and decorative arts of the last 150 years. It did not feel revolutionary, yet this new hang reflected cultural change, a shift in mindset, a new balance visible in the narratives that define this continent. Sight-lines through the display areas were bookended with a major wall-based painting, *Wall Composition in Reckitt's Blue* (2017) by Brisbane-based Indigenous artist Dale Harding (Bidjara, Ghungalu and Garingbal peoples, born 1982) and, at the other, with ten *Utopia panels* (1996) by Emily Kame Kngwarreye (Utopia, Northern Territory, c. 1910–1996). Aboriginal and Torres Strait Islander artists were visibly front and centre in this new iteration. How might this move be interpreted in relation to Djon Mundine's breakdown of the history of Aboriginal art into six phases between 1980 and 2013? He writes, "There is a wish to retain control of the discussion and definition of Aboriginal art. Although we are visible through our art, what is the place we have come to?"[13]

Harding's stencilled imagery is drawn from his country in Carnarvon Gorge, the shapes of spades and garden tools sprayed on the plaster wall in an intense blue that evokes nineteenth-century laundry whitener Reckitt's Blue and the domestic services in which his family were employed. The utilitarian nature of the manufactured tools he stencilled offer a contrast in colour and subject (but not style) to the silhouetted hands and feet of the gorge's Cathedral Cave (in its naturally derived ochre colours). His work spoke across the six galleries and two generations to the Western Desert's Kngwarreye and her hand-painted stripes of black and white, interspersed with panels of frenetic and colourful painterly swirls. Kngwarreye's joy in paint, its unsteady application and wavering lines conjure up her relationship to country. In the galleries between, two hundred artists traced their own stories of geography, place and landscape from differing cultures, times and experience. This opened visual conversations, offered a challenge to existing conventions, and choreographed an interchange of styles and cultures that travel like a series of elegant, and sometimes presumptuous, slips of time and sleights of hand.

On a feature wall, contrasting cultural views of K'gari from Fiona were juxtaposed with paintings by Sidney Nolan. It brought together three of Fiona's early photographs from the *Badtjala Woman* (1994) series, accompanied by a beautifully burnished and aged mangrove paddle from 2000, collected by her mother Shirley Foley. Sidney Nolan's much earlier paintings of K'gari are adjacent, bookended with two Eliza Fraser images. These independent narratives from K'gari are separated by their Aboriginal/non-Aboriginal perspectives, forty-five years, culture and connection. Yet Fiona finds this curatorial space, in which her work meets that of Sidney Nolan, refreshing: "It is the first time anyone has pieced the two together, with their different intellectual engagements."

Fiona's paintings of Eliza Fraser from 1990 (and not in the Queensland Art Gallery collection), were inspired by Nolan's *Mrs Fraser* (1947, now in that collection), which she first saw on the cover of a book by Michael Alexander, titled *Mrs Fraser on the Fatal Shore* (1971). In this image, Eliza Fraser dominates the picture plane within a tropical landscape. She is splayed naked, on all fours like a bestial savage, made wild and discomfited by her experience. This scene is captured within a circle, as though seen through a telescope viewfinder, evoking a vignette of something intimate, illicit or private. This painting hangs at the end of the row on the wall shared with Fiona's photographic *Badtjala Woman*. Nolan's four paintings include *Mrs Fraser and Convict* (1962–1964), with its two sorrowful figures who stagger unclothed, fragile and vulnerable, along the beach. The landscapes are double-hung. They express the pleasure Nolan took in this remote landscape, a desire to belong to this place that is noted in his nomination of K'gari as his home on wedding documents in 1948. His *Platypus Bay, Fraser Island* (1947) conjures up the mystery of this place, and *Lake Wabby, Fraser Island* (1947) records the dramatic vertiginous slope down to the green water, with the expansive sand blow behind.

The Queensland Art Gallery's collection rehang and its rebalancing of the national narrative, with greater weight tipped to the artwork and vision of Aboriginal and Torres Strait Islander Australians, points to a changing aesthetic landscape and a shifting, potential sharing, of power. It also pairs the contemporary with the historic. I am reminded that Aboriginal time is an overlay of palimpsests, in which past, present and future exist together. Yet in terms of fundamental change, given the status of culture in Australia, this may be the thinnest edge of the wedge. As Fiona has told me, the experience for Aboriginal Australia is that a door may open a crack, only to slam shut shortly after; "progress" is often one step forward, another back. Fiona's diptych *Heroes I & II* expressed the sentiment succinctly in 2003. Two large painted panels are overwritten with grey letters over a (pink) "skin colour" panel. *Heroes I* reads, "Your heroes are not our heroes", while *Heroes II* reads, "Our heroes are not your heroes".

Fiona's ambition is that Aboriginal people may be seen and granted visibility that acknowledges their longevity with this land: "We have used and loved our land—Our Island—since time immemorial. We have hosted many people on our country and we will continue to do so."[14] The generosity at the core of the Aboriginal experience of Australia is evident in their Dreamtime stories—incomers are seen as integral extensions to, and accommodated within, layers of narrative. The nature of Aboriginal legends allows for change to be reflected and embraced by evolving stories.

//

Two Notes

1 Graeme Skinner, "The Invention of Australian Music", *Musicology Australia* 37, 2 (2015): 293.

2 Ibid.

3 This section is speculative and purely fictional.

4 Ken Gelder and Jane Jacobs, *Uncanny Australia: Sacredness and Identity in a Postcolonial Nation* (Melbourne: Melbourne University Press, 1998), 23.

5 This section is speculative and purely fictional.

6 Larissa Behrendt and Fiona Foley, *K'gari: The Real Story of a True Fake*, produced by SBS with support from NITV, 2017.

7 Larissa Behrendt, *Finding Eliza: Power and Colonial Storytelling* (Brisbane: UQP, 2016), 31–32.

8 Ibid., 38.

9 Bruce Pascoe, *Dark Emu* (Broome: Magabala Books, 2014), 3–4.

10 Larissa Behrendt, *Finding Eliza: Power and Colonial Storytelling* (Brisbane: UQP, 2016), 62.

11 Joan G. Winter, "Against Their Will: A Post Contact Badtjala Heritage", in *Fiona Foley: Invisible Voices*, ed. Bundaberg Arts Centre (Bundaberg: Bundaberg Art Centre, 2000), 6.

12 Fiona Foley, "A Blast from the Past", *Periphery* 31 (1997): 165.

13 Djon Mundine, "30 Years Ago Today: 1980–2013", *Sturgeon*, 6 (2013): 48.

14 Fiona Foley, "Speech: Fraser Island", 24 October 2014.

THREE

ANCESTRY

Fiona and I stand on the jetty, looking back at the island into the dense scrub climbing steep sand hills. It is a sea of green shrubs and trees. She tells me, "Around July, you see the wattle tree in bloom. That yellow flower tells you that the bream is ready to catch."

In her early landscapes, often based on K'gari, Fiona elicits "the experiential essence of the place, juxtaposing the colours of land, water and sky … with a few small but evocative symbols of human presence".[1] K'gari is the touchstone in her life and her art, the source of symbols to which she returns. There are delicate feathers, the full moon in an open sky, shells, dingo tracks, ochre colours, spirals and diamond patterns. In the early 1990s, working in pastel, these simple drawings, often small, describe something of her own Jun Jaree (Badtjala spirit guide). They are abstracted, with a few elements over simple coloured backgrounds, and focus on animals and objects that float within the ambiguous space of memory. They are her images yet resonate with the familiarity of her ancestors in this place may inform them.

The choice of Fiona's *Black Cockatoo Feather* (1992) as a special issue Australia Post stamp in 1993 has a poetic edge. She remembers making this image very fast, sitting at her parents' kitchen table in Hervey Bay. She chose a yellow ochre colour in pastel as background, and its tonal variation is like a dreamscape. The black cockatoo is a silhouette, seated on a branch. The feather to its right is a similar length to the branch, both twice as long as the bird. The tactile qualities of the feather, its red and yellow markings on the black, are intimate, as though it had been picked up, stroked and cherished. As a stamp, her *Black Cockatoo Feather* was despatched into the world, broadcasting this private memory and her personal iconography of K'gari into a broader consciousness. Many of Fiona's pastels from this time also include postcards, either collaged to the surface, or painted in, like vignettes of place or moments of snatched recall. The idea of a postcard conveys what Fiona describes as "an idealisation of Aboriginal people and cultures, a bland repetition of the type of clichéd Aboriginal experience that most people seem to want in Australia".[2]

In this K'gari beachscape in postcard size and shape, Fiona's images are authenticated by her experience. The ancient sand mass that forms K'gari is also in a state of constant change. The sand on the island is shifting inexorably from east to west, which is particularly visible on the sand blows. As the ground shifts, artefacts from the past reveal themselves. *Dingo Skull B* (1994), also in pastel, shows a painted yellow background with visible brushmarks noting the movement of sand, divided by a thin straight horizon line. Dominating the image with its size is a large dingo skull, which recalls the unique dingoes that inhabit the island and were companions to the Badtjala people, its eye sockets black and hollow with loss. The dingo has continued to inhabit K'gari, even after its connection as companion animal to the Badtjala was disrupted when the Aboriginal people were removed from the island in the early 1900s.

In Fiona's work the dingo, solitary and alone, is sometimes a self-portrait, a reminder of the endurance of her people. Nigerian-born artist and intellectual Olu Oguibe writes in "Medium and Memory in the Art of Fiona Foley" that, "The dingo is the silent figure that calls history to account".[3] Fraser Island dingoes, *Canis lupus dingo*, are now protected as a vulnerable species.[4] Deborah Bird Rose has recorded the relationships between dingoes and their kinship with Aboriginal people, noting "the affinities between two top order predators—dingoes and humans".[5] There is a chilling parallel here: these wild dogs, seen in many parts of Australia as a pest and subsequently subject to wholesale slaughter, are targeted in a similar way to that of Aboriginal people, who were "a despised group" during colonisation. Oguibe suggests:

> In a most peculiar rhetoric of recollection the loneliness of the
> dingo encodes the savage depopulation of Fraser Island. Once
> an intimate companion for humans and a permanent party in
> hunts as well as the domestic space, the dingo witnessed the
> racial cleansing of the island at the beginning of the century,
> and today the animal wanders alone through the savannah
> and the rainforest, highly suspicious of humans, bearing in its
> mournful eyes record of what happened to the people. Foley
> adopts the dingo as both guardian spirit and signature, and
> though many may not notice it, the recurrence of the dingo

in her work reiterates that inescapable question permanently inscribed in the animal's eyes: what happened to the Badtjala?[6]

Walking at the Kingfisher Bay Resort in 2017, I find myself "fenced-in" by the dingo-proof wire within minutes of leaving our villa. Opening the gate to venture further into the forest, I wonder whose needs are best served by this ongoing separation of dingoes and people. Bird Rose notes that dingoes are self-limiting in their populations, live within family groups and adjust to environmental change: "We humans are capable of living like dingoes: we, too, have the capacity to limit our numbers and to keep our family units in balance with territory and with other species. We have the capacity to self-manage but are not handling it at all well. In fact, from an ecosystem point of view, it seems that humans are the great pests."[7]

In Fiona's early drawings, the dingo is alone, a dark silhouette, looking out, sometimes accompanied by human footprints. In other drawings the Aboriginal figure appears, with paw prints indicating the dog's shadowy presence. During our 2017 visit, prints in the sand are as close as we get to the dingo. After the removal of the Badtjala people in the early 1900s, the dingoes applied their adaptive prowess. Yet I imagine them mourning their companions, their solo hunting, and howls tearing at the darkness as evening came but the campfires did not.

THE WONDUNNA CLAN

"You didn't come from a hollow log," Shirley told Fiona.

My mother taught me

You came from me.[8]

The scourge of the stolen generations was not visited on Fiona's family. Was it luck, sheer good fortune, or something else that protected them? While children of mixed race attracted the attention of authorities in the twentieth century, Fiona grew up in a secure environment, her Aboriginal mother teaching her language and culture, a base of knowledge vested in the interrupted yet long term occupancy of their place. *The Aboriginals Protection and Restriction of the Sale of Opium Act*, 1897 offered Aboriginal people with employment important exemption from the legislation's restrictions for unemployed Aboriginal people. Fiona says, "The men in my family were involved in the fishing or the timber industry. That is how we were not really a financial 'risk to society.'" A family history notes that Fiona's great-great-grandfather, Willy "Great" Wondunna, was initiated in 1865 in the last ceremony held for Badtjala men—and was known as Coobunya (keeper of cultural knowledge).[9] Yet he obtained a Certificate of Exemption in 1942.[10] Historian Thom Blake suggests that:

> Exemption Certificates were granted only to those Aborigines
> who demonstrated to the Chief Protector's satisfaction the
> capacity to survive in the outside world. In other words, they
> were imbued with capitalist values concerning money, time
> and work. But the standards required for exemption were
> high; certificates were not freely issued.[11]

These certificates allowed their recipients to live outside reserves and missions; offering exemption from the controlling provisions of *The Act*, yet they also required a severance of ties with culture, kinship and country.[12] Ignoring severance provisions meant possible revocation of the certificate which allowed the Aboriginal recipient to live in a place and way of their own choosing (like a non-Aboriginal citizen).

We cannot know how Willy "Great" Wondunna negotiated these restrictions; he was known in the family as Headman of the Wondunna clan, and always "kept [his] connection with Fraser Island".[13] Willy Wondunna was a skilled black tracker who, it has been claimed, set off with a larger group to hunt down Ned Kelly for the Victorian police.[14] While family histories record that he was a trooper under Sergeant King, and present in Glenrowan in 1880, research by Fiona's sister Mellissa Foley indicates that Willy may have turned back, returning home before they reached their quarry.[15] We cannot know why, but I wonder if he began to feel uncomfortable in his travels so far from home.

The disruption to traditional Badtjala culture came early, shortly after William Petrie scoped this part of the mainland in 1842. It followed the end to the penal settlement of Brisbane when Moreton Bay was opened to free settlers. Fiona's Badtjala ancestors were disrupted, disenfranchised and murdered by European settlers, for whom they were at best an inconvenience; at worst a scourge to be eliminated. By the late 1840s, there was a raging war on this colonial frontier. Early observers had recorded some two thousand people living on K'gari, and noted their "unparalleled fine physique due to their exceptionally good diet: the plenitude of the fish and sea creatures in their waters, their highly developed fishing skills; and the land animals and edible plant foods on K'gari and their territories across the Sandy Strait."[16] Badtjala may be translated as "sea people",[17] with mangroves at the heart of plentiful seafood in their diet, but also as a source of other materials such as wood, and as inspiration for their legends and lore. Frontier conflict and atrocities were brought by the incoming whites,[18] with the Badtjala population falling dramatically after 1850.

"Those among the Badtjala who were not shot or driven into the shark-infested seas of the Pacific were forced into Christian missions on the Australian mainland where they were subjected ... to the Euro-Australian policy of violent 'whitification'—what Tasmanian artist Ian Anderson has described as the policy of 'fuck 'em white.'"[19] In the second part of the nineteenth century, undeclared war between the incoming whites and the Aboriginals saw Queensland as the site of the greatest loss of life and frontier skirmishes. Fiona writes:

> Badtjala people waged a twenty-year guerrilla war from the natural fortress of K'gari as the advance of white settlement moved north to the Wide Bay area. At one point, the Badtjala nation had the upper hand and raids were a daily occurrence on Maryborough town dwellers. In the *Original Maryborough Site*, Thom Blake and Richard Allom wrote that, "the prospect of the town being abandoned was real. During the crisis of 1855 at least ten per cent of the population left."[20]

However, by 1859, the balance had shifted with a campaign against Badtjala resistance using the Native Mounted Police.

> Wave after wave of frontier violence impacted. The effects of dispossession on a race and their sovereign lands were a people subdued into submission. A new co-dependent relationship formed between the colonised and the coloniser ... New

colonial systems were put in place to oversee the remnant
populations of Queensland such as *The Aboriginals Protection
and Restriction of the Sale of Opium Act, 1897.*[21]

The establishment of Maryborough as a municipality in 1861
followed the *Alienation of Crown Lands Act, 1860.*[22] After 1860, when
Queensland had gained independence from New South Wales, towns
outside Brisbane began to develop. When white colonisers arrived
in central Queensland, rape and slaughter accompanied them. Land
was opened up to white settlers. In colonial Australia, women were a
particular target for violence. The impact of this violence continues to
ricochet through the most intimate aspects of Aboriginal family life.[23]

Reverend Fuller established the first mission at Ballargan on K'gari's
west coast in 1872.[24] He was a sad witness to the declining Aboriginal
population within the mission, where Aboriginals from all areas were
quarantined. In 1872 he wrote a long private letter from Ballargan
that was subsequently published in the Brisbane newspaper, "there
are, I think, not more than 300 blacks, and yet there are no less than
19 distinct tribes. But strong drink and disease, introduced among
them by ungodly white people, have made such havoc among them that
the tribal bond, in many instances, is almost obliterated."[25]

The statistics are bald and shocking. By 1880 annual blanket
distribution recorded only 230 Aboriginals, which is only ten per cent
of the estimated population some forty years before.[26] Less than twenty
years later, in 1897, those who remained were removed to the mission
on K'gari, Bogimbah Creek Reserve. A few, perhaps a handful, evaded
capture, by hiding out in remote parts of the island. In 1904 Bogimbah
was abandoned after almost half the mission inhabitants died. Of the

168 remaining inmates (from all over Queensland), 117 went north to Yarrabah, 30 went south to Durundur and the remaining 20, from K'gari, were left to find their own way. The Badtjala nation was devastated. Joan Winter noted that "where once was paradise and a vibrant lively culture, there was silence and overwhelming loss".[27]

Shawn Foley writes, "The Badtjala people, having fought a war they did not provoke and having been forced to confront a race of greedy individuals with superior technology and battle hardened troops, were now left to pick up the pieces and patch together some sort of normality in a now shattered life."[28]

/

As a direct result of this early disenfranchisement and abuse, Australia's Aboriginal people suffer greater representation in health statistics, youth suicide, rape and sexual abuse and premature death. These past practices have propelled Aboriginal people to the margins of society.[29] Decades later, the Uluru Statement from the Heart stated, "Proportionally, we are the most incarcerated people on the planet. We are not an innately criminal people. Our children are alienated from their families at unprecedented rates. This cannot be because we have no love for them. And our youth languish in detention in obscene numbers. They should be our hope for the future."[30]

Every early death is a loss of human potential. Other symptoms of the disconnections wrought by the colonising whites are environmental damage to a fragile continent and ecosystems. And the destruction of cultural bonds established over millennia continues to reverberate with the impact of the journeying strangers in this place.

/

Fiona cast Lee-Shay Warburton, a young Aboriginal woman, as the lead in a film made in 2013 titled *Vexed*. Warburton's youth was important to the story as this poignant production deals with the breakdown of "promised marriages", a result of the historical theft of Aboriginal women by white men. Traditional Aboriginal marriages implicated kinship and multiple generations, with arrangements and promises made when children were very young: "The promised relationship created a series of lifelong responsibilities and obligations between the young man and his promised wife's relations."[31] The film's narrative unfolds in the dry creek bed of the Todd River in Alice Springs. The mournful screech of black cockatoos underscores an inexorable tenor of grief at the kinship networks disrupted and traditional marriage practices torn apart. The spoken narrative was drawn from Germaine Greer's *On Rage*.[32] Greer's acknowledgement of the theft of Aboriginal women by white men and the impact of these losses on Aboriginal men, the rage which continues to peak and ebb, is conjured in the all or nothing vocalisation of the cockatoos.

Oodgeroo Noonuccal (1920–1993), the Aboriginal poet from Minjerribah (North Stradbroke Island), writes about the melding of black and white, about relationships that bridged and divided, in "Son of Mine" (1990):

> My son, your troubled eyes search mine,
> Puzzled and hurt by colour line.
> Your black skin soft as velvet shine;
> What can I tell you, son of mine?

I could tell you of heartbreak, hatred blind,
I could tell of crimes that shame mankind,
Of brutal wrong and deeds malign,
Of rape and murder, son of mine;

But I'll tell instead of brave and fine
When lives of black and white entwine,
And men in brotherhood combine—
This would I tell you, son of mine.[33]

Entwinement of lives black and white was controversial during Noonuccal's time, but almost one hundred years before this poem was written, Fiona's great-grandfather, Aboriginal man Fred Wondunna (son of Willy "Great" Wondunna, and father to Olga and Wilf), won the heart of a white woman. Her family were high-profile Christians. Yarrabah Mission in north Queensland was the dream of their father, J. B. Gribble. It was later taken on by his son Ernest Gribble after J. B. contracted malaria. Ethel Gribble was born near Deniliquin in New South Wales in 1879 and employed by the Australian Board of Missions: she was Ernest Gribble's sister. Yet when Ethel met Fred at Bogimbah Creek Reserve mission on K'gari in about 1902, where she had been sent by her brother to assist their mother Mary Ann, they came together in a romance which was resisted by many. It caused ructions that shook their families, the Anglican community throughout Australia, and the rest of their lives.

K'GARI, 1900

Ethel's brother Ernest Gribble took over management of K'gari's Bogimbah Creek Reserve mission in 1900. This mission was started by Archibald Meston, the Southern Protector of Aborigines, whose vision was better "management" of Aborigines in Australia. He advocated for the *Aboriginals Protection and Restriction of the Sale of Opium Act*, 1897 by the Queensland government and the segregation of white and Aboriginal communities. While Queensland parliamentary speakers lauded *The Act* as "an exemplar of Christian compassion and humanitarianism: 'a determined effort to ameliorate conditions of the Aborigines' and to save a 'dying race' from extinction",[34] it represented the imposition of control over almost every aspect of an Aboriginal person's life. Forced removal to missions and reserves was integral to *The Act*. It was also a convenient mechanism for colonists, as was the widespread belief that Aboriginals were a "dying race". Colonists were keen to use land for farming and grazing without having to deal with Australia's resident and dispossessed Aboriginal peoples, many of whom were aggrieved at the theft of their country, and the destruction of their agriculture and aquaculture. Despite his reported encouragement of traditional practices, after 1897 Meston was responsible for the removal of nineteen Aboriginal language groups from their own country for despatch to K'gari. Taking Aboriginal people from their country was traumatic; the bundling together of groups with no previous association or even common language was further scarifying. The first settlement was on K'gari at Ballargan in 1872. It was later relocated further north to Bogimbah Creek Reserve after complaints from the local white population about its proximity.[35] After 1897 Archibald's son Harold

Meston was installed as the first mission manager. His regime was brutal, characterised by "beatings, intimidation, [with] terrified inmates tied-up and abandoned overnight in the graveyard, women and girls coerced into sex, violent summary punishments".[36]

/

In 2018 Fiona donated a large oil painting titled *1897 Aboriginals Protection & Restriction of the Sale of Opium Act* (2006) to the collection of Sydney's National Art School. On this dark canvas, painted in a colour that resembles dried blood, its title is created in pale sans-serif typeface. It is stark and spare and speaks to the meaning of this legislation for Aboriginal people, the absolute control it represented over their lives, the non-negotiable nature of decisions made for them by others.

/

After Ethel's brother Ernest Gribble was appointed temporary warden of Bogimbah Creek Reserve, K'gari became "another marshalling point for the Gribble family".[37] Ernest Gribble imposed the church-based regime, first established in Yarrabah, with daily chores and discipline—the routine also imposed on mission inhabitants at Bogimbah. Ethel was brought in to run the school, and his mother Mary Ann was Head Matron, responsible for ensuring that the methods Ernest had established at Yarrabah were implemented. After a brief period of establishment, Gribble returned home to Yarrabah.

Fred Wondunna, born around 1886, was seven years younger than Ethel, "dark, taciturn and handsome".[38] Ethel was, according to Ernest Gribble's biographer Christine Halse, "afflicted with the same headstrong streak of independence that cursed and blessed all the Gribbles".[39] She met Fred in her mid-twenties. She was small and slight, her prettiness masked by thick glasses through which "her eyes refused to focus properly and she could not shake off the disarming habit of seeming to look at you from two directions at once. In the full-length, high-necked dresses of the day with her dark hair in a tight knot above her neck, Ethel was the picture of a sedate, homely missionary lady".[40] In contrast, Fred was seventeen, lean and wiry, hair curled tightly close to his head. Fred was born in Dundatha (near Maryborough). Reports of his employment vary—his marriage certificate listed his occupation as storekeeper. His powerful physical presence is visible in photographs used in the Central Station educational display on K'gari, which capture the intensity of his dark eyes. Here and in other Badtjala family photographs, he looks directly at the camera, as though empowered to speak to us through history.

Before long, Fred and Ethel sought Ernest's permission to marry. Ernest was aghast. The scandal that this relationship was likely to cause prompted Ernest to send Ethel north to Yarrabah post-haste. As far as Ernest was concerned, the romance was to remain a secret and to go no further. His solution was to orchestrate Ethel's engagement to William Reeves, his reputedly "mild-mannered" deputy, who was a stone mason and bandmaster at Yarrabah. Ethel delayed, waiting sixteen months before succumbing to intense family pressure.

Finally, she wed Reeves on 12 June 1903. A photograph from this day shows an unsmiling group of six people with Ethel and Reeves at its centre. Ethel is seated with her hand resting on the shoulder of a young girl, presumably a bridesmaid. A youthful woman wearing a large straw hat stands on her other side with an Aboriginal man on the edge of the group. The photograph is not captioned, but the Aboriginal man is thought to be James Noble, who Gribble mentored to become the first Aboriginal deacon in 1925.[41] Behind Ethel stands Reeves, tall, slim and upright, his handlebar moustache distinctive. On his right an Aboriginal woman wears an outfit identical to that worn by the young white woman. The group appear sober and while the detail of Ethel's face is largely bleached by the early photographic process, her lips are set in a straight line.

Almost a year after the marriage their daughter Faith was born. Within two years Reeves, "a thin, sickly soul with a kind heart, a weak constitution and a consumptive nature" was dead.[42] The cause of death was thought to be a dramatic change to the weather caused by a cyclone. He was bedridden for three weeks and died on 29 January 1906.

By coincidence or design Fred Wondunna was not far away. He had headed north after the abandonment of the Bogimbah Creek Reserve mission in August 1904 after which some 117 people were shipped to Yarrabah. However, Fred was employed, and never an inhabitant of the mission. Shawn Foley (Fiona's brother, now Wondunna-Foley) writes that twenty Badtjala people remained at K'gari after the mission was abandoned. They were all that remained from a population of two thousand from before the coming of the white man (1770–1850).

I wonder if Ethel sought Fred out, or vice versa, but the electric nature of their earlier relationship may have been difficult to resist. Either way, the romance was rekindled; by August 1907 Ethel was pregnant with Wondunna's child. Ernest sent Ethel away from Yarrabah to conceal her pregnancy (her daughter Faith was left with Mary Ann). Unbeknownst to Ernest, Ethel and Wondunna then met up in Sydney, determined to elope.

The couple's only desire was to declare their devotion publicly by marrying. They asked Gribble to sanction their union and perform the wedding ceremony, but Gribble could see only the hopelessness of their love. At the beginning of the twentieth century, marriage to an Aboriginal man meant Ethel would be denounced as a whore and a disgrace to her sex and race. She would become a pariah, ostracised forever from polite society.[43]

They could not find an Anglican priest willing to marry them in Sydney but finally became husband and wife in December 1907, their vows heard by a Congregational minister in New South Wales. They moved to K'gari, having the first of their five children in Brisbane en route (four survived to adulthood). This first baby of their relationship was Fiona's grandfather Horace Wondunna, born 21 April 1908. Fred and Ethel settled near K'gari's Central Station, and Fred was employed in the island's logging industry.

Research undertaken by Juliet O'Conor suggests that Ethel and Fred combined traditional Badtjala belief systems with a Western education for their children. She writes about the publication of the first book of Aboriginal legends by Wilf Reeves and Olga Miller, suggesting that:

> *The Legends of Moonie Jarl* is testimony to the priority
> placed on traditional beliefs within their family and
> especially the influence of their Indigenous father. All of
> Olga Miller's publications and much of her community
> and educational work emphasises that Badtjala land and
> culture were her priority. Ethel Reeves weathered church and

society's disapproval and pursued a life with clear-sighted acknowledgement of the rights of the individual, both Indigenous and non-Indigenous. Ethel's life with Frederick is remarkable for its time, a period of immense prejudice in Australia. Ethel lived to see two of her children publish a book about Badtjala traditions. Inherent in their publication is the continuing importance of those traditions and recognition that educating children is the way to change social perceptions.[44]

This ancestral "entwine" is testimony to the strength of this couple, a trait visible in succeeding generations. Perhaps this is also the origin of the strength of the belief in education. Fiona tells me, "Ethel was ostracised from her family and had to make it on her own. She must have been a pretty strong personality to have four children to a Badtjala man. She would have been talked about: gossiped and criticised by the white people on K'gari and Maryborough."[45]

From the twenty-first century it is impossible to comprehend the maelstrom of difficulty that their love caused. In a discussion of mixed marriages during colonial times, Katherine Ellinghaus concludes that in 1900 in Australia, "Marriages between middle-class white women and Aborigines were unthinkable. Aboriginal people were not just one of many undesirable marriage partners. They were at the bottom of the scale, the extreme by which other interracial marriages were measured."[46] She compares Ethel Gribble to American humanitarian Elaine Goodale Eastman (1863–1953), who was a writer, poet and teacher. Like Ethel, Goodale was teaching at a school on a Dakota reservation in 1886, where she met and went on to marry Dr Charles Eastman in 1891. Eastman was a Santee Sioux and the first Native

American to become a medical physician. They co-authored and published books and had six children. Ellinghaus's view is that Ethel's marriage, unlike that of other rare Australian cases of young and less-educated women who married Aboriginal men, presented a much greater threat to the status quo. She writes, "When a white woman involved in an interracial marriage could not be portrayed as an oddity, it became a matter of even greater concern to Australian society".[47]

After her marriage, Ethel wrote news of it to her employers at the Australian Board of Missions. Did she want to retain her position? Was she communicating to assert her independence from her brother Ernest Gribble? Or was it important to her that they knew of her happiness? Members of the Board were reportedly incredulous; by 1910 (three years after Ethel's marriage to Fred Wondunna) measures to ensure that female missionaries did not live alone had been implemented. In the view of Ellinghaus:

> It appears that white authorities did not take kindly to
> the idea that white women, who were placed in an official
> position of power over Aboriginal people, should in any way
> compromise their social distance from their charges. Their
> middle-class status made their interracial transgressions much
> harder to dismiss as eccentric.[48]

K'GARI, 2017

Central Station, where Fred and Ethel settled in 1908, is now a large camping area and information centre, shaded by tall trees, with open areas and picnic tables below a dense canopy. A boardwalk leads down to Woongoolba Creek, a stream that runs so clear that when you look into the creek bed the water is almost invisible above the sand. The deep rainforest is dark, humid and cool. "My great-grandmother Ethel used to come down here to set the jelly in the stream", Fiona tells me. The stumps of the Wondunna house remain nearby. Fiona's cousin Shantel Ah Kit remembers:

> Uncle Horrie took us to where the Wondunna house was, where it used to be. We found the stumps from the house. We also found Nanna's old bucket. He showed us where they used to tie the boats up. It's up one of those little creeks. That tree where they used to tie them up, it still had the ring in it as well. The hook where they used to tie up to. He also showed us where they'd hunt for mud crabs. Aunty Shirley ... told us that Nanna would wear long stockings every day. And it was really hot; you know, washing and stuff like that.[49]

Driving away from Central Station toward Eurong on the surf side of the island, we pass through the forest of ancient trees; huge, gnarled and knotted, their trunks overwritten with age and etched with Aboriginal histories. Fiona's large oil painting *Scar Tree* (2000) evokes the identification she has with this place. In this work, the bark is removed from the tree and remade as a shield, carved with lines that divide it into a geometric pattern. It floats above the shadow cast by the tree and speaks to the Badtjala people's symbiotic relationship with country, their culture as ancient and as enduring as their land.

Fred and Ethel had many years together, instilling culture and pride in their children. Yet something went awry. Fiona says, "Fred went to the Tweed River area, returning to the Bay later, knowing he was going to die. That's when Mum met him—when she was a teenager [1956]. Ethel died in Maryborough Hospital when I was one [1965]." A photograph of Fred at Kirra Beach (Gold Coast) in about 1934 records a display of artfully arranged bottles of coloured sand, wares which he sold to tourists. The sign propped up in front of him reads, "Wondunna The Australian Aborigine. SAND ARTIST At Work". His physique is stocky and muscular, his hair frizzy, cut short around the back and sides and crazily wiry on top of his head. Wearing jeans and a white singlet his dark skin gleams in the sun. An interview with Shirley Foley records his last days:

> I was a bit older. You see, Nanna and Grandfather had
> parted. While we knew we had a grandfather, Nanna
> never spoke much about him to us, not much at all about
> Grandfather Wondunna ... Next thing, Uncle Wilfie heard
> that Grandfather was sick; he might've been in the Salvation
> Army home down there in Brisbane. Nanna was living in
> Cypress Street, in a flat at Urangan. So Uncle Wilfie asked
> Nanna if he could bring Grandfather home. Nanna agreed,
> and brought Grandfather home to the flat at Cypress Street.
> She sent word up to us—we lived up at Crescent Street—
> "Ah, Come down, your grandfather has come home; he's
> sick." So we went down there; we were all very excited to
> see our grandfather. We had talked about him, we had heard
> stories about him. So we went down, the family went down.
> I went to see him with my sister who was two years older
> than me. When we got there Nanna introduced us to him.

Grandfather Wondunna was a full-blood but he was very short at the time when I saw him, probably with age. After we saw him at Cypress Street they put him in the hospital where he seemed to be in isolation. I don't know what he had, maybe chest problems, or some complaint. I used to go up and see him—till he passed away. And he always had a ten-shilling note in his sandshoe in the locker for me. He'd say— "You look in the locker, there's something in there for you, in my sandshoe." So every time I used to go down there I used to get ten shillings. And I used to think—"Oh, this is great. But you know, I was very proud of him, too."[50]

Fred passed away in 1956, aged sixty-nine. Ethel died aged eighty-six, nine years later, in 1965.

Fred and Ethel's first-born son Horace Wondunna (born 1908) married Aboriginal woman Alma Mitchell in 1932. Living in Urangan on Hervey Bay, their youngest child Shirley (Fiona's mother) was born in a humpy in 1938. Horace and Alma had four children: Shirley's older siblings were Noela, Horrie and Coyne. Her father Horace Wondunna was a logger on K'gari, working in the timber industry like his father Fred before him. By the time Shirley was born he had moved his family back to the mainland to become a professional fisherman. He died at sea in 1939 when Shirley was only a year old. Fiona's cousin Bronwyn DeSatge notes,

My grandfather was working toward paying off of his own fishing boat. He didn't have that much left to pay on it, before he got lost at sea. So, going back that far, he was probably doing something that was virtually unheard of then. He, as an Aboriginal man, in a short period of time, would have owned his own business. He would've had his own fishing boat.[51]

In an interview in 1993, Shirley recalled that they moved many times during her childhood. The first home she remembered was constructed on four acres in Pulgul Street: "Our humpy was made of tin and bark and we had a wood stove."[52] All water had to be carried from the school, after school was finished for the day, "to make sure no one see us".[53] Other homes were in Childers, yet another, shared with another family, she called "the dump-house".

> And I remember there was ... this paddock with the bulls in it, and we went in it one day and I was only young, my sister and I, and the Blake kids, and the next minute this bull started to chase us in the paddock. And there's a bit of a dip there, and my sister said to me—laid me under the dip and she laid on top of me and the bullocks went straight over us, like that, jumped straight over us. Oh, God, we were daring in those days. And then one of the boys, Benny Blake, found a bit of gelignite or something down the dump and he brought it home. We had an open fireplace and we had a kettle there. I just threw it in the fire, like, and the kettle went everywhere and the ashes went everywhere.[54]

In another interview, Shirley recalled:

Mum married again when I was about seven, or something like that. She married Fred Davis. They had no children, so it didn't complicate things, then. But in the war years, it was still very tight. Things were very hard to get, you know. And we had to move up to Childers, because the Army and that, along the coast.[55]

Moving back to Hervey Bay, she recalled school at Urangan fondly, noting that in this time "there was no prejudice".[56] Her mother Alma could afford to educate only one of her children. She chose Shirley's older sister Coyne, who became a nursing sister. Her son Russ said, "My Mum, Coyne, was probably one of the first registered Aboriginal nurses. She had registered herself as Reeves, she didn't register herself as Wondunna. I suppose that was understandable at the time."[57] Wilf too used Reeves (as did Ethel throughout her married life).

Shirley finished her formal schooling in grade six. She loved learning. She told Boscott during the recording of an oral history: "School was good, though, very good, you know. Played every sport, every sport you could think of."[58] Fiona does not know how her mother felt about the cessation of her schooling but said that Shirley was likely to have been accepting. "They all knew they were poor. Alma was a single mother with four kids." Rowan Foley was the Park Manager of Uluru-Kata Tjuta National Park and is currently the CEO of the Aboriginal Carbon Foundation (AbCF). He describes Shirley's motivation as "poverty". During a TEDx Talk about his work with the AbCF, he said, "The number of teeth you have is one measure of poverty. Both my parents grew up in poverty, but my mother grew up in extreme poverty living on a rubbish dump for four years as part of the 'dump-house mob' and leaving school after grade seven to become a domestic servant. By the age of sixteen she had lost all of her teeth."[59] He adds, "My motivation in creating carbon economies on Aboriginal lands is as a vehicle to overcome [this type of] poverty."[60]

Shirley's family maintained its independence and connections with culture, living in Badtjala country in Hervey Bay. They were, however, aware of their lands over the water on K'gari, and Shirley never lost her awareness or desire to rekindle the relationship with the island. In 1999 she remembered, "I didn't go to the island until I was twenty-one years of age. We never had transport or anything, before that … Nor did I go over there when 'Great' or Uncle Wilfie were alive. Uncle Wilfie used to go over though, because he could come up from Maryborough, being a man, come down on the Forestry boat."[61]

As a young woman, Shirley set off with her best friend. They travelled through Australia, spending most of their time in the north, looking for seasonal work, fruit-picking and whatever else they could get. They took on available jobs, moving to the next town when the work dried up. Her niece Rachel Killer remembers,

> Attitude, that's in the spirit of the Wondunnas. It's always
> been like that. Well, Aunty Shirley, she has always had high
> hopes of everyone. But so [had] Nanna. In their family, they
> were like that. Aunty Coyne, as well. They all had some sort
> of profession behind them. And they set good role models for
> us. In our family, the majority of us have always worked, and
> earned good wages.[62]

After meeting and marrying Barry Foley in Perth, Shirley had four children. Fiona, born 1964, was first, followed by Shawn (1965),

Mellissa (1966) and Rowan (1968). Shirley instilled a belief in education in each of her children. Shawn told me, "A university education was non-negotiable for us all. One of Shirley's mantras was, 'You can't fight the white man with a spear and boomerang: you need to use education'. This was at a time when people did not necessarily subscribe to the view that you had to get educated."[63]

Shirley always dreamt big. In her work for Australia Post in Sydney, she developed award-winning visual learning methods to train staff from different cultural backgrounds. When living in Mount Isa she often looked after a white baby, driven by her love of children and her independent spirit. Equally, children were drawn to her.[64] She had educated herself about Montessori methods, finding parallels in them with traditional Aboriginal teaching methods. In 1996 she completed a dictionary of Badtjala–English words, now lodged with the National Library of Australia and relaunched in Hervey Bay in 2018.

What became her life's work was securing access to land. Her ability to negotiate and deliver may have been inspired by her dreams for K'gari. Rowan remembers, "My mother was a community leader. Back in the day, she thought, 'I want to build a culture centre on K'gari, so who do I need to speak to?' She had brains and personality, not the formal education, but strategy and diplomacy. She was formidable, not daunted by being poor and black and female, coming from a long way back in the pack."[65] Her aunt and uncle, Olga Miller and Wilf Reeves, published *The Legends of Moonie Jarl* with Jacaranda Press in 1964, the first book of Aboriginal stories by Aboriginal authors published in Australia. A print run of five thousand was distributed in schools and bookshops. O'Conor noted the authors' confidence, attributing it to the fact that, "Reeves' and Miller's parents and grandparents expressed social convictions contrary to popular thought during their lifetimes".[66]

A photograph of Olga Miller and Wilf Reeves from around 1964 captures Olga's positivity and openness. She looks up at the photographer, chin lifted, high forehead, large eyes and curly hair bearing a strong resemblance to Fiona. Her dress is structured around a triangular yoke with a large feature button at the front. Below the belted waist, which emphasises a slim build, her long fingers hold a narrow, rectangular clutch. Wilf appears quiet, more guarded in his eye contact, and wears a suit with bow tie and badges on his lapels. His face is lined. In an interview, Shirley said:

> Uncle Wilfie was a very, very funny man, you know. I said to him once, because you don't ask him too many rude questions, you know, because you respected your elders, and I got a bit cheeky one day, and I said to him, "Uncle Wilfie," I said, "Why haven't you ever got married", because it was puzzling me, you know, and he turned around and he said to me, "Well, you show me the woman that can eat grass and I'll marry her". He was sort of like that sort of person, a dry wit. He was good but very introverted he was. You wouldn't know he was in the house.[67]

She also remembered his goodness, and the advice he offered. On another occasion, Shirley was complaining to Wilf about a boy she knew from school. She recalled:

"Gee that Georgie Barney makes me wild", I said to him one day. I said, "You say something to him and he thinks he knows everything". [Wilf] said, "Look, you find people like that". He said, "What you do is you just shut your mouth and don't say anything". He said, "Let them bust themselves telling you what you already know, because they think they're doing a good job, but you know different, so just keep your mouth shut and don't say a thing. They'll come undone themselves," he said. "That's all you've got to do, but you know differently", he said. I never forgot what he said.[68]

Shirley's vision of regaining access and custodianship of land on K'gari was shared with her family and community. Glen Miller, Fiona's cousin who was closer in age to Shirley than Fiona, said,

[We] had a big meeting out at Queensland University. Peter Lauer was the curator of the Anthropology Museum; he'd done a lot of work with [Olga Miller] on Fraser Island. He actually organised a meeting for all of us to get together to talk about a land claim on Fraser Island, back in 1980. We all just turned up, but Shirley had a plan—as she always does. To give the Badtjala people a base over there. I guess, ten out of ten for Shirley, all she's ever wanted was something on Fraser Island.[69]

Shirley managed this feat later, during the years of the conservative National Party government, in 1989, which makes her achievement all the more striking. She found a sympathetic ear in Maryborough-born

Lin Powell, despite his government's long-term political intransigence. Powell was a member of the National Party and represented the state seat of Isis (which included Hervey Bay and K'gari) from 1974–1989.

A Special Lease over a six-hectare site was made available (under the *Land Act*, 1962–1989), dated 15 March 1990. The Leasee is described as Thoorgine Educational and Culture Centre Aboriginal Corporation, and the term was twenty years from 1 January 1990.[70] Shirley established the Thoorgine Educational and Culture Centre in 1989, with plans to host bird-watchers, schools, architects and other students of culture on her country of K'gari. Fiona relates, "Her vision for the Badtjala people was to have a centre on the island that they could use for education, and to celebrate our culture. It was always about the next generation, and employment of Badtjala people, to elevate their economic destiny."[71] The cultural exchanges were interspersed over a number of years:

> The Maningrida women's weaving workshop saw Arnhem
> Land women teaching Badtjala women to weave for the first
> time. Following that, Badtjala men went to Maningrida.
> They lived on an outstation and stayed out bush with their
> host families. There were cultural exchanges where four
> Pitjantjatjara Elders from Uluru came to K'gari and saw salt
> water for the first time. They sang in their language—on our
> land. They painted and made boomerangs. They spoke of
> dreams that they had of our Old People. There was a weaving
> workshop that invited the Palawa women from Tasmania to
> spend time with our Badtjala women, finding new species of
> vines from the rainforest at Lake Allom. I remember making

a basket from hoya vine, and other Badtjala women used different plant species.

Shirley made these particular contacts through her children. Rowan was working as a ranger for the Mutitjulu community at Uluru and he travelled with two senior couples to K'gari from Uluru. Fiona remembers, "I introduced Mum to [curator] Diane Moon and Djon Mundine. Diane brought women from Maningrida [where she was working as art adviser] to K'gari. In 1996 when I undertook a residency in Tasmania, Shirley met the Palawa women who later travelled to K'gari for a cultural exchange and taught us to weave using their techniques."

/

Shirley's full life was cut short in July 2000. On a mild winter afternoon, she collapsed in her Hervey Bay garden, a beautiful and darkly greened environment under mature trees. Fiona was overseas, flying back from Japan where her work had been shown at the first Echigo-Tsumari Art Triennale in Niigata. Shirley required regular dialysis for kidney disease, but it was a heart attack that felled her. "The last thing she said to Dad was, 'I love that tree'. It was a cherry guava." Fiona said, "I rang from Japan the day before and she was in town with my cousin. So I spoke to Dad and then Sunday I started travelling back to Australia, arriving home in the early hours of Monday morning. She died on the Sunday afternoon, at about five. My cousin Narelle picked me up from the airport. I got to Dad's place and he came out to the front door. He was in tears." Even fifteen years later Fiona's emotion is evident: "My mother's loss was such a shock; she was the glue that kept us all together."

/

In August 2018 Fiona returned to live in Hervey Bay. This was a stressful move; with financial pressures and conflicting demands following the completion of her PhD. On 16 September, Fiona sent me a photograph of a roosting frogmouth in the rafters of the studio that sits amongst tall trees and back from the road on her half-acre block. "View from my studio today", she wrote. I knew she would find comfort in this beautiful bird inhabiting her shared environment; frogmouths remind her of her mother.

Fiona invoked her mother's memory on 24 October 2014 when the Badtjala people's Native Title Claim for K'gari was handed down. It had been an eighteen-year battle for acknowledgement of their custodianship, one that Shirley had begun, yet the rights that were so hard won on that occasion offered significantly less than the potential of the land that her mother had secured in 1986, that she envisaged as the Thoorgine Education and Cultural Centre. Again, in Hervey Bay on 9 November 2018, Fiona spoke at the launch of the reprinted *Badtjala–English/English–Badtjala Word List*.[72] In front of her Wondunna clan and supporters of the Wondunna Aboriginal Corporation, she made a heartfelt claim for acknowledgement of her mother's achievements. With her sister Mellissa Foley and her brother Shawn Wondunna-Foley in the crowd, she noted that Shirley Foley's legacy "carries on in her children—and in this publication. I am so very proud of my mother's research."

K'GARI, 2017

In May 2017 Fiona and I visit Thoorgine, renamed the Thoorgine Centre Eco-Camping Ground (on 17 July 1995), but colloquially known as "K'gari Camp". These days it is a rudimentary camping ground of unpowered tent sites surrounding a communal kitchen and toilet facilities. It is modest; a long way from the scope and ambition of Shirley's vision for this place. A few open-sided bush-pavilion buildings sit on the land, back behind the dunes on the surf side of the island, north of Happy Valley. Shirley's choice of this parcel of land was informed by her awareness of K'gari's hammering winds, and Thoorgine is beautifully located, sheltered from the shoreline on the ocean side. The architectural plans for this site dated 1993 include an art gallery, cultural education facility, administration buildings, camping areas, accommodation for a ranger and manager, and a cafe. These facilities have not been built. We do not spend very long at the site—Fiona is uncomfortable in this place of such high hopes, lost to the family in 1994.

Shirley chose her eldest son Shawn Wondunna-Foley to manage Thoorgine's development after the land was made available in 1986. The Thoorgine Educational and Cultural Centre Aboriginal Corporation was incorporated in 1986 under the *Aboriginal Councils and Associations Act, 1976*. Shawn resigned from his job in maritime electronics at CSIRO in Hobart to return home to Hervey Bay where he and Shirley worked together on the project. It was an amazing time. They published *The Badtjala People: A Cultural and Environmental Interpretation of Fraser Island* in 1994.[73] The acknowledgements in the book assert that the corporation is "Executively managed by the Badtjala people" with its purpose, "to fulfil educational, cultural, social and economic needs of the Badtjala people" and its mission: "To assist Australians to experience, appreciate and support Badtjala people's culture and relationships to traditional homelands through cross-cultural educational interpretive activities, programs and information packages."

Yet Thoorgine was lost to the Wondunna-Foley vision. Later in 1994, a coup for control of the site emerged from long-term generational clan conflicts. Rowan Foley, whose experience in Aboriginal communities is extensive, suggested, "When a community does not have community development and other professional skills to draw on, difficult situations can often simply be dismissed as 'politics'. It may be that the available tools were insufficient to work through points of conflict." He added, "In time the vision may be realised by the next generation".[74]

In Hervey Bay in 2017, I meet Shawn in the local Mary Ryan's coffee shop. His eyes are very blue against his fair skin and beige workwear; I'm not sure if I imagine an air of defeat. He remembered, "The Thoorgine journey itself was incredible … Nobody else has been able to achieve anything like that since. Our family has tended to be doers, if we say something then we commit to making it happen. The family bore the brunt of what happened and our relationships with each other suffered."[75] Rowan writes, "Thoorgine … consumed the whole family. It was just, like, absolutely everything was dedicated to this visionary project. It was a real attempt to bring the community together within the Bay. Through that organisation, we did encounter and overcame a lot of black and white political differences, but in the end it was perhaps too visionary and ahead of its time."[76]

During the years of Thoorgine, Fiona and her family transformed the land granted to them. Barry Foley recalled, "Where that land was, the lantana was twenty feet high, a mess! We cleaned all that up and put in the windmill, the underground water."[77] After its loss, Barry's disillusionment and despair was so great that he left Hervey Bay, moving to Tasmania where he spent a full year. Fiona told me, "To lose the project was momentous for both my parents. Shawn stayed away from the family for years. He can't see the enormity of what he did." At K'gari's Central Station, the educational display (dated 1996) describes Thoorgine as facing an "uncertain" future. Yet at Thoorgine itself, a brass plaque announces its "official opening" in 1995. The air of neglect is pervasive; if this is victory it feels Pyrrhic.

/

The Native Title Consent Determination granted to the Butchulla people on 24 October 2014 was also hard fought.[78] Native Title offers little tangible benefit to its community without significant management. Fiona moved from Brisbane to Hervey Bay in February 2015 to assist her community with its potential. While Native Title recognises Aboriginal rights and interests to land and waters according to their traditional law and customs as set out in Australian Law, the bundle of rights offered to claimants vary. Fiona was keen to assist with the necessary structures to deliver the best possible outcomes from the Butchulla Native Title claim. This move also gave her time to spend with Barry during these last years of his life in a place that will always be her home.

Ultimately, Fiona spent just over a year in Hervey Bay, finding herself restless. Brisbane was not a place to which she really wanted to return, and ultimately she chose Lismore, moving there in early 2016, influenced by a friendship with Aboriginal artist Karla Dickens. Perhaps there was too a familial echo in Lismore. Her great-grandfather Fred lived in the northern New South Wales city for fourteen years and made his living there working the deep-sea oyster beds on the nearby coast.

Lismore is in a beautiful part of New South Wales, located in Bundjalung country. It is a small city with a university, close to unspoiled beaches and Byron Bay. Fiona bought a three-level house surrounded by mature trees in Goonalabah. From the kitchen and living areas it looks west over Lismore, with vistas to the hills on the other side. Its steep and rocky site became a garden, with resident koalas, frog mouth birds and snakes. Lismore was the place where much of the study toward her doctorate took place, a retreat that allowed her to research, write, plan and make. Yet in 2018 Fiona moved again—this time from Lismore back to Hervey Bay. She describes as constant "the pull to Hervey Bay ... it's still my home". This relocation and the responsibilities that await, remind me of an intriguing experience that a colleague recalled years before in an email to Fiona:

> I had gone to Hervey Bay to open an exhibition and the
> woman running the gallery organised a dinner afterwards at a
> restaurant on that street that runs along the water. She invited
> you as a local artist she thought I should meet, but I already
> knew you a bit at that stage.
>
> Your mother had died some time before and you
> were talking about her and her activism. I asked you in a
> conversational way whether you were going to take over and
> become the senior woman. You gave a non-committal answer
> and at that moment I heard a voice, which I immediately
> knew was your mother, saying "not just yet". I was a bit
> spooked and did not know what to do. I did not feel
> confident to tell you at that stage.[79]

On her Lismore veranda, Fiona is framed by the tall, ghostly eucalypts that shrug their bark into the garden below. The rocky slope the house sits on leans in to embrace the building. A pond occupies the flat area below the house, and the top storey's deck extends into the tree tops, a vertiginous three stories. Dress Circle Lismore offers spectacular views over the township out to the mountains beyond—the sunset has been a daily ritual for Fiona since she moved here.

Shirley's death in 2000 pushed Fiona toward a realisation. "After the funeral and the scattering of the ashes on K'gari (with Dad, Rowan, Mellissa and [her nephew] Blayde), I was aware that there is no enduring residue of a human life after they die. But gardens can endure—putting plants into the earth, crafting, building and improving land may outlast our time in this place." In Lismore she transformed the exterior of her house in two years, moving away the rubbish, growing hardy bromeliads and Indigenous plants: bat flowers, two grevilleas, casuarinas, Fraser Island vines, passionfruit, staghorns, elkhorns, ornamental gingers, crow's nests, native frangipanis, native gardenias. She also planted two fig trees in the area's red volcanic soil, creating more vegetation to support the steeply sloping land, and to protect the koalas, snakes and frogmouth birds that regularly move through this territory.

Fiona's father Barry had died a month prior. His battle with cancer was short but intense. Fiona had spoken to him on New Year's Day, when he told her he was in hospital in Brisbane. "He was not well. But we had a chat." That day she had discovered dog food, laced with glass, just inside the fence which divides her property from the spare allotment next door. She believed that this bait had been intended for her German Shepherd, Pir'ri. Fiona told Barry about her call to the police, her suspicion about the culprit. He listened to her frustration with the limitations of the police processes. Two days later his wife Cleo phoned Fiona: he was not good. Barry could not speak when she arrived at the Brisbane hospital: "His face lit up but he couldn't say anything." This final struggle to breathe, the inexorable shutdown of his body, his pain, and the loss of his company, remains another sadness etched into Fiona's psyche. He passed away in the early hours of 7 January 2017.

Fiona and Barry were in touch regularly by the end of his life. "Any worries I had I could talk to him about; he always gave good advice. He believed in what I was saying. And I know he was proud of my achievements; but he didn't say so—in so many words." The echo of Barry's unselfconscious baritone, singing from an opera he had written inspired by the plants and animals of the place that became his home, feel like his love letter to K'gari and the Bay where he spent so much of his life. In my last conversation with Barry Foley while he was in Wesley Hospital, his dryness, and the flat delivery, utterly without pretension, reminded me of Fiona.

"Cleo told me that Dad said, 'Fiona had the most courage.'" Arriving home to Lismore after her father's funeral in Hervey Bay, Fiona found koalas and the frogmouths roosting in her trees. On this summer day they were surrounded by the swelling song of the cicadas. A card sent to Fiona to mark her twenty-first birthday (1985), included Barry's handwritten words:

> Here's to my Fiona Dove,
> who I know loves to Run
> with wind in her hair.
> Barefoot on golden sand
> with a fishing rod in her hand.[80]

Fiona's courage and determination were modelled by her Badtjala mother and the support of her father. With their passing, the responsibilities of leadership passed formally to Fiona; yet she had already stepped up.

JUNE 2018

It was a crisp winter afternoon with lowering light when Fiona arrived at my house outside Brisbane. She was on her way north, on one of many trips between Lismore and Hervey Bay over that period to facilitate her relocation. She drove her car in under the house and, after the engine stopped, she emerged from the driver's seat. I saw her first from the back. Her head was shorn of its lengthy curls to reveal a close cap of hair, a mixture of dark and white. As she unloaded an overnight bag from the heavily laden car she turned around to greet me. She said, "I got tired of dying my hair. I think it's time to embrace the salt and pepper." Looking at her face, framed by a clippered number four cut, it seemed that the time for her colleague's prophecy had arrived. Perhaps letting her hair grey was Fiona's outward embrace of the role of a senior woman.

//

Three Notes

1 Benjamin Genocchio and Djon Mundine, *Fiona Foley: Solitaire* (Annandale, NSW: Piper Press, 2001), 56.

2 Cited in ibid., 43.

3 Oguibe, "Medium and Memory in the Art of Fiona Foley", 52.

4 Save Fraser Island Dingoes Inc. "The Fraser Island Dingo", http://savefraserislanddingoes.com.

5 Deborah Bird Rose, "Dingo Kinship", *Wildlife Australia* 50, 2 (2013): 35.

6 Oguibe, "Medium and Memory in the Art of Fiona Foley", 52.

7 Bird Rose, "Dingo Kinship", 36.

8 Fiona Foley quoted by Mundine, "Seeing Black", 52.

9 Wondunna Aboriginal Corporation, "A History of the Wondunna Clan" (Hervey Bay: Wondunna Aboriginal Corporation, 2000). Unpublished.

10 Ibid., 62.

11 Thom Blake, *A Dumping Ground: A History of the Cherbourg Settlement* (St Lucia: UQP, 2001), 136–137.

12 Judi Wickes, "'Never Really Heard of It': The Certificate of Exemption and Lost Identity", *Indigenous Biography and Autobiography*, http://press-files. anu.edu.au/downloads/press/p119111/mobile/ch06.html.

13 "A History of the Wondunna Clan", 62.

14 Educational display, Central Station, Fraser Island, visited 9 May 2017.

15 I was unable to discuss this with Mellissa Foley.

16 Winter, "Against Their Will", 8.

17 Fiona Foley and Julie Ewington, *Fiona Foley: Pir'ri–Mangrove* (Brisbane: Queensland Art Gallery, 2001), 3.

18 Winter, "Against Their Will", 8.

19 Oguibe, "Medium and Memory in the Art of Fiona Foley", 51–52.

20 Fiona Foley, *Biting the Clouds*, 60.

21 Ibid., 64–65.

22 The Maryborough township was founded in 1847.

23 Among other seminal research, Aileen Moreton-Robinson's *The White Possessive: Property, Power and Indigenous Sovereignty* (Minneapolis: University of Minnesota Press, 2015) makes a compelling case for the way in which colonisation and white possession and its disregard of Indigenous sovereignty continues to impact and marginalise Australian Aboriginal people.

24 Fiona Foley, "Biting the Clouds", 86.

25 Reverend E. Fuller, "The Fraser Island Aboriginal Mission", *The Brisbane Courier*, 7 September 1872.

26 Winter "Against Their Will", 8.

27 Ibid., 10.

28 Shawn Foley, *The Badtjala People: A Cultural and Environmental Interpretation of Fraser Island, a Unique Land and Seascape to which We Belong* (Hervey Bay: Thoorgine Educational and Culture Centre Aboriginal Corporation Inc. 1994), 15.

29 Ibid., 16.

30 National Consitutional Convention, Uluru Statement from the Heart (Uluru, 2017).

31 Australian Government: Australian Law Reform Commission, "Recognition of Aboriginal Customary Laws", *ALRC Report* 31 (1986).

32 Germaine Greer, *On Rage* (Melbourne: Melbourne University Press, 2008).

33 Oodgeroo Noonuccal, "Son of Mine" (1990), accessed Australian Poetry Library.

34 Christine Halse, *A Terribly Wild Man* (Crows Nest, NSW: Allen & Unwin, 2002), 38.

35 Fiona Foley, "Biting the Clouds", 98.

36 Ibid., 58.

37 Ibid., 59.

38 Ibid., 82.

39 Ibid.

40 Ibid.

41 Ibid., 102.

42 Ibid., 82.

43 Ibid., 83.

44 Juliet O'Conor, "*The Legends of Moonie Jarl*: Our First Indigenous Children's Book", *The LaTrobe Journal* 79 (Autumn 2007): 80.

45 Fiona Foley, interview by the author, 14 and 15 August 2016.

46 Katherine Ellinghaus, *Taking Assimilation to Heart: Marriages of White Women and Indigenous Men in the United States and Australia, 1887–1937* (Lincoln: University of Nebraska Press, 2006), 149.

47 Ibid., 162.

48 Ibid., 165.

49 Shantel Ah Kit, "Mount Isa", in "A History of the Wondunna Clan" (Hervey Bay: Wondunna Aboriginal Corporation, 2000). Unpublished.

50 Shirley Foley, "Hervey Bay", in "A History of the Wondunna Clan", 48–49.

51 Bronwyn DeSatge, "Mount Isa", in "A History of the Wondunna Clan", 33.

52 Shirley Foley, oral history with Hilary Boscott, 1993. Unpublished.

53 Ibid.

54 Ibid., 4.

55 Foley, "Hervey Bay", in "A History of the Wondunna Clan", 52.

56 Shirley Foley, oral history with Hilary Boscott, 1993. Unpublished.

57 Russ Simkins, "Townsville", in "A History of the Wondunna Clan", 15.

58 Hilary Boscott assisted Shawn Wondunna-Foley with the preparation of *The Badtjala People: A Cultural and Environmental Interpretation of Fraser Island, a Unique Land and Seascape to which We Belong*. This included recording an oral history with Shirley Foley.

59 Rowan Foley, "How a Market for Ethical Carbon Revealed an Indigenous to Indigenous Model", TedX Talk (Brisbane, 18 December 2018).

60 Rowan Foley, interview by the author (telephone), 3 January 2019.

61 Shirley Foley, "Hervey Bay", in "A History of the Wondunna Clan", 53.

62 Rachel Killer, "Mount Isa", in "A History of the Wondunna Clan", 42.

63 Shawn Wondunna-Foley, interview by the author, 12 May 2017.

64 Fiona Foley, "Speech: Fraser Island".

65 Rowan Foley, interview by the author (telephone), 3 January 2019.

66 O'Conor, "The Legends of Moonie Jarl", 76.

67 Shirley Foley, oral history with Hilary Boscott, 1993. Unpublished.

68 Ibid., 1314.

69 Glen Miller, "Brisbane", in "A History of the Wondunna Clan", 27.

70 This lease was renewed for another thirty years in 2010.

71 Foley, "Speech: Fraser Island".

72 Wondunna Aboriginal Corporation, *Badtjala–English/English–Badtjala Word List*, 3rd ed. (Hervey Bay: Wondunna Aboriginal Corporation, [1996] 2018).

73 Foley, *The Badtjala People*.

74 Rowan Foley, email to the author, 14 January 2019.

75 Shawn Wondunna-Foley, interview by the author, 12 May 2017.

76 Rowan Foley, in "A History of the Wondunna Clan", 8.

77 Barry Foley, interview by the author, 19 January 2015.

78 Badtjala is also spelt Butchulla. The latter spelling is used in the Native Title Consent Determination. Fiona Foley and her family prefer Badtjala.

79 Email from a colleague to Fiona Foley, 17 September 2012. I have been unable to secure written permission to use this text from a private email to Fiona Foley. Without formal permission I have chosen not to use their name.

80 Fiona Foley archive.

FOUR

BECOMING

Across the sea from K'gari, Fiona spent her earliest years in Hervey Bay. As a five-year-old she remembers "sitting on the beach at Urangan looking across to K'gari and asking my grandmother why there weren't any *giviids* [Aboriginal people] living there. She didn't have a satisfactory answer and got a little bit gruff with me."

At home Fiona says they spoke "Badtjala in the family home with my extended family",[1] learning the traditional boundaries and geographical landmarks of Badtjala country—K'gari, Double Island Point, Tin Can Bay, Bauple Mountain and north to a point at the mouth of Burrum Heads. She pored over *The Legends of Moonie Jarl*, its stories handed to her great-uncle Wilf Reeves and great-aunt Olga Miller by their father Fred Wondunna, who imparted his knowledge and "correct behaviour".[2] Reeves tells us in the introductory pages that, "These are the stories that belong to all Australian children, for their own birds and animals are the subjects of legends which have been handed down since the First Time". His words explore the origins and importance of all living things, and the meaning attached to the natural rhythms of Badtjala places. They describe spirits good and bad, a Jun Jaree for everyone, to keep them from harm. The Jun Jaree is like "the fairies and pixies ... a good spirit which can belong to you alone".[3]

The book also shares behaviour protocols and knowledge of Badtjala places. "I knew it was rare—most Aboriginal people did not have stories published. I felt lucky, culturally enriched really, to have that object in our home and our stories of K'gari recorded."[4] Shirley Foley's 1996 dictionary of the Badtjala language was also an important precedent, that "allowed us to conceive of writing our own history".[5] In 1984, when Fiona was at art school, she found an answer of sorts to her five-year-old self, in C. D. Rowley's *The Destruction of Aboriginal Society* (1970) in which she found accounts of the "intentional" violence directed at Queensland Aboriginal populations for more than sixty years. The tragedy was massive, with many deaths, and the decimation of Badtjala populations.

/

When Fiona began her schooling, she found an excluding ethos:

> My earliest interactions with "outsiders" were when I
> attended the local primary school at Urangan, Hervey Bay
> where I intuitively sensed there was a point of difference.
> I found that difference coming from other school children
> and my classroom teacher, who I was fearful of. They were not
> *giviid* like me. I was made to feel different from a very early
> age in an environment that was not my home. As I found out,
> being from the Aboriginal race meant also being scrutinised

by others on a daily basis. As Frantz Fanon writes, "I was responsible not only for my body but also for my race and my ancestors".[6] This scrutiny seemed to penetrate all aspects of life. It was a much larger societal embrace that I could not articulate at the time.[7]

Always being the "new kid" can't have made it easier, as her family's many moves saw Fiona attend at least six primary schools. By the time she reached high school, her family were in Sydney. Living in the northern suburb of Hornsby, she was sent off to the local Asquith Girl's High, a public school with about one thousand students. Fiona said, "I was pretty middle of the row. My mother used to say I was a plodder; I would get there in the end. At some point I also realised that I was very determined. My mother insisted that we all did our Higher School Certificate. I passed psychology and I got an okay mark for art (for the practical side)." She gained entry to an art certificate course at East Sydney Technical College (now the National Art School). Her first year involved three hours of travel every day, from Hornsby to Randwick and back.

> I was still living with Mum and Dad. In the first year, I got three Cs and a B, and my mother said to me, "If you don't pick up your grades, you are going to be a primary school teacher". I thought, "No way José!" So I picked up my grades and, in second year, at East Sydney Tech, the course was run out of the old jail in Darlinghurst, up near Oxford Street. The trip was a bit less in distance. And it was a great environment: I had two really good lecturers, Bruce McCalmont in sculpture

and Geoff de Groen in drawing. I majored in printmaking and sculpture and then, when I finished my two-year certificate, I thought, "I'll do my BA". I applied for two schools and I got into both. I kicked off at Sydney College of the Arts. The first year was the foundation year and years two and three we could major. You only had to do one major, but I like to push the limits. I did a double major, once again, printmaking and sculpture. I thought, "I won't go into painting, because there are a lot of Aboriginal painters". I wanted to be a bit different.

Aboriginal protocol gives rights to particular stories to families, groups and lineages, a lesson Fiona internalised at art school. In 1983—during her second-year at East Sydney Technical College—"I was making an etching, and copied a drawing by another Aboriginal artist, a bark painter. I remember birds and water lilies. As I peeled back the paper of the etching plate I felt this falsehood."

She was aware of a difficulty: she wanted to represent her Aboriginal heritage visually but was without symbols. Given the disruption to Badtjala culture, traditional skills and iconography had been lost. Her parents told her: "You have to be true to your culture." And she had a realisation: "I started to understand that I have remnants of a traditional culture—some of which is in museum collections. That *was* my traditional culture and I could draw upon it. It felt like a huge jigsaw puzzle." And she found herself with company on this journey: "At that time, artists on the east coast were creating a new visual language. I became part of that."

Shirley discovered three shell necklaces from K'gari, held in the South Australian Museum. When Fiona visited the museum, she noted their beautiful shapes, one a moon crescent, the second squarish and the third elliptical. She interpreted them as *Pearl Shell Necklaces* (2000), a triptych on canvas in which the shiny opacity of the pearl shell is rendered over a golden background, contemporary paintings of exquisite traditional objects from her Badtjala heritage. "At a deeper level I understood I had to talk about my history. It was a lesson from my mother about cultural authenticity, being true to your culture, not feeling you have to copy another Aboriginal culture to represent yourself."

Amongst the lessons Fiona learnt from her family was activism. Rowan Foley suggests that the Wondunna mob "always seem to be a fairly cluey, switched on mob [with] a bit more of an understanding of society, perhaps more of a philosophical outlook … to retain our own integrity".[8] In 1985 the highly regarded, mostly biennial, survey exhibition *Australian Perspecta* opened at the Art Gallery of New South Wales. It did not include artists of Aboriginal or Torres Strait Islander descent, despite the intense and growing interest in artists such as Trevor Nicholls, Lin Onus, Banduk Marika, Turkey Tolson Tjupurrula and Johnny Warangula Tjupurrula, all of whom had been featured, with Fiona herself, in the *Koori Art '84* exhibition held the previous year at the nearby Artspace. Fiona, a first-year student at Sydney College of the Arts, acted on her own initiative: "One Sunday morning, before opening time, I took some blackened stick figures I was working on from my studio to the steps of the gallery. I had painted a large canvas like the Aboriginal flag." She set them up with the canvas "flag" spread out over the broad sandstone steps leading toward the gallery's classical facade (built 1896–1909), with five stick figures standing like sentinels in front of it. Behind, and to one side of the gallery's central Ionic columns, she placed a single white figure. "It was prior to the opening at 10 a.m., one Sunday morning. There weren't many people around," she recalled. "I took some photographs."

Taking on the hallowed architectural halls of the Art Gallery of New South Wales and the colonial outlook it represented would have daunted most people, particularly students. Her later art dealer, Brisbane-based Lance Blundell who showed her work in Brisbane at Savode Gallery, remembered the incident and its impact: "It drew attention to her personally and it did the broader movement great assistance."[9]

The same stick figures were used the following year in her sculpture *The Annihilation of the Blacks* (1986). Overall this sculpture is 207 cm tall and 267 cm wide. It features two forked sticks connected to each other with nine black figures, simply rendered, strung from the horizontal support between the sticks. The rope is secure around their necks. On the ground, a single white figure stands firm, its shadow long. This artwork was inspired by Fiona's knowledge of a massacre that occurred on the Susan River in Badtjala country, Hervey Bay. The incident was hushed up. This particular massacre (one of many in the area), followed the death of a number of white colonists during battles that waged following their arrival between 1840 and 1850. Badtjala and their Gubbi-Gubbi neighbours (further south) resisted the theft of their country. Shawn Foley writes that by 1850 Commandant Frederick Walker convened a Native Mounted Police Force: "By this time brutalities included open and indiscriminate massacres and an early form of chemical warfare in which flour was laced with arsenic."[10]

On this day, the fear must have risen like the heat from the iron-shod horses' hooves on grasses around the Susan River. I can only imagine the broken bodies, the blood and wounds, a crumpled child sliced by bayonet, the stench of acrid sweat, and the dismembering grief that followed. Winter writes, "In late 1857 vicious European attacks assisted by native troopers unleashed a wave of such relentless horror that the tribal peoples of the region could never again rise to defend themselves and their country. Mass murders, drownings and poisonings are well documented. Land seizures, massive clearances, urban, agricultural and pastoral developments had a devastating impact."[11]

In *The Annihilation of the Blacks* the loss of Fiona's Badtjala ancestors' grasp on their country fuels its starkly sketched emotional power and political message. It marks a consolidation of working with her own narratives, intuiting the oral history told to Fiona by her mother. Its achievement was recognised with its purchase by the National Museum of Australia while Fiona was still a student, one of their earliest acquisitions from an urban Aboriginal artist.

CITY & COUNTRY

Fiona first saw Aboriginal art curator Djon Mundine speak at Sydney University. He had curated what is now known as The Ramingining Collection for the Power Institute Gallery between 1981 and 1984. An exhibition was commissioned and shown in 1984 (subsequently acquired for the JW Power Collection). Fiona was a student and remembers that she was shy to introduce herself. Later they spoke on the telephone. He had seen Fiona's work at *Koori Art '84* at Sydney's Artspace. *Koori Art '84* was one of the earliest exhibitions to recognise urban Aboriginal artists, and featured artwork that was informed by a different aesthetic and stimulus to the acrylic paintings on canvas by artists from regional areas, which had become well known and widely exhibited in the 1980s. It was shown at Artspace, Sydney, 5–29 September 1984. The catalogue includes writing by sociologist Vivien Johnson and her (then) husband artist Tim Johnson.[12]

This exhibition is identified as the beginning of the urban-based Aboriginal art movement, with other artists whose work might (under different circumstances) have been considered for the 1985 *Perspecta* exhibition. Onus, Nicholls, and Marika were largely resident in regional areas, although their aesthetic was individual and diverged from the more collective-based desert painting style.[13] Fiona contributed two etchings, monoprints that she had made at Sydney College of the Arts. They depicted the gum leaves she had loved since childhood, and a lizard. Djon remembers liking her work and gave Fiona and her friend Michael Riley his address in the Northern Territory. He was working as art adviser at Milingimbi and then moved to Ramingining, between 1979 and 1995. Djon offered a point of entry to a traditional community.[14] Fiona imagined Ramingining as a place where she might experience culture and set about to find a way to embrace the opportunity, hoping to see how traditional Aboriginals lived and understand how it was to be whole.

/

In the 1980s Sydney had dynamism and political vibrancy. The national funding authority, the Australia Council for the Arts, was established in 1967 and given statutory authority in 1975. The first Indigenous Director of the Aboriginal Arts Board was Gary Foley (appointed 1983). Fiona had written to every art and craft centre in the Northern

Territory to secure places to visit and, in 1985, then a second-year art student, went to Foley's office to seek funds to assist a field trip to remote communities in the Northern Territory.

"I was a little intimidated by him, as he spoke to me while leaning back in his director's chair with his boots up on the table. Then he asked me, 'Are we related?' My comeback was 'maybe on the Irish side'. I didn't want to be like some little pushover." Weeks later she received a letter from the Aboriginal Arts Board, and was "surprised" to have received her first grant. Fiona had made previous applications without success.

She arrived in Ramingining on an oppressively humid day in 1985, "filled with romantic ideas about traditional Aboriginal culture". After a week on Bathurst Island, a place where the heat is ameliorated by a breeze from the sea, she felt discomforted even walking across the gravel airport strip under the baking sun to waiting cars. Djon did not immediately prove a kindred spirit. She remembered:

> He didn't meet me at the airport, so I got a lift in the back
> of a ute and travelled in the open air. I was dropped at the
> side of a dirt road. There was nothing: a huge Eucalyptus
> forest, straight trees, ironbarks, cycads and tall grass. It was
> December and the driver just pointed to a track through
> the bush. I could hear Tina Turner's "Nutbush City Limits"
> blaring. I walked through the bush to find his house, then
> the art and craft centre, a "donga". I could smell the Pandanus
> mats inside, piled high. And Djon's desk, piled with paper

just as high. My job, the first times I went up, was to file that paper, to deal with the mess on his desk, sort it into a functioning pile. By the end of my time there I had some order in it. When I came back, the following trip, Christmas 1986–1987, the pile was back, just as high!

While I was there we would go to outstations ... I got to meet the artists in their homelands, the women who were weaving, the artists' wives and children. It was still a polygamous society. David Malangi, whose art was on the one-dollar bill, had four wives, all sisters, and children from the various mothers. He lived on this huge billabong. I met Jimmy Wululu, another famous artist, and Paddy Dartingu. I saw Djon's special relationships with all of the artists. He worked every day for that community.

There was no TV in Ramingining, so we had radio or videos. I was in my early twenties and unsure of myself, and really shy around traditional Aboriginal people. I didn't know how to converse with people in these communities. At the same time, Djon was walking around with his dreadlocks, shirtless, in army pants or long shorts, and barefoot. He had a clapped-out four-wheel-drive vehicle that would sometimes work and sometimes not ... Yet his relationship with senior Aboriginal people was visible in the way he interacted with them. Paddy Dartingu was there; he wasn't painting much anymore, and had a handkerchief patch over one eye. He would come to Djon's house and Djon would shave him. There was an immense level of respect and trust between Djon and Paddy.

I also went to Milingimbi, an island off the mainland.
I remember a sacred site—a beautiful waterhole, quite large,
and tamarind trees around the edge. But the water was
completely polluted, full of shopping trolleys and 44-gallon
drums. I was devastated—and shocked—at the treatment of
this site of significance. That was a reality check. Before that
I had romantic notions of what traditional Aboriginal people
were like. This trip blew all of that out of the water. I had to
rethink what Aboriginal society was in remote communities:
they are no different to elsewhere. There are strong culture
leaders and then people affected by colonisation, similar to
my community back home. [15]

This was the first of the regular trips Fiona made to Arnhem Land
and Maningrida, also on the coast of the Northern Territory (where
arts adviser and curator Diane Moon was working), until 1993. She
travelled north the second time with Avril Quaill, whom she met at
Sydney College of the Arts.

The year 1988 was significant: it marked the bicentenary of the
"discovery" of Australia and arrival of the First Fleet on 26 January.
Fiona attended the historic demonstration in Sydney where forty
thousand people "black and white Australians together in harmony"[16]
became the largest march in Australia since the Vietnam moratorium.
She also attended protests in Brisbane at Expo 88, a march that ended in
Musgrave Park. Later that year she was invited to the Barunga Festival
in Katherine (Northern Territory),[17] where the Barunga Statement was
presented to Prime Minister Bob Hawke. This historic document called
for a treaty and Hawke's signature at the festival was only symbolic; the

statement was never presented to Parliament yet is on permanent display in Canberra. Yothu Yindi's global hit "Treaty" was inspired by this event.

Like others of her generation, Fiona's connections with traditional Aboriginal people were motivated, at least in part, by making sense of the loss of her own cultural heritage. At the heart of this drive is her mother's research into Badtjala culture. "Mum loved meeting traditional people and spending time with them. They would show her things that she didn't know about because that connection had gone for us. For her it was a way to understand how to collect Pandanus and make a dilly bag and much more."

/

In 1987 Fiona spent seven months living in Ramingining. It was a pretty lonely life: "I was printing T-shirts while I was there. It was supposed to offer work for the Community Development Employment Projects program, but no one came to work while I was there—for seven months! And Djon was away a lot." Then she was offered the first dog that was hers alone:

> The builder was going to shoot him if no one wanted him.
> "Ben" was a ten-year-old German Shepherd and he took a
> while to get used to me; he wasn't accustomed to a female.
> Ben and I would do a biggish walk around the whole
> township of Ramingining, on the dirt road each afternoon.
> While we were in Ramingining, one of the nurses was given
> magpie goose chicks from the nest, and she gave one to me.
> The chick would follow Ben everywhere, even for our walk
> around Ramingining. But the little chick was taken one day,

from a box outside the house in the sun. I came out and it
was gone. Must have been a snake or bird. When I left, Ben
came back to Hervey Bay with me.

It was at this time that Fiona realised her own symbols and an
individually driven mode of art-making: "My trips to Arnhem land made
me realise that I had to create things anew. In this place I found my voice.
Looking back, I had to do it that way. There were no people who had
gone before to bounce ideas off—we were the first out into the world. In
the beginning, we had no one, no female Aboriginal artists I could go to
in Sydney. The only people I had support from were my parents."

The example of her parents was both formative and influential.
Rowan suggested, "They charted their own course, and led by
example".[18] Shirley's quest for land on K'gari dominated family life and
in the book produced by Thoorgine Education and Cultural Centre in
1994, she writes,

> For too long people have abused our culture. They have raped
> our culture, and they've used it to their best advantage, so I
> think it's about time now that we turned the clock around
> saying, well, we're the Indigenous people; we'll tell our story
> the way it was told to us. You learn our culture from us, not
> from anyone [else].[19]

Avril Quaill is a Noonuccal woman who has worked as an artist,
curator and arts administrator. She was recently Creative Director
of the Quandamooka Festival and since 2019 has been Acting Head of
Aboriginal and Torres Strait Islander Engagement at the Queensland

Museum. In the 1980s she was a student at the Sydney College of the Arts (SCA), a year ahead of Fiona. She also recalls a dearth of guidance at art school: "I was a painting major and there was no Aboriginal art teacher—apart from Tim Johnson who was not Indigenous. I remember him showing us photographs from his last trip to Papunya! I really struggled to find iconography to use."[20] Despite the nascent explorations of their Aboriginal students, the SCA teaching staff were strongly resistant. Fiona recalls that work from her second exhibition *Urban Koories* (1986) at Willoughby Workshop Arts Centre was assessed harshly by SCA academics:

> SCA sculpture lecturers Tom Arthur, Nigel Helyer and Bronwyn Oliver didn't understand the context of Aboriginal society. They slammed me. I was devastated.
>
> My parents were really supportive and said, "Just keep going". The validation came when the National Museum of Australia wanted to buy *The Annihilation of the Blacks* in 1986. Then, at the end of my third year, in 1987, I installed work titled *Art Bites* for my graduation show at Pier 2/3 [at Sydney's Walsh Bay]. During the assessment they slammed me again, suggesting that what I was doing was, "a passing fad and will only last five years". I could hear the lapping of the waves under the pier. I had no voice to respond. I could feel tears welling up and all I could think to myself was, "don't let a tear drop". I turned up every day, Monday to Friday, nine to five. I was also the only student in my year who was doing a double major (in sculpture and printmaking—etching).

Fiona created *Men's Business* (1987) in response to viewing a boy's public ceremony at Ramingining. The three drawings that comprise the work map the dance ground over which the full moon rose in ochre colours. A serpentine line represented the dancers, a rectangular blanket covered the initiates, and two conical hats sprout feathers from the top. The ceremony went through the night. She remembers, "I was awake all night; it becomes like a dream state. You are sleeping in the open, watching the moon rise and the stars come out. And, in your ears, the boomerangs are clapping and singers singing. There are about twenty dancers. You sleep and wake, you become part of it. I was only asked to leave close to dawn."[21] This drawing, shown by Roslyn Oxley9 Gallery, Sydney, in Fiona's first solo exhibition in 1988, was acquired by the Art Gallery of New South Wales. After the earlier acquisition of her sculpture by the National Museum of Australia, it marked her as an artist of significant promise.

Fiona had seen the way in which art centres operated in the Northern Territory. She had observed the relationships that existed amongst the artists, their shared studios, the community they offered each other and the impact of a united front. The city-based exhibitions that Fiona participated in—*Koori Art '84* (Artspace) and *Urban Koories*—received a decidedly mixed reception. The work of city-based Aboriginal artists often did not have the romance, colour and movement of the better-known art from the desert. Its newness, innovative aesthetic and uncompromising political edge meant its reception often echoed the type of response that Fiona had experienced from her art school lecturers.

In 1986 she joined fellow artists Michael Riley, Euphemia Bostock, Fernanda Martens and Jeffrey Samuels (each of whom had been in both shows), to look for support on their way forward.

> We started to come together. Artists came from the College of Fine Arts, and Sydney College of the Arts. Michael Riley was pivotal. I remember the meeting at Fernanda's house where the phrase "to strike while the iron's hot" was used, and we went flicking through an Aboriginal dictionary. We four chose the name Boomalli—Fernanda, Jeffrey, Michael and me.
>
> We met at people's houses—at mine in Glebe or Fernanda's in Alexandria. There were only five or six of us at the beginning, and the last to join was Brenda Croft.

Boomalli means "to strike" or "make a mark" in at least three Aboriginal languages—Bundjalung, Gamilaraay and Wiradjuri.[22] Boomalli Aboriginal Artists Co-Operative included so many artists who have become influential, notably Tracey Moffatt and Fiona herself, but also Bronwyn Bancroft, Brenda Croft, Michael Riley, Arone Meeks, Euphemia Bostock and Avril Quaill.

They became a co-operative, developing a group environment in which young urban artists were able to muster support for a new style of Aboriginal art, present exhibitions, and broker a different genre into a marketplace more familiar with regional styles. Eric Michaels writes that, "During 1987, the Australian press reported frequently that Aboriginal art, especially Western Desert acrylic 'dot paintings', had become flavour of the month in New York, Paris, and Munich."[23] In 2000 Benjamin Genocchio suggested, "For many people, Aboriginal art still conjures up ideas of a craggy old Elder, somewhere in the interior sitting on the hot earth painting up a story—not a young, hip urban artist making videos, installation or even pastels."[24] In contrast, Fiona and her colleagues "had to sing into being a language from a disrupted history".[25]

Michael Riley found the first rental space for Boomalli and the Australia Council provided seed funding. The first opening was huge, attended by performer Lydia Miller, a Kuku Yalanji woman who later headed up the Aboriginal and Torres Strait Islander unit of the Australia Council, and Aboriginal activist Charles Perkins (1936–2000), who was at that time Permanent Secretary of the Department of Aboriginal Affairs. Michael Riley made a film, *Boomalli: Five Koorie Artists*, which recorded that first event, in which journalist John Newfong declares the group significant because "Aboriginal people have been defined by others for too long".

Fiona recalled, "We did it for and by ourselves". In a photograph of the founding members, Fiona is at the heart of the group, with Tracey Moffatt holding a bunch of flowers on her right, Brenda Croft is holding back Fiona's long curly hair while Euphemia Bostock, grinning excitedly, grasps the sleeve of Fiona's shirt. Michael Riley, tall, good looking, stands to her left, arms folded, while Avril Quaill peers around Tracey to engage with the camera from the back of the group. Avril remembered later that curator Diane Moon, then arts adviser in Maningrida, sent black cockatoo feathers to Fiona to celebrate the group's formation. Avril used the feathers as a symbol for signage and corporate identity during the first exhibition at Boomalli: "The ten feathers represented the number of artists in the collective."[26] Bernice Murphy noted that this group consolidated the understanding of what urban Aboriginality might look like, writing that, "Many urban artists brought a stringently critical view of Australian cultural history to their work. This may be traced in Fiona Foley's reworking of the motifs of colonial dispossession in her two-dimensional works and mixed-media installations."

It was a time of dynamic change. In an essay for *Michael Riley: Sights Unseen* at the National Gallery of Australia, Brenda Croft recalls,

> What a productive time the late 1980s were, particularly
> around the establishment of Boomalli: Fiona Foley was
> picked up by Roslyn Oxley9 Gallery; Bronwyn Bancroft had
> established a small fashion boutique, Designer Aboriginals,
> in Balmain; Tracey Moffatt's career rocketed skyward at a
> phenomenal rate shortly after Boomalli's first exhibition
> in late 1987; and other south-eastern artists such as Brent
> Beale, Gavvy/Kevin Duncan, Robert Campbell Jnr, David
> Fernando, and Sheryl Connors either joined or had their
> work exhibited at Boomalli. Concurrently, Indigenous visual
> and performing arts organisations were being established
> across Australia in Brisbane, Darwin, Perth and Melbourne.[27]

Boomalli celebrated its thirtieth anniversary in 2017. Its legacy is visible in the recognition for city-based artists who make work about their Aboriginality. In recent years other city-based collectives have emerged to support Aboriginal artists in urban areas, most notably ProppaNow (established in Brisbane in 2003). The influence of urban Aboriginal artists has also been extended by the establishment of specific courses such as Queensland College of Art's Bachelor of Contemporary Indigenous Art,[28] their prominence in notable prizes such as the

Telstra National Aboriginal and Torres Strait Islander Art Awards (NATSIAA) (since 1984),[29] and exhibitions such as the National Gallery of Australia's National Indigenous Art Triennial (since 2007).[30]

/

For an artist institutional acknowledgement is crucial. Having work acquired for major institutional collections or being included in significant survey exhibitions is noted by colleagues, art professionals and the market. Fiona's 1989 invitation to be part of the prestigious contemporary exhibition hosted by the Art Gallery of New South Wales titled *Australian Perspecta* followed the acquisition of her 1987 drawing by the host institution. Invited artists are often commissioned to create new work on such occasions, and Fiona's contribution to *Australian Perspecta* (1989) included *Aboriginals Excluded 1985 Perspecta vs Token Aboriginals Included 1989 Perspecta* (1989). These two tone works drew attention to her earlier protest about exclusion of Aboriginal artists in 1985, with twin paintings of a single silhouetted figure over this divided background. They meet like a horizon line that conceals the figure's groin area, with the second painting showing the figure's spread fingers also touching the point that the land meets the sky like a talisman, implying that the constraints on the limits of the artworld should be broader. Along the bottom of these drawings, photographs of her protest on the steps of the Art Gallery of New South Wales are collaged.

In 1990, Boomalli refused to participate in the Queensland Art Gallery's ground-breaking exhibition *Balance*, curated by Marlene Hall and non-Aboriginal curator, artist and dealer Michael Eather. *Balance* brought together black and white artists to examine "influence and appropriation, collaboration and theft, and the crossroads inherent between them". Eather's memory of this project was "walking through a lot of cultural landmines".[31] Yet Fiona's view was that *Balance* "seemed ... behind in terms of its paternalism toward Aboriginal artists and curators".[32]

> We were demanding shows be curated by Aboriginal people. Years later, Marcia Langton called us "young black fascists"[33] because we didn't go in that show. It has never been properly acknowledged that the generations of Aboriginal curators [visible in institutions now] had to be fought for. Those institutions didn't open their doors automatically.

This quest to be acknowledged was part of the stimulus for the formation of Boomalli in 1987. This required a level of demand for recognition of urban Aboriginal artists and forced confrontation with institutions and gatekeepers. Yet for Fiona, taking up the fight was integral to her method of operating, influenced by the depth of involvement in Aboriginal politics at her mother's knee:

> I don't see myself as courageous, but [to me] that is the normal thing that you do. You stand up for your beliefs. We formed Boomalli so that we weren't pushed around anymore. We wanted to be independent and curate and write and challenge institutions to show our work. We all had a bit of that chutzpah.

Boomalli brokered the introduction of Aboriginal curators into institutions to work with collections of Aboriginal and Torres Strait

Islander art. Having Aboriginal people involved in writing, curating and making space for Aboriginal art empowers Aboriginal people to manage their own material. Fiona was the first Aboriginal person interned as a curator in the 1990s at the Museum of Contemporary Arts. Boomalli was also central to placing Aboriginal curators at the Art Gallery of New South Wales.

Fiona's first project was a co-curated show with Djon Mundine. She remembers their second show, when they acquired funding, "$80,000—for a show to travel to the Havana Biennial". *Tyerabarrbowaryaou II* was curated for the 5th Havana Biennial following its predecessor titled *Tyerabarrbowaryaou* (the first exhibition of contemporary Aboriginal art) seen at the Museum of Contemporary Art, Sydney, 19 February to 17 April 1992. Given the struggle to achieve such milestones, Fiona believes that subsequent generations, younger Aboriginal artists, "have walked into this privilege without realising that it has been a challenge to get us in those institutions. And the level of curating today is a little disappointing. Boomalli was set up to be edgy and question the status quo. Now, most Aboriginal curators are stuck in a mindset and play it safe."

This may be because the activism that was part of the Boomalli journey is not necessarily part of the journey for younger generations. Avril Quaill recalls:

> We were not just at art school by day but also out and about
> at night, having discussions at the Toxteth Hotel in Glebe,
> going to rallies, etc. There were "Rock against Racism"
> concerts happening in Chippendale. The Warumpi Band
> arrived in Sydney and we put them up in our Glebe house.

> We were in Sydney, it was something new, it was Aboriginal,
> everyone came! People like Watters Gallery also came to look
> at our shows—there were only a handful of art galleries in
> Sydney, but their directors and staff all came—Roslyn Oxley,
> Garry Anderson, Utopia Art Gallery.[34]

Zoe Pollock writes:

> The expression of a modern, urban form of Indigenous art
> was central to the cooperative's aims and as a result much
> of the work produced there was political in its message.
> The 1988 *De Facto Apartheid* exhibition echoed the call of
> Indigenous academic and activist Marcia Langton's paper
> of the same name, for acknowledgement of Australia's black
> history. In 1989 *Taken Away* by Sally Morgan addressed the
> issues faced by the stolen generations.[35]

Tracey Moffatt was a member for only two weeks, although she remained
part of a social and collegiate network. Moffatt (born 1960) was the
Australian representative for the Venice Biennale in 2017. Thirty years
prior, in 1987, she had declared, "I'm Aboriginal but I'm an artist. I'm
an artist but I'm not an Aboriginal artist." Mundine suggests that this
means Moffatt was "in effect refusing to be stereotyped, pigeonholed,
and definitely never disrespected as a token".[36] Like Moffatt, Gordon
Bennett (1955–2014), another successful Aboriginal artist from this
time (who lived and worked in Brisbane), rejected the tag of "Aboriginal
artist". In contrast, Fiona identifies strongly and says that her mother
would be furious about any disassociation of her race, having raised all

four of her children to be proud. "I was born in Maryborough Hospital, raised on Country, had holidays on K'gari as a child for a month at a time. Aboriginal mothers are a force to be reckoned with."

Moffatt and Bennett had different experiences of Aboriginality to Fiona. Moffatt was the eldest of four children, fostered out and raised in a white suburban home in Brisbane. Bennett was, like many of his generation, unaware of his Aboriginal identity until he was in his early teens. Richard Bell writes that when Bennett found out "it triggered an identity crisis". His work is a strenuous reaction against the racism which he witnessed throughout his life, using art as "a tool to articulate the denial of his Aboriginal identity".[37]

For Fiona, Boomalli was a significant crucible, a launching point for her work, and a collegiate network that still, to some extent, exists around her. The unity of the initial group did not last long and by 1993 a changing dynamic made her uncomfortable. Ten founding artists had initially comprised the board.[38] Prior to Fiona's departure for a Boomalli exhibition in Budapest, Brenda Croft made significant changes. "She started putting her friends on the board (including her father). I had left as Boomalli curator and Hetti Perkins followed me into that role. At the same time, Boomalli moved into another premises, in Abercrombie Street. I wrote a three-page letter of resignation before leaving Sydney." The professional, personal and artistic associations—but also conflict— were powerful within the group. Boomalli was comprised of colleagues and friends who became rivals, and as individuals they were all political, strong-minded and opinionated. Fiona's relationship with Brenda Croft, which had been close since they were teenagers, was a casualty.

Their teenage exchange of girlish letters, which remain in Fiona's archive some thirty-five years later, is a poignant reminder that conflict may arise within professional rivalries. Within Fiona's generation of Aboriginal artists and curators, there are divisions of friendship, and many lines scored around allegiances, so many of which date back to Boomalli. Brenda Croft writes,

> Those of us who were fortunate enough to be a small part of these exciting times were unaware then that we were making history; we were just having fun and learning as much from being with each other as from any tertiary-accredited study. We were growing into our Aboriginal identity as well as our adulthood and we were lucky to be able to share this together.[39]

Bronwyn Bancroft, who was one of the founding members of Boomalli and recently organised the thirtieth anniversary of the Sydney gallery, also remembered:

> The disagreements and arguments about decisions re hierarchy at the time. It was hard to be a manager. The repository for how you employ people changed, all predicated by individuals. Then the accent of who was in shows and who wasn't was a fundamental philosophical difference. I walked away several times.[40]

Notable for Bancroft is Fiona's courage in continuing to speak out: "It is a lot to take on the establishment; they silence you by including you in the shows and that shuts you up or peeves you. Or they exclude you. With Fiona her dedication to political activism has permeated all her career. She wouldn't know how to be any different."[41] Rowan concurred: "She has always been outspoken."[42] Yet working as a curator, trying to make art as well, attending meetings and events, coupled with the busyness of a politically active life in inner Sydney, Fiona finally felt that "I could not do both successfully". She left Sydney to live in Hervey Bay in 1995, a place where she has lived, off and on, ever since.

HERVEY BAY, 1995

Fiona arrived with her career heading into the next phase. She had achieved a Bachelor of Visual Arts degree at Sydney College of the Arts (1986) and added a teaching degree with a Diploma of Education at University of Sydney (1987). The DipEd she had found tough going. She was encouraged by Fernanda Martens, who, according to Fiona, insisted she "keep at it—get your degree!" It had been a struggle to even gain entry to the course, with Fiona recalling, "Linda Burney helped me. She mounted a case as to why they should take me." At the heart of her difficulty, apart from the sheer pressure of work, the meetings and curatorial activity with Boomalli that coincided with the draining business of prac teaching, was "the doing of something that I wasn't passionate about". For Fiona, teaching was a fall-back position, "so that if I failed as an artist, I had something to go back to". So far, Fiona has not entered a school classroom since those prac teaching days. Yet she is driven to educate, her work the vehicle, albeit within galleries, museums and universities, and, increasingly, in the public sphere. Her first public art project at the Museum of Sydney, *Edge of the Trees* was delivered on the eve of her departure from Sydney, a collaboration with Janet Laurence.

Fiona's involvement with Boomalli Aboriginal Artists Co-Operative from 1987 gave her a leadership role amongst her generation. By 1988 she was offered representation by Roslyn Oxley9 Gallery, a coup for an artist straight out of art school. Oxley recalled that, before she started the gallery in 1982 "we went all over, took a year looking for people, and so then we started off with really young people, artists who hadn't shown in Sydney before, a whole new bunch of people. Our people."[43] Fiona recalls her cheekiness at their first meeting. "She asked me about some of my imagery, in particular the dugong bones. Roslyn asked, 'What's that?' I said, 'If you don't know, don't ask.'" Fiona's promise, however, was cemented with this level of commercial backing, together with the imprimatur of exhibitions like *Perspecta*. Fiona exhibited with Roslyn Oxley from 1988–2006—her 1988 exhibition sold out.

In 1991 an exhibition titled *By Land and Sea I Leave Ephemeral Spirit* was shown at Roslyn Oxley9 Gallery in Sydney. It was inspired by Michael Alexander's 1971 book *Mrs Fraser on the Fatal Shore* which featured a Sidney Nolan painting of Eliza Fraser (*Mrs Fraser*, 1947) on its cover. In this exhibition, she wrote the Badtjala position back into the K'gari narrative. Fiona's art had become a vehicle for her educative message and her curatorial experience had taught her to negotiate institutions, yet it was her Badtjala country that continued to nourish her progress and inspire her to new heights.

//

Four Notes

1 Fiona Foley, "Biting the Clouds: *The Aboriginals Protection and Restriction of the Sale of Opium Act,* 1897", Exegesis, Queensland College of Art, 2017.

2 Miller and Reeves, *The Legends of Moonie Jarl*, 4.

3 Ibid., 43.

4 Quoted in Louise Martin-Chew, "Fiona Foley Courage", ed. Redcliffe City Art Gallery (Redcliffe: Moreton Bay Regional Council, 2014).

5 Ibid.

6 Frantz Fanon, *The Wretched of the Earth* (New York, Grove Press, 1963), 14–15.

7 Fiona Foley, in *Defying Empire: 3rd National Indigenous Art Triennial* (Canberra: National Gallery of Australia, 2017), 57.

8 Rowan Foley, in "A History of the Wondunna Clan", 7.

9 Lance Blundell, interview by the author, 2017.

10 Wondunna-Foley, *The Badtjala People*, 15.

11 Winter, "Against Their Will": 9–10.

12 Vivien Johnson is an important early writer on Australian Indigenous art and Tim Johnson an early collaborator with Aboriginal artists. His practice explores spiritual connections between his own and other cultures.

13 Zoe Pollock, "Boomalli Aboriginal Artists' Cooperative", *Dictionary of Sydney* (2008), http://dictionaryofsydney.org/entry/boomalli_aboriginal_ artists_cooperative.

14 Fiona later spoke on the phone to Mundine to gather the information she required to write a letter to Ramingining to secure an access permit (and permission to visit) from the Northern Land Council.

15 Fiona Foley, interview by the author, 11 and 12 February 2016.

16 Melanie Pose, "Indigenous Protest, Australian Bicentenary, 1988", *Museum Victoria Collections*, https://collections.museumvictoria.com.au/ articles/2835.

17 In 1988 Fiona judged the weaving section of the Barunga Festival art competition with Hazel Hawke.

18 Rowan Foley, interview by the author (telephone), 3 January 2019.

19 Shirley Foley, "Living on the Island and in the Bay", in *The Badtjala People*, 19.

20 Avril Quaill, interview by the author, 2017.

21 Michael Riley and Paul Humfress. *Boomalli: Five Koorie Artists. Ethnographic Video Online, Volume 3* (Acton, ACT: National Film and Sound Archive of Australia, 1988).

22 Pollock, "Boomalli Aboriginal Artists' Cooperative".

23 Eric Michaels, *Bad Aboriginal Art: Tradition, Media, and Technological Horizons* (Minneapolis: University of Minnesota Press, 1994), 147.

24 Ben Genocchio, "Lick My Black Art", in *Fiona Foley: Invisible Voices* (Bundaberg: Bundaberg Arts Centre, 2000), 4–6.

25 Ibid., 12.

26 Avril Quaill, interview by the author, 31 May 2017.

27 Brenda L. Croft, "Up in the Sky, Behind the Clouds", in *Michael Riley: Sights Unseen* (Canberra: National Gallery of Australia, 2006).

28 QCA Bachelor of Contemporary Indigenous Art alumni include Gordon Bennett (1955–2014), Gordon Hookey (born 1961), Dale Harding (born 1982), Robert Andrew (born 1965), Vernon Ah Kee (born 1967), Tony Albert (born 1981), Bianca Beetson (born 1973), Ryan Presley (born 1987), Carol McGregor (born 1961). Fiona Foley was awarded her doctorate by QCA in 2018.

29 The Telstra National Aboriginal and Torres Strait Islander Art Awards were established in 1984. Notable urban Indigenous artists who participated in the first award included Fiona Foley, Lin Onus, Arone Raymond Meeks and Jeffrey Samuels. Winners include Lin Onus who received the 1988 Museums & Art Galleries Award, Julie Dowling won the 2000 Telstra General Painting Award, Richard Bell won the 2003 Telstra First Prize, Danie Mellor the 2009 Telstra Award, Judy Watson the 2006 Telstra Works on Paper Award, and Tony Alberts the 2014 Telstra Award.

30 *Defying Empire: 3rd National Indigenous Art Triennial* (NGA, 2017) responded to the 50th anniversary of the 1967 Referendum which recognised Aboriginal and Torres Strait Islander people as citizens of Australia. At least 75 per cent of this exhibition were urban Aboriginal artists. Amongst these were Tony Albert, Brook Andrew, Daniel Boyd, Megan Cope, Karla Dickens, Blak Douglas, Fiona Foley, Julie Gough, Dale Harding, Jonathan Jones, Archie Moore, Reko Rennie, Yvonnie Scarce, Judy Watson and Jason Wing.

31 Louise Martin-Chew, "Integrating Culture and Community: Global Arts Link (Ipswich) and FireWorks Gallery (Brisbane)", *Art and Australia* 37, 3 (2000): 424.

32 Fiona Foley, "Just Little Bits of History Re-Repeating", in *Volume One: MCA Collection* (Sydney: Museum of Contemporary Art, 2012), 29.

33 Marcia Langton used this term in conversation with Fiona Foley when Fiona was employed as a curator at the Museum of Contemporary Art, Sydney (1991–1994).

34 Avril Quaill, interview by the author, 31 May 2017.

35 Pollock, "Boomalli Aboriginal Artists' Cooperative".

36 Djon Mundine, "In Praise of Shadows and Otherness", in *Tracey Moffatt My Horizon*, ed. Natalie King (Surry Hills: Australia Council for the Arts, 2017), 20.

37 Richard Bell, "Gordon Bennett: Richard Bell's Tribute to the Passing of an Australian Art Great", *The Guardian*, 14 June 2014.

38 Bronwyn Bancroft, Euphemia Bostock, Brenda L. Croft, Fiona Foley, Fernanda Martens, Arone Raymond Meeks, Tracey Moffatt, Avril Quaill, Michael Riley and Jeffrey Samuels.

39 Croft, "Up in the Sky, Behind the Clouds".

40 Bronwyn Bancroft, interview by the author, 23 March 2017.

41 Ibid.

42 Rowan Foley, interview by the author (telephone), 3 January 2019.

43 Quoted in Michael Hutak, "On the Couch: Roslyn Oxley", *Art Collector*, April–June 2017.

FIVE

EMBODIED

T'our bodies turn we then,

That so,

Weak men on love reveal'd may look;

Love's mysteries in souls do grow,

But yet the body is his book.

John Donne[1]

HERVEY BAY, NOVEMBER 2018

We walk down the stairs onto the beach, the timber rail flaking its white paint in curls, reflecting the tops of the waves. The beach slopes steeply toward the water but the wind is muted, sheltered by the groyne. In front of us, a fisherwoman's line extends slackly into the sea, and we walk up a little way, sinking in sluggish sand. Large yellow grains of granite move lazy around our feet. A bank sits proud of tiny waves that flurry onto the shore, and we place our towels, then clothes, up out of the way of the water. I stand for a minute, looking out at the flat horizon, the sea which extends into infinity. Fiona stands, thigh deep, a few metres from the shore. "It's cold!" she says. I follow her out, and it is, but when she dives under the water's surface, I do too. The sea is beautifully clear and calm over the sandy bottom. I float—immersed in blue. After a few minutes I head back to the beach, wrap myself in a towel and sit on the bank. Fiona is still swimming, cavorting like a dolphin, her small round frame bobbing up and down, diving and resurfacing. In her pleasure I see the child that she was, the weeks every year on K'gari, in a time when the ocean functioned as both a place for fun and as a refrigerator. These memories are encapsulated in her skin, her muscles, her lungs and her antics celebrate and enact them anew.

SYDNEY, 1994

Fiona put her body and herself into the (photographic) frame early in her career. She has used it to render history personal by echoing the archival evidence of her ancestry. Her physical courage in *Badtjala Woman* (1994) evokes my memory of our immersion into the cool water of Lake McKenzie, the warm calm of Hervey Bay, and the rougher ocean beaches near Lismore. In revealing her body, Fiona celebrates her power, family and ancestors, and connections to country. In the early 1980s Fiona found an image of a young Badtjala woman dated c. 1899 in the archives of the State Library of Queensland captioned, "Aborigine, Fraser Island". She was aware that this young woman was photographed without the dignity or recognition of a name, tagged simply "Badtjala Woman". Language is a cultural artefact; naming a political act that identifies individuals within their cultural group. Fiona wondered about this Badtjala woman's life and reality, the circumstances that might have led her to pose for the photographer. It stimulated a protective desire on behalf of her ancestor, to give her character as a woman beyond an anonym. "She had a name, and a birth year, and a role in society. She had a day that she died. There was no information at all with the photograph. She deserved more. I thought, 'I could recreate that image. I'd have to reveal myself, to do it bare-breasted'."

In another image from this series (collectively titled *Native Blood*), Foley's eyes meet those of the viewer, her gaze steady and measured. Long curly hair shrouds her shoulders, necklaces made of reeds and shells rest between her exposed breasts, and she wears a grass skirt that gathers softly around her waist. Her feet are encased in twenty-first century black platform sandals and her eye contact with the viewer is direct, confident, bold. In its insouciance it reminds me of the Édouard Manet *Olympia* (1865), the painting that scandalised society less for its portrayal of nudity or a courtesan than for the young woman's direct gaze at the viewer. Yet in *Native Blood* Fiona is both Manet's Olympia and the black servant carrying flowers to her mistress. To reveal your body, to offer it up to the record permanently, even in visual art, a realm that David Marr suggests is a rare territory "where nakedness can be celebrated in public",[2] requires courage. In this image Fiona becomes a silent witness, her presence absorbing the situation and setting as if to imprint the history anew, her courage matching that of her Badtjala ancestor. When the series was shown in *Australian Perspecta* at the Art Gallery of New South Wales (1995), Fiona recalled,

> My mum came to the opening. Tracey Moffatt was there, looking stunning in a Chinese cheongsam. Michael Riley

and my friend David Prosser were there too. Mum walked past my photographs to be with them—she got on really well with my friends—but she said to me when she was going past, "I didn't bring you up to be like that!" I think secretly she liked the images, but she had a prudish morality. She was half-stirring, and half laughing.

These photographs were released in an unlimited edition. In them, Fiona changes her stance, at times looking out to meet the gaze of the viewer. Her aura is dramatically different to the original "Badtjala Woman": she is named as the artist and subject, proud, empowered. Her motivation was potent:

> I knew first-hand about the deep held fears and hatred held towards Aboriginal people. In our generation, why be silent? We've been allowed to have a voice. In my mother's generation, they didn't have that. They lived with the possibility of being removed—Palm Island was a real threat.

Palm Island in north Queensland is also known by an Aboriginal name, Bwgcolman. A tropical island with significant natural assets, it was used during the nineteenth century as a place to relocate Aboriginals deemed disruptive or guilty of simply having Aboriginal and non-Aboriginal heritage. It has ongoing social issues; notorious as the site of the tragic 2004 death in custody of Mulrunji (Cameron Doomadgee) at the hands of local policeman Chris Hurley.

In this way, using photography and her body, Fiona has explored two hundred and thirty years of violence directed at Aboriginal people, and particularly against Aboriginal women. Since its beginnings, she has scored into her practice the continuing repercussions of this violence, making her body the site, the vessel of these cicatrices. The body of Fiona's practice draws together the ongoing dysfunction that spins outward from the way Aboriginal people were evicted from their land and their traditional ways of life, noting not only the downward spiral, but the lack of acknowledgement that continues to chafe at the open wound of colonisation.

HERVEY BAY, 1995

Back in Hervey Bay, Fiona was looking around the world at the work of other female artists. She remembers, "Ana Mendieta, the Cuban artist, had developed new ways to represent the feminine. There are universal ways of depicting female genitalia. Many things over the years fed into that, including seeing rock engravings at Carnarvon Gorge. Perhaps there is a type of understanding that is innate." Fiona developed a new series of textile artworks called *Black Velvet*. They are confronting, the gentleness of the *Badtjala Woman* banished. Michael Riley's 1987 film footage taken earlier on K'gari records Fiona building a sand sculpture on a sand blow high up behind the beach. The inner section of this sculpture, coloured with red sand and the same elliptical shape as she later used in *Black Velvet* (1996), sits inside a protective outer rim. She says, "Aboriginal stories often have an inner and an outer story ... The inner story is like a woman's fertility." Her *Black Velvet* textiles possess an edge in their depiction, yet the shape used echoes that moment on the beach from some nine years before.

Fiona stitched a series of nine cotton dilly bags with a stylised red and black vulva shape. They are a receptacle, a carrier, vessels titled for a euphemism. Aboriginal women were referred to as "black velvet" by the invading white men who did not resist their sexual attraction to the women. Sandra Phillips writes, "Men on the frontier sought to control Aboriginal lands as well as women's bodies—with or without consent".[3] Fiona decided that this shape "was how I would represent the feminine". First shown at Savode Gallery in 1997, the *Black Velvet* dilly bags were acquired by the Queensland Art Gallery in 2001. Andrew Baker said that these works are like a "steel fist inside a velvet glove. Appliquéd dilly bags, they are beautiful to look at, yet chillingly realistic in their portrayal of what happened to Aboriginal women."[4]

/

In Riley's film, *Boomalli: Five Koorie Artists* (1987) Fiona defines herself "first as an Aboriginal, secondly a woman, and thirdly an artist. My priority is my Aboriginality." As the *Badtjala Woman* images make clear, she is protective of those from the past who could not defend themselves. In her own life, her art and its ability to educate has remained front and centre. Now in her fifties, she increasingly steps into her community.

/

The most enduring relationship of Fiona's adult life has been a friendship. She met curator Djon Mundine in 1984. Their shared history and understanding is tangible, as is their mutual respect. On 14 August 2018, Fiona was invited to address the National Association of the Visual Arts *Future/Forward18* symposium on the topic,

"Working the Public Space", in conversation with long-term colleague Nick Mitzevich, recently appointed Director of the National Gallery of Australia. Djon caught the train from Sydney to hear Fiona speak. Her presentation was powerful, her commentary about the deterioration of the art market, and her candid remarks about diminishing opportunities for artists along with slower commissions for public sculpture, flavoured so much of what came after at this event. At Canberra's Polish Club that night, Djon and Fiona entertained curator Virginia Rigney and me with stories of Aboriginal art, artists, places and exhibitions. I had a real sense in their presence of the dynamic nature of Aboriginal history that is unfolding in the art of our times.

At the forum the next day, Fiona told me that she and Djon speak on the phone almost every day and have done so for much of their three decade-long friendship. "Djon says that he has spent more time talking to me over the years than he has spent talking to partners, family, other friends. Sometimes we don't speak for long—but there is always something to say." Their connection within a highly factionalised Aboriginal art world may be, at least partly, the glue, as is shared humour and ethics. Djon told me, "Aboriginal people get tired of how many times you can point at the obvious. Niceties should give way to manners. Aboriginal artists should be in shows; but nothing is changing, no matter what people say." On any measure theirs is an extraordinary friendship, important to them both. He describes it as, "a real relationship, a sounding board; we can be critical of each other". Their support for each other, he told me, is "solid".[5]

Other friendships have sustained Fiona over the years. When she returned to Sydney from one of many trips to Ramingining (1985–1989, 1993) she moved into a house in Glebe:

I started socialising with other artists. By 1987 I was finishing my Diploma of Education at Sydney University. I was hanging out a lot with Michael Riley. We were both single—mates. He had other women friends that he was mates with too. He was an interesting character. I was living by myself and he would come over and crash the night. He had an itinerant lifestyle in the city and he had these female friends, Aboriginal woman like Linda Burney, and Raelene Delaney (she has passed away now). He would rotate from house to house, staying one or two nights at your place then going to the next one. He was so familiar; he would come in, open your fridge, go through what was there and then pick up your phone and start ringing people. He did that with all of us.

Michael Riley made photographic portraits of his inner circle, including an image of Fiona. Some of these have been exhibited as *Portraits by a Window* (1990). In his image of Fiona, his characteristically dark background and low light highlights her dark eyes and high forehead, and it conjures the comfort of their relaxed friendship. About the series, he said, "It's a collection of portraits of young Aboriginal people who were striving to do things in their own fields differently. I suppose you could call them 'movers and shakers'—people who get out and do things, want to change things, change themselves, want to move on, sort of break away from the stereotype."[6]

In 1993 Fiona met Nigerian-born art historian Olu Oguibe in London. Her work was in the *Aratjara: Art of the First Australians* exhibition at the Hayward Gallery. Visiting the *Third Text* office,

Olu was there: "Immediately there was this synergy between us." He visited Fiona in Sydney twice; she took him to Hervey Bay and K'gari. They had a joint exhibition at Roslyn Oxley9 Gallery in Sydney in 1994. Their long-distance relationship ended, but Oguibe's writing about her work is reflective and insightful. When a review of her work in the *Myall Creek and Beyond* exhibition (2018) quoted his words, she said, "It gave me a jolt. I'd forgotten how well he understood."

BRISBANE, 2002

Brisbane was Fiona's home for twelve years. She moved from Hervey Bay in 2002 to a townhouse near the Brisbane River in New Farm. This inner-city location offered her close enough access to Hervey Bay with the cultural life of a capital city. Yet this period, in which her promise was consolidated and major opportunities came her way, delivered both pain and heartache.

In 2003 she delivered the powerful *Red Ochre Me* within the Queensland College of Art Gallery. A major work within this exhibition, *Stud Gins* (2003) reclaimed the language of the frontier. Fiona screenprinted the terms used to describe Aboriginal women and girls onto old woollen blankets which were hung on the walls. Words were drawn from Christine Halse's book narrating the history of missionary Ernest Gribble:[7]

> The women were the most vulnerable. For colonists reared
> in repression and restraint, the luminous, black nakedness
> of Aboriginal women was tantalisingly bewitching, and
> their flagrant ignorance of British prudery was a potent

aphrodisiac. They were known as "black velvet" and "stud-gins". In a world where the physical gratification and restraining influence of white women was in short supply, Aboriginal women were coveted sexual spoils of conquest.[8]

The trajectory of the words on the seven blankets—"Aboriginal, Women, Property, Defiled, Ravished, Shared, Discarded"—are confronting. Now in Canberra, they are displayed in the contemporary Aboriginal galleries at the National Gallery of Australia (2017), their prosaic greyness and scratchy wool medium juxtaposed with the vibrant painterly celebration of Sally Gabori's *Outside Dibirdibi* (2008). They hang opposite Vernon Ah Kee's *If I was White* (2002) which confronts the disparity in the life outcomes of Aboriginal and non-Aboriginal Australians.

These Aboriginal galleries evoke the power of a living history. So many of the influential image-makers are artists from Fiona's generation, with a new generation who have followed their lead. Judy Watson's paintings are unframed, and canvases move like the water that flows through her Waanyi country as viewers pass. Tony Albert's capture of the kitsch and racist Aboriginalia which he has collected since a boy becomes something other in his *Brothers (Unalienable)* (2015). Its decorative collage and paint prettify an Aboriginal figure with a target on his head and chest, identifying young Aboriginal men as easy marks in the eyes of authority figures. Richard Bell's *Psalm Singing* (2007) has a vibrant surface with optically confusing changes of style. The words on the painting are almost illegible: "I live in the valley of the shadow of death." The text evokes the harsh reality of the Indigenous mortality statistics expressed so succinctly in Ah Kee's *If I was White*.

Fiona's *Stud Gins* is stark, even in this context, without the reassuring succour of beauty or the seduction of visible hand-crafting. The words, printed in a sans-serif typeface on government-issue blankets, scarify. Anna Haebich describes them as "a terrible, composite narrative of the life trajectories of many women".[9] When these blankets were first shown, as part of *Red Ochre Me* (2003), they were juxtaposed with *Anal Tantric Sex* (2003), photographs of naked male buttocks with cheeks spread to the camera, and an installation called *Sacred Cunt Juice* (2003) which was evocatively raw and arguably, even more confronting.

This exhibition was a distillation of focussed research over the exploitation of Aboriginal spirituality. Fiona read an exposé written by journalist John van Tiggelen about a course of "Advanced Shamanic Training" in remote central Australia. At the end of his ten days, he claimed to have been initiated into the Wanampi Dreaming of Uluru. Van Tiggelen described "an invented jumble of anthropology, Carlos Castinados without the drugs, appropriated spiritual techniques and group therapy".[10] For this he paid $2,000 to a facilitating "shaman". To Fiona, this uninvited invasion of Aboriginal women's places, ritual and ceremony, demanded a response. The artworks she made as *Anal Tantric Sex* and *Sacred Cunt Juice* (bottles of red liquid containing ochre, sealed, on rows of small vulva-shaped shelves under low light), pilloried this exploitation. Each of these works deal with the subject of sexual exploitation of Aboriginal women by men, and her *Why Do They Hate Us* (2005) seems the saddest epitaph. Written in silver letters on a black background (like a tombstone), these words are arranged in a cross shape, a symbol of the Christianity that was central to the mission system which decimated Aboriginal familial and marriage systems.

Sitting amongst the other works were a series of *Bone Boxes*, made from timber to replicate the stacked cardboard boxes in which the Queensland Museum had returned Badtjala skeletal remains to the Badtjala people some years before. The small box on top echoed the smallest box; it had contained a skull. Fiona and her mother were involved in the repatriation. They collected the boxes from the airport in Hervey Bay and she remembers, "We handled the bones; the skulls had all their teeth. They were perfect—with no cavities. The next day we wrapped all of the remains in tea tree bark and transported them to K'gari. Mum had selected the location for their burial and the Queensland Parks and Wildlife Service dug the graves for their return. Each clan played a role. We all joined in singing 'K'gari gin'di yin'na mi' into the ground."[11]

The reception to the work of *Red Ochre Me* was quiet, and the story of the *Bone Boxes* received little attention in the context of the other works. This remains a source of disappointment. Fiona remembered,

> Matt Foley [then Arts Minister] opened the exhibition.
> It was packed—there were about four hundred people there.
> I anticipated that it would be a trigger for discussion but it
> elicited the opposite response. I learnt many lessons about
> Queensland that year.
>
> I was shown a wall of passive resistance. I had been made
> Adjunct Professor at Queensland College of Art that same
> night. No one would talk to me about the work, apart from
> [QCA lecturer] Russell Craig and QCA Gallery Director
> Simon Wright. Simon commissioned and paid for Anna
> Haebich to write about that show. Before that exhibition in

2003 I was a celebrated artist and after that no one wanted to talk to me. My life became very quiet in Brisbane.

For an artist, the public exhibition of a body of focussed research, distilled as sculpture, artwork and installation, provides a public testing ground of their ideas and their visual expression. For a body of work as confrontational as *Red Ochre Me* to emerge into a void, to elicit very little response and a dearth of discussion left Fiona feeling isolated, particularly when its subject matter, while undeniably difficult to confront, unearthed important issues. It is possible that at least some of her audience felt shame and disquiet, but were unable to address their feelings directly at this time. What is evident is that, in *Red Ochre Me*, Fiona noted the new-age movement seeking out and cheapening Aboriginal spirituality, another form of colonisation. The conceptual and aesthetic strength of what she produced endures, even if it was little discussed at the time.

/

Fiona's most significant studio art of recent years is in the medium of photography. She has used it to engage with cultural stereotypes within her practice. This has become a defining element of her oeuvre. Having Aboriginal people behind the camera facilitates a self-made definition of their own image and identity: "Firstly replacing the documenter, then creatively reinterpreting their photographic history."[12]

By stepping into her body, she creates work that elicits emotion. In this mode, Foley is empathising and identifying with others in a way that extends her identity into a broader, internationally political realm. In these exotic places she may try on another persona to take the temperature of the experience of other Indigenous peoples. Often her work allows an exploration of fixed expectations, an escape from the racist treatment that has impacted her since her earliest school years. One of her most successful series, now in a handful of institutional collections, is *HHH (Hedonistic Honky Haters)* (2006). This work was photographed during a residency in New York. It sees a group of black Americans (plus Fiona) assembled in patterned hoods made from fabric prints which use the traditional African Dutch wax technique. This hooded group offers a reversal of the well-known KKK who espouse white supremacy. It was shown at each of her representative Australian commercial galleries and also in London, where its global message was easily translated. Linda Carroli wrote:

> Foley is throwing down a gauntlet, endeavouring to stop
> meaning inscription in its tracks through a challenge to its
> own sense of virtue. Certainly, it is possible to read these
> images as representations of race and colour—black hoods,
> richly "ethnic" patterned robes, brown skin and eyes—and
> to read them through a veil of radical chic or uncanny
> encounter. But this is not the point and Foley inquires into
> the processes of telling and performing other histories in
> other languages in an art world that either continues to reject
> them or defaults to the vapid recidivism of "backlash" or
> culture wars.[13]

Fiona later cast herself as a Muslim woman in the background of a staged confrontation between youthful black and white men, drawing attention to the racism directed at other marginalised groups in Australia. This racism hit the front pages of national newspapers following Sydney's Cronulla riots in 2005. Titled *Nulla 4 Eva* (2009), this series of photographs represents Australia's current multi-cultural nature, with Asian people, Aboriginal figures, Indians, Muslims in concert with the clichéd Australian associations (XXXX Beer logos, bronzed surfers, sand and surf). Vestiges of less well-known history are also visible with a reclining smoker and opium pipes evoking the prohibition of marriage between Aboriginals and Chinese in Queensland in the nineteenth century that was enshrined in the 1897 *Act*.

Racism is based on hierarchy, with degrees of acceptance doled out according to a shifting and artificial scale, and cultural values. The position at the base of the pyramid is enforced by those above, with each group party to the system able to reinforce their own position by keeping others beneath them. Racism is described as an example of a "wicked" problem,[14] "complex problems that are highly resistant to solutions and that are characterised by high difficulty and disagreement about the nature and cause of the problem and their potential solutions".[15] It is base human behaviour that relies on dominance, requiring the evolutionary power and pack language of animals, but also cultural values and beliefs. Racism, "as a legacy of colonisation and slavery, has had profound intergenerational effects on health, social and economic outcomes".[16]

/

In 2011 *The Oyster Fishermen* saw Fiona develop a photographic narrative that was personal as well as political, exploring the violence that may sit inside relationships. This series opens with the arm of a woman (Fiona), holding a nautilus shell over the horizon, pouring water into the sea. The photographs are sepia, with spot colour used to highlight the dress worn by the woman, which stands out as an intense deep blue stitching the narrative together. Its inexorable progress echoes the small swell that washes into shore on the island's east side. The second image focuses on the skeleton and head of three fish which have been left on the sand, remains of a meal. The third image is calm; the three fishermen relax on the beach with their boat and the fourth shows a man looking out to sea. The fifth is a man reading a bible, and in the sixth and seventh we begin to develop a sense of these men as individuals. The eighth is a detail of a box, bible and beer bottles. In the ninth the woman emerges again, the bottom of her dress visible in the coastal scrub. Her feet nestled into mangroves on the beach, is a peaceful image (ten), but in eleven her head is thrown back, hands tied, and she is on her knees, abject, as a fisherman drags her up the beach. The brutality accelerates, with the woman tied to a tree, beaten, and finally, she lies in the sea floating lifeless, seen from above with her head facing down. The trajectory of this narrative is compelling. Our early introduction to these apparently cultured men is disarming, for we feel that we know them, these gentle souls with their Western accoutrements of music and books. Yet they turn, all three complicit in the violent death of an Aboriginal woman.

Fiona brought a group of men to Kingfisher Bay to act *The Oyster Fishermen* (2012). One of the men involved in acting this story apologised to Fiona for his ancestral past. Focused on delivering the work, she was surprised: "I was not asking him to bear the shame or the sorrow. Getting white guys to be 'in character' is hard—they don't really want to act the bastard—they are polite, middle class. I selected them for their potential look—like a colonial man."

Involvement in these narratives has the potential to be draining, but Fiona is able to distance herself from the violence in the content: "I don't take on the persona of what I'm acting out. I don't let it enter me too deeply. You are there, in it, for a time and that's it. It is like in the film world. At the end that is a wrap for the day. You walk away." For others, particularly the men that she chooses for their "look", most of whom are not professional actors, her narrative can trigger a sense of guilt by association, even in the innocent. Carl Warner, who photographed the series with her on K'gari, recalled:

> Convincing white boys to play racists is really hard; they
> don't understand that that is not who they are. These issues
> are new to them, but not to Fiona. It is a pretty common
> thing with people in those situations, who may end up
> thinking about endemic issues like racism. They might go
> into apology mode and no one needs to hear that apology.[17]

Badtjala Woman was the first of Fiona's collaborative projects in which she worked with a professional photographer and the themed series is an approach which Fiona continues to use today. The first *Badtjala Woman* images were photographed by Greg Weight in Sydney. In subsequent work, Fiona has sourced the location, found the props and costumes, and directs what is recorded by a photographer. Her most recent series *Horror has a face* (2017) was also photographed by Warner, with whom Fiona has regularly worked for ten years. *Horror* was her most ambitious shoot, with a cast of nineteen, four photographic sites, and significant props and costumes. As Warner sees it, "the photographer disappears in that situation. You should be invisible, with the focus on capturing the narrative. That is the perfect balance point for this kind of work. I like Fiona's strong Indigenous perspective and working with her in this way has helped expand some of my own ideas."[18]

A watchful presence is vested in Fiona's aesthetic. She is all too aware that balance is difficult to achieve and that small stumbles may be dangerous. At an artists' camp convened by Gold Coast City Art Gallery and hosted on Minjerribah/South Stradbroke Island, Fiona was the group mentor and artist Delvene Cockatoo-Collins, a Quandamooka woman, was part of the emerging artist group. *School's In* and *Black Velvet* (2015) were made there, and Cockatoo-Collins modelled for this photograph evoking the violence of the schoolroom, the site of Fiona's first experience of racism. Fiona approached Cockatoo-Collins to be in this work as a young beautiful Aboriginal woman.

School's In (2015) sees the young woman, wrists tied with red tape (with its bureaucratic associations), hiding her face in the trunk of a huge dead tree, an archetypal 1960s timber school chair propped nearby on a magnificent tree root. The tree stands between the beach and the bush, a metaphor for the educated Aboriginals of Fiona's generation, caught between tradition and integration, drawn to the beauty and connections of their Aboriginal past while required to meet mainstream benchmarks in order to fulfil their potential within a different cultural milieu. The model's black cotton shift and the vintage wooden chair speak to Fiona's early school experiences of a different reality and racism. *Black Velvet* (2015) was spelled out on a beach in discarded clothes, similar to the op-shop-sourced detritus of the "white trash" image in 2005 for *Signpost II*.

/

In late 2014 the Badtjala Native Title claim on K'gari was awarded following an eighteen-year fight, many iterations, and a great deal of compromise. Nonetheless, the spirit of Shirley Foley was summoned when the consent determination was handed down at Kingfisher Bay at K'gari. It was the stimulus Fiona needed to move out of Brisbane and back to Hervey Bay. She wanted to assist her community with the process of reclamation of their land. In *Black Velvet* and *School's In*, there is a sense of leaning into culture, country and community to lend support. The beach (at South Stradbroke) marked with the words "BLACK VELVET" stretches into the distance and out to sea. Jo-Anne Driessens was asked to buy the second-hand clothes for the making of the work. She recalled,

> a similar approach; revealed only at the time of creating the work. The only thing she discussed that morning with the artists was to bring along any of their own clothes to add to the actual creating of the work on the surf beach. Industry guests were able to witness the whole process. Carl Warner took the final image—with a ladder![19]

It is not visible in the image, but the stretch of ocean between South Stradbroke and the Gold Coast is The Spit, known for a narrow strip of treacherous water that has ensnared many.

/

Our bodies change faster than the earth. They are the vessels that define us, central to our ability to express ourselves—physically, visually, emotionally and sexually. They contain the evolving biological imperative and can create our descendants. Unlike the evolution of a continent over centuries and millennia, human bodies morph over days, weeks, years and decades of life, impacted by diet, exercise, changing conditions, age, environment—and race. They carry the previous generations, with characteristics like courage, leadership and grit handed down. Connection to place, and country may also be implicit. Kim Mahood writes, "I believe that geography shapes who we are and how we think, and the time I've spent in this remote tract of [the Tanami] desert among both its original inhabitants and its second-settler latecomers has only served to reinforce that belief".[20] In artistic traditions, it is the body that remains at the heart of traditional skills. The body exposes foundational structure, so expressive of the fundamentals of human experience.

Contemporary mores, such as the way we reflect the power of the cerebral over the physical, are a telling conductor of current insecurities. Yet the body sits underneath all else; on it we depend utterly. In death, it is abandoned, a carapace. The body is the common vehicle for humanity, and is shared between cultures. Art has reflected the human journey through time and place and, in our need to create, separates humans from animals. Its changing nature reflects historical change in knowledge, ideas and ideologies. The body is a subject for art as old as Aboriginal culture; as subject and object its depiction reveals the psyche as tellingly as any physical realities.

Fiona's journey is reflected in her body and the evolution of her artwork builds and reflects the changes and trajectories of her ideas and experiences. Time marks our bodies, and I can trace my own life experiences on my skin, scars and flaws expressing meaning for me alone. On another time scale I am reminded of the ancient trees that define K'gari's Central Station, their age expressed in their size and the knots and depths that are etched over their surfaces into deep time.

//

Five Notes

1 John Donne, "The Ecstasy", in *Love Poems* (London: Phoenix, 1996), 46.

2 David Marr, *The Henson Case* (Melbourne: Text Publishing, 2008), 134.

3 Sandra Phillips, "Black Velvet: Redefining and Celebrating Indigenous Australian Women in Art", *The Conversation*, 9 May 2016: https://theconversation.com/black-velvet-redefining-and-celebrating-indigenous-australian-women-in-art-56211.

4 Andrew Baker, interview by the author, 19 August 2016.

5 Djon Mundine, interview by the author, 2017.

6 Michael Riley, *Portraits by a Window* 1990, http://www.michaelriley.com.au/portraits-by-a-window-1990/.

7 Ernest Gribble was Fiona's great-grandmother's brother.

8 Halse, *A Terribly Wild Man*, 26.

9 Anna Haebich, *Red Ochre Me* (Sydney: Casula Powerhouse, 2006), 13.

10 John Van Tiggelen, "Once were Emus", *Good Weekend Magazine, Sydney Morning Herald*, 9 February 2002, 15.

11 "K'Gari gin'di yin'na mi" is a song known to Aboriginal people throughout south-east Queensland. It is thought to originate on K'gari (hence its title).

12 Tim Morrell, "Collector's Dossier: Fiona Foley", *Art Collector*, 50 (2009).

13 Linda Carroli, "Fiona Foley – No Shades of White", Roslyn Oxley9 Gallery, 31 March 2005.

14 Horst W. J. Rittel and Melvin M. Webber, "Dilemmas in a General Theory of Planning", *Policy Sciences* 4 (1973): 155.

15 Heather Came and Derek Griffith, "Tackling Racism as a 'Wicked' Public Health Problem: Enabling Allies in Anti-Racism Praxis", *Social Science & Medicine* 199 (2018): 181.

16 Ibid.

17 Carl Warner, interview by the author, 15 May 2018.

18 Ibid.

19 Jo-Anne Driessens, personal communication with the author, 27 May 2018.

20 Mahood, *Position Doubtful*, 9.

SIX

NOTORIOUS

A century ago Australian public squares and city streets were decorated with bronze statues, usually featuring explorers, British kings and queens and memorials to war. By the second decade of the twenty-first century we are more accustomed to fluorescent and LED-lit shapes, video, graffiti and ephemeral experiences, along with the large objects in metal from the 1980s and 1990s, a bridge perhaps between these sculptural movements. Creating these manifestations in public spaces reflect the multiplicity of current ideas. Contemporary public art has changed the game for Australian visual artists and offers audiences contemporary narratives of relevance to our time.

Sculpture in the public realm is increasingly used to curate contemporary narratives to its community and visitors alike. It creates urban places as relevant to their function and current audiences. Public art may define the activity and atmosphere designed to occupy a precinct or area. In the last thirty years this work has allowed an artist's solo practice to become more viable, for these projects may yield significant income streams for an artist (albeit only for the duration of the project) and insulate them against the vagaries of art sales alone as an income stream. *Edge of the Trees* was commissioned for the exterior of the Museum of Sydney in 1995. It was a collaboration between Fiona and artist Janet Laurence (born 1947). It was Fiona's first public artwork, and she learnt important skills. She also emerged with a jaundiced view of curatorial exercises that combine black and white artists.

SYDNEY, 1995

Museum of Sydney curator Peter Emmett suggested Janet and Fiona collaborate for a high-profile site at the new museum building on the site of Sydney's First Government House. He was keen to involve an Aboriginal artist. Fiona recalled,

> Janet and I put ideas together and co-presented to a committee of nine people, with Hetti Perkins as the Indigenous board member. Janet found the poles at one of the old wharves and the sandstone came from Gosford Quarry. She designed the lighting and I did the sound. I had Aboriginal students from Tranby College pronounce the words [for the soundtrack] and recorded them at the ABC studio in Ultimo. I had never had that experience before and I was assisted by Lorena Allam.
>
> I made oyster middens by first eating the oysters, putting the shells in a bucket of water and using a toothbrush to scrub each one to get the mussel remains out of it. I had a space at

what is now the Walsh Bay Arts precinct in Sydney. I spent a lot of time down there, scrubbing the oysters and tipping the water used in the sea, then crushing the oysters and putting oxide and ash in with them.

Located near Sydney's Circular Quay, the Museum of Sydney is a stone's throw from where Fiona was then employed at the Museum of Contemporary Art. Described as both a public artwork and an exhibit of the museum, *Edge of the Trees* is a holistic experience, evoking the site's present museum function and Aboriginal past through materials such as sandstone, timber and steel. An aural "map" records Koori voices, naming their Aboriginal places of occupation from around Sydney, symbolised by the forest of twenty-nine timber, steel and sandstone columns through which visitors can walk. Its title came from words written by historian Rhys Jones, who described the first contact moments of invasion/colonisation in 1788:

> The "discoverers" struggling through the surf were met
> on the beaches by other people looking at them from the
> edge of the trees. Thus the same landscape perceived by the
> newcomers as alien, hostile, or having no coherent form,
> was to the Indigenous people their home, a familiar place,
> the inspiration of dreams.[1]

This installation draws together the botanical, historical and physical past. Laurence's website describes *Edge of the Trees* as "a symbolic space—a membrane where two cultures looked through to each other— here they mingle and intertwine, a weaving towards the future".[2]

While Fiona admired Laurence's significant experience and skills, once the project was in train (with Fiona also working full time in her curator's position), she felt that,

> Janet Laurence got the upper hand. Towards the end of the project Laurence tried to stipulate that we sign a contract. Her name had to come before mine in any written material— she wanted to identify me as the assistant artist. I didn't go along with that. But she made $50,000 out of the project, and I made $16,000. I didn't know my rights and got railroaded.

It was during the installation of the work that Fiona was disenfranchised. She remembered,

> There was a crane on site to lift each element in place, and Laurence was directing proceedings, changing her mind about things. Then she said, "Let's have a lunch break", but after I left she stayed to direct the remainder of the placement. We were given the Lloyd Rees Award for Urban Design, but the experience was no collaboration.

"One had more power than the other", Fiona told me. The collaboration was "an opportunity to ride on an Indigenous person's coat tails". In her view, the power differentials were impacted by the closeness of the relationship between Emmett and Laurence. Fiona sensed that she was "never going to get an equal hearing". While *Edge of the Trees* remains a powerful entry to the museum, and its aesthetic and conceptual longevity is impressive, Fiona felt, "Like the black bunny required to legitimate their process". Historian Naomi Parry was working at the Museum of Sydney at this time and was involved in the project's execution. Her memory, in 2018, of the way this sculpture evolved remains fresh. She tells me that Fiona was indeed "done over" and had every right to feel manipulated by a senior artist.[3]

Despite this rocky beginning, Fiona has contributed substantially to public sculpture in Australia. A series of six major works for Mackay's Bluewater Trail (2009), a playscape and memorial in Sydney's Redfern Park (2008), reading rooms and a major sculpture for the atrium space within the State Library of Queensland (2006), a seminal sculpture for the Roma Street frontage of the Brisbane Magistrates Court (2004), and *The Lie of the Land* for Melbourne Museum in 1997 have all been integral to the building of her reputation as a substantial contributor to Australia's public realm. However, she has consistently turned down collaborations where black and white artists are asked to collaborate. The situation, in which black artists may be seen to be propping up or empowering white artists, is noted by academic Adam Geczy, who writes,

> To see a desert painting on a white wall in a clean air-conditioned room is tantamount to conversing with a desiccated corpse. This incongruity becomes more complicated when Aboriginal art is placed together with non-Aboriginal art in some kind of curatorial conversation. Who is legitimating whom? And what kind of correspondence is being set up?[4]

Recent interventions such as the new Queensland Art Gallery Australian art collection rehang (2017) seek to prise open these power differentials for discussion.

LAKE MCKENZIE, K'GARI

In 2005 Fiona used the Lake McKenzie beach where we swam in 2017, far away from the tourists, as the site for an installation. A photograph recorded this installation, the words "white trash" in the foreground, laid out on the sand. "White trash" is from the American vernacular, referring to the social status of poor white people, a working class without education or property. Nancy Isenberg's *White Trash* gives a list of other descriptors: "Waste people. Offscourings. Lubbers. Bogtrotters. Rascals. Rubbish. Squatters. Crackers. Clay-eaters. Tackies. Mudsills. Scalawags. Briar hoppers. Hillbillies. Low-downers. White niggers. Degenerates. White trash. Rednecks. Trailer trash. Swamp people."[5] This sub-group did not see their fortunes rise over the nineteenth and twentieth centuries although, as Cowie points out in a review of Isenberg's book, they have not suffered alone. In the Australian context, the terms "redneck" and "bogan" are also used to refer to a poor underclass.[6] Cowie writes, "blacks and native Americans suffered even more" than the white working class.[7] Sub-groups may also look for solidarity. The racism in the Australia of Barry Foley's youth was also directed at the Irish. I can only wonder if his attraction to Shirley may have recognised a sense of being similarly marginalised; certainly, they shared fierce independence and a fighting spirit.

Foley's use of this term is provocative. Yet "white trash" is also literal, as her words are built from the discarded garments of locals, the majority of whom are white. They also symbolise the detritus of European capitalism. Using this term also evokes history, a status reversal and reminder of a period when Aboriginals on K'gari were briefly winning the war. The proud history of the Badtjala includes guerrilla warfare on the colonising whites during the second half of the 1800s. Fiona writes that, "Badtjala warriors used stealth on the township of Maryborough and retreated to the sanctuary of K'gari when needed".[8] This was a battle that, with Badtjala knowledge and bush skills, they were winning—until the Native Police were brought in.

The *Signpost II (White Trash)* image looks back toward the area where the tourist buses deposit their cargo, with small groups of people scattered along the beach opposite. The ugly words and their raw materials are patently out of place here. The sky and bush overshadow the words, with building grey cloud an implication perhaps of the dominance of nature over the human. The image captures a brooding disquiet, racial tension encapsulated in its contrasts of dark and light, the human-made within such a pristine natural environment.

It was created and photographed during an artist residency, over two weekends in 2005, under the auspices of an initiative through the Great Sandy National Park (K'gari). Nine artists from the Hervey Bay area worked under Fiona's direction and mentorship. On the first weekend she assisted them with their own projects, and the following weekend they helped her create two installations. Early into the second day there was tension. Jo-Anne Driessens, the artist photographer who assisted Fiona and bought the second-hand clothes, said,

> Fiona keeps her cards close to her chest. She had asked me
> to photograph the whole weekend of art-making with the
> artists and I was unaware until the final afternoon what
> purpose the bag of clothes had (I noticed them in the four-
> wheel drive when we were heading over on the ferry). Fiona
> didn't start making the work until everyone had had a swim

in the beautiful Lake McKenzie; they were relaxed. Once
the group realised what was going on, two people walked off
immediately. They refused to have anything to do with it.[9]

Fiona recalls, "The term, 'WHITE TRASH' created a bit of a discussion point. Some people got their noses out of joint. Making art you have to deal with other peoples' psychosis, some of it is not rational. The racism came out. One of the local artists admitted that she'd used those exact words, directed at her neighbours in Hervey Bay." Fiona has owned property in Hervey Bay since 1988; these words are inflammatory. What may be most reassuring to those near the bottom is the insulation of a group below them. I wonder if the use of the term "White Trash" by a Badtjala woman, directed back across the water to the whites of Hervey Bay, is what was at the heart of the disquiet they created. Yet Fiona's intention was not to incite hostility (although clearly debate and controversy do not inhibit her making and showing). Later, National Parks administrators became concerned about exhibiting the work at the local Hervey Bay Regional Gallery. "I had to get solicitor Michael Drummond involved—ultimately, the work was exhibited."

MCKENZIE'S JETTY

Fiona's first installation at McKenzie's Jetty in 2006 was less contentious. This site is about two kilometres up the beach from K'gari's Kingfisher Bay Resort and is adjacent to North White Cliffs. It is a place close to where Fiona's mother's ashes were scattered in 2000, "a place for us to cling to". The jetty was built in 1918 as part of the early timber-getting industry on K'gari, constructed with local satinay timber, *Syncarpia hillii*. Hepburn McKenzie purchased the timber rights for some four thousand acres of adjacent land and a tramline was constructed to haul the large logs from the McKenzie mill to the jetty. The tramline operated until 1925. These trees were thousands, possibly millions, of years old.

The jetty is also adjacent to the site of the first mission on K'gari, established at South White Cliffs in 1870 by Reverend Edward Fuller. The mission was short-lived, as the difficulty of growing vegetables in the island's sandy soil coupled with antipathy from local whites, saw it abandoned by 1873. According to Fuller's letter published by the *Brisbane Courier* in 1872, the mission was a personal initiative, established at his own "risk, cost and responsibility".[10] He mentions "Mr Pierson and his party", timber-getters working on the island close by.

In 2005 Fiona chose to put another layer of communal history over McKenzie's Jetty, albeit temporarily. *Signpost I*, a photograph of the aged timber structure of the jetty at low tide, is the enduring record of this installation. The jetty's substantial posts are connected to each other with red tape that Fiona had bought from Bunnings in Hervey Bay. The tape forms a tangled, messy web of sticky plastic that erodes the timber structure's appearance of solidity, forging a newly distracting facade.

At the time, Fiona and her extended family were many years into a legal process toward recognition of their clan's ownership of a small parcel of land on K'gari. She recalled, "I let the artists wrap McKenzie's Jetty any way they wanted. They were locking it up, putting red tape around the entire process. The jetty was in the Wondunna claim area at that stage, before we had to come in as one language group. We were within a long, legalistic process." The photograph is taken low to the ground, with the blocking shapes of the jetty and the bright-red tape a tacky screen that foregrounds the forested cliffs behind. It casts the island as resistant to cultural incursion from foreigners. Shadows of the jetty loom large on the sand in the foreground, an ironically fruitless exercise to privilege the human-made over the natural and a puff of white cloud marks the sky.

In 2017 the jetty stretches across the beach at low tide, its shadows dramatic in a way that echoes the *Signpost* image. Fiona brings me here at the end of the day, on our way back into Kingfisher Bay after hours of negotiating the hired four-wheel drive through irregular sand tracks across the island and her family stories. There is an educational display, with faded images of Shirley, her siblings and Olga Miller. I know that, for Fiona, their presence here is much more significant than these images can project, and the wind shifts as we look into the blurry outlines of their faces. Down on the beach, a strange iron structure, probably part of an old tram carriage, is embedded on one side of the jetty, dwarfed by the sandy cliffs behind. Fiona and I walk barefoot on the beach nearby, through a tidal puddle, and suddenly the soft underside of my bare foot presses into a jagged piece of rusty iron. The cut is deep and bleeds copiously; I cannot remember when I last had a tetanus shot. Fiona's shoes are back at the car so she chooses to walk to the resort along the beach. My wound grows sticky with sand as I walk and run alone, back along the track through the forest, as the sky darkens above the canopy of the trees. I feel a bit spooked, the bush which felt so benign earlier, under the sunlight, is less open to my passing in the graininess of the early evening light. The day slips away, fading as I reach the four-wheel drive we left on the road just outside the resort. I drive the trusty little vehicle into the hire facility a few minutes short of the 6:00 p.m. deadline as my phone pings with a text message: "Having a sundowner on the beach—come down when you're ready: F." Even now, the scar on the underside of my foot endures, marked by a foreign element that has risen through the sand to the surface. The memory of the sunset at the jetty which rendered the old carriage on the beach an unnatural, intensely red hue, takes me straight to the mineral dark sand, the salty wind, and the sense of something restive that stirred to smite me in that place.

SYDNEY, 2010

The auditorium in Campbelltown in the greater western region of Sydney was full on 21 May 2010 for a rare Biennale of Sydney event held outside the inner city. Fiona stood slowly and walked the lectern. Her paper described a suite of her photographic works included in the Biennale titled *Bearing Witness* (2009). Her images, shown in the colonial quarter on Sydney's historic Cockatoo Island, included characters drawn together to represent the powerful in Australian settler society, a "who saw what" on the frontier. In one image, a colonial woman is dressed in heavy blue velvet, tea cup in hand, standing adjacent to a table with a lace tablecloth and the platters laid for afternoon tea. Behind her is a green pot filled with dried poppy heads (the source of opium) and a large white shell rests below the table cloth. Around her neck is a breast plate of the type Aboriginals were forced to wear, which reads COLONIAL WOMAN. She looks at the viewer, face neutral, impassive. The cup she holds and the teapot on the table are printed with an elegant poppy arrangement. It is pretty, its fragility loaded with historical weight: the powerful destructive forces directed at Australian Aboriginals included opium. Other figures included in *Bearing Witness* include the priest in an elaborate red and black costume, gold cross heavy on his chest, the Aboriginal warrior wearing the cockatoo feather in his twine headdress, the barrister in his traditional garments holding the wig, and the Elder whose breastplate bears words from Sophocles, "Ignorant men don't know what good they hold in their hands until they've flung it away". In another image, the frontiersmen who instigated this war stand with a gun pointing down at a young Aboriginal woman. She hides, partly covered by a government issue blanket printed with the word "Defiled". One of these two men stares out at the audience, eyes wide, frightened by his actions.

These individual portraits represent the culpable, all of whom had borne witness to and were complicit in the brutal treatment of Aboriginal Australians. Each of these individuals make eye contact with the viewer, appearing in front of an all-white background, literally white-washed of a past, and removed from context outside the dress and accoutrements of their position; a blank slate. Yet in these careful representations of her oppressors, Fiona also evokes an understanding of each individual, each caught in the context of a brutal net. The display of *Bearing Witness*, in rooms built for convicts on Cockatoo Island, was beautifully choreographed.

The day before the North–South Dialogue Forum, "curatorial duo" (Indigenous Canadian) Gerald McMasters and (European-born and American resident) Catherine de Zegher, were appointed joint Artistic Directors for the following Biennale, in 2012.

The forum itself was convened by then Campbelltown Arts Centre director Lisa Havilah, who invited Djon Mundine to facilitate a panel discussion on the 17th Biennale, *The Beauty Of Distance: Songs of Survival in a Precarious Age*. The discussion explored one of the Biennale's sub-themes relating to "First Peoples and Fourth Worlds". A Canadian delegation of First Nations representatives were paired with an equal number of Aboriginal artists. During earlier Biennale activities, an eagle feather had been presented by the Canadians to acknowledge Aboriginal artist and curator Brenda Croft, following her involvement with a previous Australian visit to Banff, in Alberta.

As convenor of the panel, and the first speaker, Djon presented an irreverent parody of the Australian arts and funding scene, a send up of the personalities, situations and corruption that he sees as endemic to the sector. Djon later recalled both the amusement of Biennale of Sydney 2010 director David Elliott, and the mortification of the Canadians. "They were very stiff", he remarked. At the conclusion of her speech, Fiona took a fluffy white cockatoo, commercially made for tourists, out of the plastic bag. With ceremony, she presented it to Djon Mundine. "I just sat there with it on the table, cradling and stroking it, for the rest of the event", he told me. There was a buzz of consternation and confusion from the audience.

Fiona was making the point that the Biennale was overdue for an Australian Indigenous director. Yet the slight hit home—the Canadians noted the connection to the cultural practice that had been enacted with ceremony during the Biennale official reception at the Canadian Embassy. Fiona said recently, "Australia would wait another ten years for the appointment of an Aboriginal curator of the Biennale of Sydney (with Brook Andrew's appointment). This is the type of institutional racism we face in this country. The Canadians do not understand because of their privilege and elevated status when being hosted in this country."

/

Djon told me this story as we sat at a cafe in Kings Cross's Springfield Avenue one morning in March 2017. The Cross was as busy at 9:00 a.m. as at 9:00 p.m., although the crowd is different, with city commuters heading for the station, nightclubs closed up, and doors of the many cafes open and welcoming. Petrel Kitchen had been dark and umbrella-less the night before when my friend Kathryn had walked me past it on the way home from the theatre. Despite grey skies and occasional drizzling rain, the umbrellas were now unfurled, tables ensconced underneath. As I arrived I saw Djon on the pavement, sitting under one of the umbrellas, talking to a thin, blond woman, middle-aged, casually dressed. As she left, the waitress appeared, also greeting Djon by name.

I met with Djon, on and off, throughout that Friday, first at 9:00 a.m., at 12:30, then again between 3:00 and 4:30 p.m., between his other commitments. His experience and incredible recall of events, personalities and perspectives are informed by decades of involvement. A constant stream of passers-by greeted him, stopped for a chat, and sometimes sat down for a while, including anthropologist John von Sturmer and Sydney College of the Arts academic Brad Buckley (who remembered Fiona as a conscientious student). Writer Susan Charlton waited patiently for her turn. Djon's running commentary diverted after each interruption to the context of these other relationships. His "hood" has history, undercurrents that run strong and deep.

About 5:00 p.m. after I had left him for the last time that day, Djon phoned to apologise for the interruptions and to reiterate his admiration for Fiona's integrity, her commitment to "the cause, beyond her own self and financial interests". Fiona's commitment is indeed unrelenting. Later, in her archive, I found a letter from Fiona to Luca Belgiorno-Nettis. He had reprimanded her after her address to the 2010 Forum and she felt the need to refute his claims:

> Firstly, I would like you to know that every time I am asked
> to speak publicly I put much time and thought into the
> topic or questions being asked of me ... I do not take these
> engagements lightly but rather consider the issues proposed
> by the forum organisers. Your comment to me that "I am a
> shit stirrer" is simply not valid and was rude in its dismissive
> nature. My public statement that there were no Australian
> Aboriginal writers for the 17th Biennale of Sydney catalogue
> was not plucked out of thin air. After reading essays by
> Ngahiraka Mason, Gerald McMaster, Skeena Reece and
> Jimmie Durham I still believe my criticism holds true as a
> glaring omission ... Why are there no essays by an equivalent
> Aboriginal curator or artist from Australia?[11]

As I spoke to Djon on the phone on that day in 2017, I was walking near Elizabeth Bay Marina, overlooking the harbour. Its edges were blurry in the light drizzly rain. The implication of his remarks was clear: those more committed to their own financial destiny than the Aboriginal cause are common—and Fiona stands apart.

In recent years "the culture wars" have made regular appearances on the front pages of newspapers, in politician's Twitter feeds and mainstream television. By 2017 the debate was about acknowledgement—of the violence of our histories, and the cultural artefacts (statues and monuments revering Captain James Cook, and explorers like Lachlan Macquarie and John Batman) that obscure this repressed history. Yet within this debate, art has an ability to infiltrate with stealth. In late 2015 Andrew Baker showed me images of Fiona Foley's *I.O.U.* This new body of work was first shown in Perth as part of *Kurlkayima Ngatha— Remember Me* in February 2016.[12] Large stainless-steel letters, as tall as she is, were created as receptacles—"I" on the wall, honey (O), and ash (U). The materials are meaningful—ash meant death in colonial histories because bodies were often burnt after massacres, to dispose of the evidence. It is also a by-product of opium, traded with Aboriginal people in Queensland for wages. Opium was (mis)used to quell rebellion and to cultivate submission and passivity. Honey is significant in Aboriginal ceremony and song and was intrinsic to Fiona's conversations with traditional Pilbara land owners when she was conceptualising this work during her travels in Western Australia in 2015. On a personal level, ash has the death knell of finality for Fiona—as the last frontier of a physical connection to life.

Fiona's installation mingled the aromatics and slipperiness of ash with the stickiness of the honey, evoking memories of the way each of these materials feel when rubbed between the thumb and finger. The scent and stickiness of the honey seemed to quiver with tension at the lip of its rigid receptacle. Yet each of these materials were confined by the unmoving hardness of its container, and the stark cold message in the steeliness of the I.O.U.

The core of Foley's artistry brings together uncomfortable layers of history—national debts not settled, treaties not yet negotiated—with familiar materials that take us into an organic realm of touch, smell and early memory. It is a down-the-rabbit-hole transformation that feels magical even as, at the same time, it debates the rotten core in the history of Australia's occupation. Yet in bringing this history into the light through her art, Fiona is marked as notorious, rather than celebrated.

//

Six Notes

1 Rhys Jones, "Ordering the Landscape", in *Seeing the First Australians*, eds Ian Donaldson and Tamsin Donaldson (Sydney: George Allen & Unwin, 1985), 185.

2 "Edge of the Trees", *JanetLaurence.com*, http://www.janetlaurence.com/edge-of-the-trees/.

3 Naomi Parry, interview by the author (phone), 7 January 2019.

4 Adam Geczy, "The Air-Conditioned Desert: Curating Aboriginal Art", *Art Monthly Australia*, 250 (2012): 44.

5 Nancy Isenberg, *White Trash: The 400-Year Untold History of Class in America* (New York: Penguin Books, 2017), 605.

6 Jacqueline Zara Wilson, "Invisible Racism: The Language and Ontology of 'White Trash'", *Critique of Anthropology* 22, 4 (December 2002): 396.

7 Jefferson Cowie, "The Great White Nope: Poor, Working Class, and Left Behind in America", *Foreign Affairs* 95, no. 6 (2016): 150.

8 Foley, *Biting the Clouds*, 61.

9 Conversation with the author at an exhibition of Driessens' photographs at Redland Art Gallery, Cleveland, 27 May 2018.

10 Fuller, "The Fraser Island Aboriginal Mission".

11 Letter from Fiona Foley to Luca Belgiorno-Nettis, Chairman, Board of Biennale of Sydney, 25 May 2010. From the artist's collection.

12 FORM, *Kurlkayima Ngatha–Remember Me*, Perth, February 2016.

SEVEN

FRONTAL ATTACK

Fiona understands loss, its finalities and the journey inherent in grief. It took her three years to recover her equanimity after the death of her mother in 2000. In January 2017 the death of her father was another wrench. As an Aboriginal woman, Fiona's life has been a litany of loss, with too many family and friends lost to illness, connections both close and distant, gone too soon. The gap in life expectancy of seventeen years between Aboriginal and non-Aboriginal Australians remains a chasm. Michael Marmot, chair of the Commission on Social Determinants of Health (for the World Health Organization) writes, "Differences in access to health care matter, as do differences in lifestyle, but the key determinants of social inequalities in health lie in the circumstances in which people are born, grow, live, work, and age. These, in turn, arise from differential access to power and resources."[1] He goes on: "Striking among the causes of premature mortality among Indigenous Australians are the high rates of cardiovascular disease, diabetes, kidney disease and cancer—diseases that are closely linked to social causes, which are not well understood by simply grouping them as 'poverty'."[2] When I talk to Fiona about the deaths of people in her network, and what took them so young, she says simply, "Aboriginal health issues". These are ongoing, a fact, integral to the surreal blur of loss which colours and infiltrates her life. Its origins lie in the way in which colonisers used Australia's Aboriginal peoples. In Fiona's ancestral history, the health of the Badtjala people—their tall physiques, strength and vitality was noted in the early years of colonisation; within a few decades, ninety per cent of them were dead.[3]

In 2004, the early loss of talented Aboriginal artist-photographer Michael Riley aged only forty-four was desperately sad for his colleagues, friends and family, and the promise of his artistic vision. He had kidney disease, a condition that is two and a half times more prevalent in Aboriginal and Torres Strait Islander communities than in non-Indigenous communities, due to high levels of traditional risk factors (diabetes, high blood pressure and smoking). Other factors include inadequate nutrition, alcohol abuse, streptococcal throat and skin infection, poor living conditions and low birth weight (which has a relationship to reduced nephron development).[4] Shirley Foley also suffered from kidney disease. Djon Mundine writes in a 2018 exhibition catalogue on Riley's work that,

> An image of a discarded bible in a muddy puddle signals a
> cynical rejection of organised Christianity and its promise.
> It is still a fact in some Aboriginal communities that by the
> time the generations of sons have reached thirty they have
> no role models to guide them, owing to their fathers' dying.

To lose someone so gifted is a loss for all of us who knew him, and a loss to all who appreciate art.[5]

Sadly, in the Aboriginal community, these sorts of losses are all too frequent.

THE PUBLIC REALM

Fiona is mindful of the power of public sculpture to provide a platform to convey messages to broad audiences, even into the mainstream. When she was offered the opportunity to create a public artwork at the new Brisbane Magistrates Court (BMC), two years before the State Library commission, she was offered a high-profile site on Roma Street. Jay Younger was the public art commissioning curator for the court. She told me that all fourteen artists were offered a direct commission and assigned their own site and budget. While the BMC Roma Street access is a relatively quiet part of the central business district, there is passing traffic, both vehicular and on foot. The work Fiona created for this commission, *Witnessing to Silence* (2004) was seminal within her oeuvre and in its reception.

Art in public places was galvanised in the late 1990s in Queensland, when the incoming Beattie Labor Government embraced a "two per cent for art policy" in public buildings from mid-1999. In the thirteen years between then and the change of policy that came with the election of the Newman Liberal National Party Government in 2012, art was integrated into new government buildings.

Fiona was offered the largest allocated budget. Younger tells me, "Her site across the road from Emma Miller Place formed a particular political and spatial relationship between the courts and Emma Miller Place." Emma Miller (1839–1917) was a union organiser and suffragette. "The site of Emma Miller Place has been a historical meeting place for Land Rights and activist marches. Fiona was chosen for the site at the courts across from there because she is a politically motivated, critically engaged practitioner."[6] However, she found the committee approvals and negotiation process on this project tough going. Ultimately, finding the attitude from "the suits" confronting, and after a breach of contract that may have resulted in her being underpaid, she engaged a lawyer to attend meetings with her. She found that there was resistance from the committee (including the architect) that requested new concept designs based on their misreading of her work—as manacles.

Finally, she negotiated the form and concept of the proposed artwork with subterfuge, concerned that her concept would not be approved if she disclosed her artwork plan and its meaning. She presented the 94 place names etched into the foundation stones (which were later revealed as sites of Queensland's massacres) and the materials used (water and ash, two methods used to hide Aboriginal bodies after massacres) under the more benign guise of environmental disasters (flood and fire). However, the real impetus behind *Witnessing to Silence* required sharing, and she took her story to *The Australian* newspaper in 2005, three months after the work was installed and secure.

This artwork opportunity saw Fiona commission significant research to develop, for the first time, a comprehensive statewide listing of sites of Aboriginal massacres since the settlement of Queensland. The etching of the place names into pavers on the ground plane evokes the grave stones we might see in a cemetery, yet makes the point that the Aboriginal people and communities slaughtered are unacknowledged victims of the violence of the Frontier Wars. Ash is visible behind glass in the grey stainless steel pillars that stand like silent sentinels, a marker of Aboriginal loss, grief and sorrow in the face of unlawful deaths. Together, with the misting spray of water that was part of the original artwork, the materials speak to the methods of disposal of the people murdered by colonists—their bodies burnt or submerged in water courses. These losses, memorialised in this significant artwork, mark the Indigenous peoples sacrificed to the colonisation of Australia, an illegal act of dispossession of peoples resident on this continent for close to 70,000 years.

The siting of this work, at the contemporary site of the adminisation of law in this state, is a sombre reminder of the injustice that continues to be visited on Australia's First Peoples as a direct result of this violent dispossession. Fiona writes, "Disproportionate violence moved against sovereign nations ... There was no respect afforded to the original peoples or indeed any effort to compensate them for the occupation of their lands or the taking of their resources. It was wholesale brutality, murder and theft."[7] This public artwork, from 2004, has also been important in paving the way for other artists to explore, in their subject matter, other histories of Australia's violent past that remain little known.[8]

Witnessing to Silence (2004) possesses a deathlike stillness that hovers within the three elements facing the street. Laminated ash is encased in five glass and stainless-steel pillars that sit inside a circle of marble pavers. The adjacent circle encloses a group of lotus stems in cast bronze (representing water but also evoking the Buddhist use of the sacred lotus lily and enlightenment), with its original iteration including a misting device which sprayed the lilies every fifteen minutes. This element was decommissioned during the Brisbane drought in 2005. The circles suggest the dance grounds or bora rings that are part of traditional Aboriginal ceremony. Dark pavers are scattered like grave stones through both circles, inscribed with the names of places at which massacres occurred in Queensland during the Frontier Wars.

This is a public artwork of which Fiona is proud. Many years later, Younger (who learned about the subterfuge in *The Australian*) told me that all BMC artworks were extraordinarily scrutinised, and "six others were scrutinised alongside Fiona's, and if any artist was at risk of censorship there were other artists more at risk of censorship than Fiona".[9] It was a tense time in the Department of Justice and Attorney-General, with the jailing of Chief Magistrate Di Fingleton in 2003 and the government keen to avoid any further negative attention.[10] Younger remembered, "When Fiona presented her advanced concept, I remember the prickliness of the room, and Fiona's discomfort. Then the client representative saw [what was then proposed] as two circles and a line as manacles. I saw this as scales of justice."[11]

Younger acknowledges: "I certainly understand her view that her work may not have been able to proceed if she was upfront [about its meaning]."[12] During the BMC artwork launch in November 2004, the Daniel Templeman sculpture at the front of the building attracted most of the media attention. Younger interpreted Fiona's actions in taking the issue to the press as a way of activating the artwork politically. I was then Brisbane visual arts critic for *The Australian*. "I've got a story for you", Fiona said to me down the phone. Then her throaty laugh. As a freelancer, I offered it to *The Australian*; the story was ultimately written by arts editor Miriam Cosic.

It is so often work in the public realm that draws ire and comment. Younger recalled that Anna Bligh's response as Arts Minister of the day was that, "Fiona is considered a foremost artist, and this is an appropriate place for issues of justice and injustice". Bligh's statement acknowledged the professionalism of artists and offered them licence to make the work they felt pertinent for the occasion.

Aaron Seeto sums up Fiona's approach, "In tackling histories that are mostly hidden from mainstream view, Foley's work demands not only a public declaration of their disappearance, but subtly and powerfully, she engages the process of public art and the institutions that commission it. In this sense, public art … can be read as a tool describing Foley's artistic and political intention."[13]

OPIUM

———

The role of opium in the history of Queensland was little known until the publication of Rosalind Kidd's book, *The Way We Civilise* (1997). Fiona remembers, "Mum had read the book and told me to read it. Each Christmas I read new books being released. It's usually a quiet time for me, when I can read and not be distracted." Kidd's research drew on documents preserved in the State Archives and *The Aboriginals Protection and Restriction of the Sale of Opium Act*, 1897, which is housed in the State Library of Queensland.

Fiona's first exhibited works on this theme were *Black Friday* (2006). Sombre and dark panels are overpainted with words or phrases; some include images of poppies below the words. The narrative thread throughout the exhibition was strong: the phrase "£30,000 Annually Queensland Government" referred to profits flowing from the opium trade. Red petals add poignancy to the quavering line of the poppy stems, hinting at the human cost to Aboriginals as a direct result of opium addiction. In *Opium Permits* an image of a pipe and drifting smoke in gold noted the valuable nature of this drug to both settlers and the government's implicit role. Titles such as *Opium Permits* and *Opium Dregs* take on a double meaning to underscore the power of the subject. In the paintings, the qualities of brushstroke and surface become places for the eye to wander freely, at odds with the unsettling truths they describe. A series of etchings repeat some of these forms. Their shadows and secondary echo evoke the pall of the past over the present.

Fiona has been making work about opium, specifically the 1897 *Act*, since 2001. The history of opium connects to K'gari and renders it personal. Aboriginal people were sent to Bogimbah Creek Reserve mission on K'gari from across the state in 1897. In her book titled *Biting the Clouds* (a euphemism for being stoned on opium), Fiona writes,

> Queensland maintains and hangs onto a collective amnesia
> regarding race relations in their state. One could even say
> that intellectual ignorance is celebrated ... My truth has
> been to challenge white patriarchal society and ask them
> to look at themselves, their hypocrisy, arrogance, silences
> and denial. Very rarely has this legislation been covered
> by Queensland artists. During 2003, Shaun Weston
> acknowledged my art as offering "truths we may only come
> to realise after encountering Foley's work".[14]

In 2006 Fiona's major sculpture *Black Opium*, which comprises 777 poppies assembled in an infinity symbol, was installed on the ceiling above the public spaces at the State Library of Queensland. It was one of only two public artworks commissioned as part of the redevelopment of the library and Queensland Art Gallery at South Bank.[15] Permanent and public, it offers a fitting memorial to Aboriginals whose families, welfare and future have been impacted by the past, in this place where histories are found and rewritten. The poppies hang, heads down, installed on the fourth level but visible from the building's sheltered vestibule. It can be seen from much of the library, even after hours when the library itself is closed but its exterior spaces are occupied (given the 24/7 wireless internet access it offers). Fiona's aesthetic continues to extend sorrow and empathy over generations of losses.

Fiona also created a series of "mood" rooms, accessible from the fourth floor. Again, there are seven in number. Small and intimate places, they are meeting or study areas for one or two people, evocatively furnished like bespoke Wunderkammer. They explore, visually and conceptually, the relationships *The Act* sought to prevent between Aboriginal Australians and the Chinese people in north Queensland. An overt government agenda sought to outlaw sexual contact between Asian and Aboriginal peoples, with the idea of maintaining "racial integrity".[16] In quiet solitary spaces, individually named for their dominant influence—Bliss, Shrine, Mangrove, String, Silver, Gold and Slow Burn—the visitor may surrender to the multiple histories that Fiona has combined within a pleasurable aesthetic. We are physically embraced, implicated, immersed and immobilised by the revelatory nature of the histories which unfold. They progress from one to the next and through this process elements of history, emotion, beauty, ideas and visual cues offer a multi-layered understanding. To journey through each room makes for an experience as poetic as it is political, into greater understanding. Alison Kubler writes,

> Here again is the number seven. Plus one makes eight: the integer of infinity. Is this symbolism intended or accidental? Is Foley a contemporary seer, divining meaning from the blackest of histories? There is indeed a deeply embedded symmetry and symbolism that speaks to the very heart of Indigenous culture, its richness, longevity and historical tenacity. In this light, we might approach the rooms as seven steps to a kind of enlightenment.[17]

The mood rooms offer a journey through Queensland's histories, experienced like a symphony Fiona conducts, through history, emotion, beauty, and visual cues. Their impact is cumulative, poetic and political, offering a place to know the past and spend time with what Henry Reynolds described as "this whispering in our hearts".[18]

Kidd's book *The Way We Civilise* was also the starting point for Fiona's first art film *Bliss* (2008), which is featured in one of the mood rooms. The film's aesthetic echoes the seduction of the drug in its meditative capture of the movement of opium poppies. Pink swathes of flowers sway in the breeze, their beauty a foil for the drug's deadly capabilities. Opium was regulated in Queensland history with the 1897 introduction of *The Aboriginals Protection and Restriction of the Sale of Opium Act*, the first formal list of strictures used to render Aboriginals compliant during the settlement of Queensland. As Fiona relates, "It was detrimental to Aboriginal people, dictating the way in which they lived their lives by the state government. It described who they could and couldn't marry, where they lived, allowed them to be quarantined into missions, severed relationships with Country, and broke down the laws that had governed their society previously."

Fiona's research into opium and the ramifications of *The Act* continues. Just as it proved a game changer in the destruction of Aboriginal families, systems and nations, *The Act* has seeded Fiona's art for eighteen years. In 2006 she wrote, "Haunted by our continent's Indigenous forebears, the brutality has a lingering residue—it leaves memories. Ironically, it is these memories that have shaped and given meaning to a new era of Australian art and culture."[19]

"Opium and its relationship with Aboriginal people took me into a journey to find out about Aboriginal lives. I am still dumb-founded that white Australians don't know about their own history. While it is not my role to teach them, I have taken on the slow process of illuminating people through my art practice."[20]

Bliss includes text that appears like a subliminal script. Filmed in Tasmania where poppies are legally grown, it provides vignettes of text which expose the malignant effect of the offer of opium (usually ash or dregs) to Aboriginal people in return for free labour. Highly addictive, the drug ensured loyalty or enslavement to employers. The aesthetic of the film also seduces the viewer, its aesthetic and soundscape capturing the changing wind conditions on this open landscape. Words with harsh and ugly meanings taken directly from history overwrite the images of poppies from time to time, and the drama of their movement, occasional stilling, and changes in scale and viewing vista, lull us into a sense of bliss at odds with the historical realities. It remains powerful, its medium part of its message.

Bliss was acquired by both the University of Queensland Art Museum and the Museum of Contemporary Art in Sydney and became the stimulus for *Fiona Foley: Forbidden,*[21] a major survey exhibition that toured both venues. This exhibition and its display in Sydney, where Fiona had trained and made such strong early strides, and Brisbane, where her work continued to provoke, was a powerful affirmation of her contribution in the year of her forty-fifth birthday.

Anna Clark describes "historical consciousness" in her book *Private Lives, Public History* as something "learned, studied and critiqued. It is also gossiped, chattered, whispered, imagined and laughed."[22] Fiona might add that history is visible and engaged with physically, emotionally and intellectually. Like the bump in the leaves she selected as a child, her work renders history tactile, and capable of developing, in its audience, a consciousness, perhaps even a conscience. It is in her public art that her audience is largest, most potently educative. It is a space that she examines, particularly in her own country.

Robust debate about public sculpture, or any art, is rare enough in Australian cultural life. In 2011 Fiona took the lead again, hand-picked for the opportunity by the bureaucracy of Arts Queensland. She was asked to speak at a forum which addressed public servants and the broader arts community "Creative Capital: Arts and Culture Strategic Directions for Queensland". When she was approached, she told Arts Queensland that she *would* be critical. The invitation to speak was quickly confirmed.

Just before the forum, an Arts Queensland press release drew attention to a paper published with the same title: *Creative Capital:*

Arts and Culture Strategic Directions for Queensland. Noting the fifth anniversary of the highly successful Gallery of Modern Art (GOMA) and the redeveloped State Library of Queensland at the Cultural Centre, South Bank, then Arts Minister Rachel Nolan asked Queenslanders to contribute to the way forward.

Fiona took the stage. She was nervous; Djon Mundine had flown from Sydney to be in the audience. The topic she tackled was public sculpture in and around Brisbane's Queensland Art Gallery/Gallery of Modern Art (QAGOMA) precinct. First, she drew attention to the way in which the public art processes in Queensland were side-stepped to secure a $1 million commission for a major sculpture for the exterior of the Gallery of Modern Art (GOMA).[23] This commission, announced the month before, was awarded to New Zealander Michael Parakowhai for *The World Turns* (2011–2012). Fiona believed that this was a bad decision, for the reasons she articulated:

> Government policy was put to one side. The Art+Place panel
> of experts was sidelined. Their decision-making powers were
> taken away from them, along with $750,000 of their budget,
> which was moved across to the Premier of Queensland
> Sculpture Commission. A new committee was created to
> oversee the process and select the winner. It would be chaired
> by the Director of GOMA, along with the Deputy Director,
> a sitting member of the GOMA Board of Trustees and the
> Deputy Director General of Arts Queensland.

She noted that only three out of the seven appointees to this especially convened committee were truly independent.[24] The second part of her argument related to the investment of Aboriginal artists in creating aesthetic experiences in their own places, to highlight "the systematic erasure" of Aboriginal art and culture:

> Civic spaces are a reflection of who you are and where the bureaucratic community wishes to see itself echoed around the world. When the landscape at South Bank, Brisbane could as easily be substituted for South Bank, London then something is amiss. What makes us different to any other place in the world? The answer is obvious ... It's Aboriginal and Torres Strait Islander culture. When Brisbane's South Bank is visually barren of Indigenous art, it says to me and every other visitor—that Queenslanders do not value, respect or take pride in the original nations that they have replaced. The foundation of Australian culture must begin with including the aesthetic of Aboriginal and Torres Strait Islander peoples. If their art and presence is nowhere to be seen in designated cultural spaces, then the commissioning of public art by international artists only adds another layer to the erasure of Australia's Indigenous people.[25]

Regarding the Parakowhai commission being awarded to an artist of Māori descent from New Zealand, she stated:

> The Gallery of Modern Art currently has three works in its public art collection. They are by Scottish artist Martin Boyce, Taiwanese artist Lee Mingwei and Brisbane-based artist Scott Redford. In December, the deputy director of

> GOMA stated that in relation to their fourth commission
> by artist Michael Parekowhai, "International artists are in
> the minority so it's an opportunity to have an international
> artist make work".[26] The irony is that three out of four is not
> a minority.[27]

In terms of an artist's practice, public art allows a rare opportunity, given its scale and budgetary scope, to realise an aesthetic ambition. Internationalisation of contemporary art was also part of a change in the public art policy in 2007, when Art Built-in ceased and Art+Place: Queensland Public Art Fund was brought into effect. This created a situation in which opportunities were even more tightly contested. The Parakowhai issue had collateral damage. In terms of international relations, John Stafford, who was at the time the senior arts bureaucrat in Queensland, described Fiona's criticism as "genuine and influential. However it read as an unmitigated cultural disaster in regard to our relationship with our close international neighbours, New Zealand. The new minister was ill-equipped to deal with these issues, resulting in a trifecta of cultural gaffes, a series of uninformed and regrettable messages to send to the international arts community."[28] Yet Fiona's comments were on target in their identification of a significant oversight. Two years later, incoming Queensland Art Gallery director Chris Saines (from 2013) was "determined to remedy" the lack of public artworks by Indigenous artists in Brisbane's South Bank cultural precinct.[29]

As a cultural leader, Fiona is prepared to take on the heat generated by discussion of these issues. On this occasion, given the importance of the issue to other Aboriginal artists, she sought support from Brisbane-based arts collective ProppaNow, "set up in Brisbane in 2003 to give urban-based Aboriginal artists a voice".[30] She asked members Tony Albert and Megan Cope for a letter of support from the group; they declined because "they were going to New Zealand later that year". While ProppaNow trades on outspokenness, self-described as "a unique and controversial perspective of black Australia which is sometimes confronting and always thought provoking",[31] Fiona found ProppaNow's disinterest disappointing. Her remarks were well received but resented by QAGOMA management.

> Arts Queensland knew I wouldn't speak favourably of the QAGOMA. I am very judicious about the research I do for public presentations. I scoped outside the building to be confident of my point. And I had scoped what was on inside the building, all of which was donated by the James C Sourris AM Collection. I received a standing ovation. Paul Keating gave the lunchtime keynote, introduced by Anna Bligh. The room was abuzz with what I presented. There was a bank of the QAGOMA staffers: Julie Ewington, Bruce McLean, Suhanya Raffel staring at me.

The fallout from this event was small-minded. In the week that followed, I reported Fiona's remarks in a small article on the Arts Queensland Forum (2011) in *The Australian* newspaper (16 December 2011). A phone call from the head of marketing at the Queensland Art Gallery lambasted me for alleged misrepresentation of the Queensland Art Gallery's position. It reinforced a perception that the Queensland Art Gallery found any coverage that came without praise unacceptable under its then management.[32]

/

In 2016 Fiona released her third film as part of an exhibition at Andrew Baker Art Dealer. Called *A Quintessential Act* (2016) it features an interview with historian Professor Raymond Evans, relating details from Queensland's Frontier Wars. It takes place in front of Fiona's seminal sculpture *Dispersed* (2008) which, in charred timber and metal, spells out the word "DISPERSED", the "D" filled in with gleaming bullets. In the course of their interview, Evans describes "dispersed" as the ultimate weasel word, transformed in the course of Australian settler history from the verb which means "to scatter" into a euphemism for mass murder and theft.

Foley, dressed in slick newsreader garb, cradling a large microphone, asks Evans a series of questions about the impact of invasion on Aboriginal people, the role of white women, his view of *Dispersed* and revisits *Witnessing to Silence* (2004), which was inspired in part by comments in a conference paper delivered by then Queensland Art Gallery curator Tim Morrell that Fiona interpreted as, "Australia being settled peacefully".[33] The interview segues to Foley and Evans standing, shifting gear to be conversational, with Foley becoming relaxed and smiling. The final footage sees her standing alone in front of *Witnessing to Silence,* on the footpath of Brisbane's Roma Street, a Badtjala warrior in corporate garb, a uniform to solicit understanding.

The power of *Witnessing to Silence* and its location within the court which facilitated the death and destruction of ninety-five per cent of the Aboriginal population in Queensland marks the end of this short film.

Fiona is also a convincing warrior, arguing for the power of humanity over history. She insists on authenticity, staking a claim for the art made to speak to this place in the world and to be distinctive.

/

Fiona's critique of the public sculpture around the Gallery of Modern Art was addressed in 2016. In June of that year, an Indigenous Sculpture Commission was announced for the public realm within Brisbane's cultural precinct and unveiled by November, in time for the *GOMA Turns Ten* celebration. In its budget and scale, this new work remains dwarfed by the $1.2 million Parakowhai commission (which celebrated GOMA's fifth birthday). GOMA director Chris Saines suggested that the smaller ($250,000) budget and footprint of this new work was ameliorated by its prominent placement at GOMA's entry. He also conceded that the cultural climate by 2016 had been impacted by shrinking government investment.

Fiona was invited to pitch for the sculpture commission. Her experience with public art has governed her personal rule to steer clear of opportunities with budgets under $300,000. An artist fee may come down to five or ten per cent of the entire budget, and concept development and delivery may take years and is a significant workload. She believes that:

> Other artists are the beneficiaries of my speaking up, writing
> articles, constructing an intelligent argument, speaking publicly
> at conferences, doing radio interviews and being devalued by
> GOMA over many years. There are some people that "do"
> and there are some artists who remain silent, and benefit.

The final commission was delivered with poetry by Judy Watson. Her *tow row* (2016) evokes the fishing practices used by Aboriginal people in the adjacent Brisbane River. This butterfly shaped fishing net is cast in bronze, casting light and shadow with its form at the building's entry (depending on the time of day).

Chris Saines was appointed QAGOMA director in 2013. Within months of assuming his new position, he acquired *Dispersed* (2008) for the QAGOMA collection. He invited Fiona to meet with him to acknowledge that her work had been "overlooked". In April 2014 he opened a survey exhibition of her work at Redcliffe City Art Gallery titled *Courage.* He spoke knowledgeably and without notes about the power of her artwork and its contribution.

In 2017 she was appointed by Arts Queensland to the Board of the Queensland Art Gallery. Her professional journey has confronted many who created obstacles and resisted her pace of cultural change. While other artists may share an interest in probing uncomfortable histories with aesthetic explorations, and note contemporary injustices privately, Foley is on her own in terms of making public criticism of major collecting institutions, other artists and cultural flashpoints.

Political acts outside art-making have become part of Fiona's artistic pattern. They form, as Jay Younger suggested, a way to complete the project that may jettison a sculpture out of the realm of the art world and into the mainstream, rather like a grenade into a paddock. This has become, at one level, simply what she does, a way in which she negotiates a path into and through the obstacles thrown up by the wider world. Its other layer is driven and purposeful, her subjects wide-ranging but drawing on injustices done to her as a Badtjala woman from K'gari, her family and forebears, and the history that has been imposed upon them.

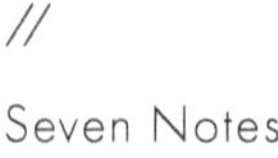

Seven Notes

---

1 Michael Marmot, "Social Determinants and the Health of Indigenous Australians", *Medical Journal of Australia* 194, 10 (2011): 512.

2 Ibid.

3 Joan Winter writes, "In 1867, 1,000 aborigines had gathered for the annual government blanket distribution, by 1872 the number had dwindled to 435 and by 1880 it was just 230." In "Against Their Will", 8. Shawn Foley also writes in *The Badtjala People* (16), that between 1850 and the disbanding of the mission on K'gari 1904, the Badtjala population plummeted from 2,000 to 20.

4 W. E. Hoy, P. Kincaid-Smith, M.D. Hughson et al., "CKD in Aboriginal Australians", *American Journal of Kidney Diseases* 56, 5 (2010): 983–993.

5 Djon Mundine, Introduction to *Michael Riley* (Albury: Murray Art Museum Albury, 2018): 8.

6 Jay Younger, interview by the author, 15 February 2017.

7 Foley, *Biting the Clouds*, 41–42.

8 The Centre for 21st Century Humanities has developed an online map which continues to research and document massacres all over Australia. It builds on Australia-wide research begun by Bruce Elder's 1988 book, *Blood on the Wattle*: https://c21ch.newcastle.edu.au/colonialmassacres/introduction.php.

9 Ibid.

10 In 1999 Diane Fingleton was the first woman to be appointed Chief Magistrate in Queensland. She approached the position with a reform agenda particularly with regard to Aboriginal recognition. A magistrate's transfer dispute saw her tried and convicted on a charge of retaliating against a witness in 2002. In 2005 her conviction was quashed by the High Court of Australia when Justice McHugh argued that "it would be hard to imagine a stronger case of a miscarriage of justice in the particular circumstances of the case".

She subsequently became a magistrate of the Caloundra Magistrates Court, and retired in 2010. National Library of Australia, "Fingleton, Di (1947–)", Trove (2008) https://nla.gov.au/nla.party-579027.

11 Ibid.

12 Ibid.

13 Seeto, "Ground Cover", 33.

14 Foley, *Biting the Clouds,* 7.

15 *Black Opium* was commissioned under the Queensland Government Art Built-In initiative (1999–2007).

16 Rosalind Kidd, *The Way We Civilise* (St Lucia: UQP, 1997), 45.

17 Alison Kubler, "Fiona Foley and Her Fearful Symmetry", in *Black Opium: Fiona Foley*, ed. Ian Were (Brisbane: State Library of Queensland, 2010), 33.

18 Henry Reynolds, *This Whispering in Our Hearts* (Sydney: Allen & Unwin, 1998).

19 Fiona Foley, "A Touch of the Tar Brush", in *The Art of Politics/The Politics of Art: The Place of Indigenous Contemporary Art*, ed. Fiona Foley (Brisbane: Keeaira Press, 2006), 24–27.

20 Fiona Foley, "An Act of Largesse", presented at *Race, Whiteness and Indigeneity: An International Conference*, Gold Coast, 6–8 June 2017.

21 Fiona Foley, *Fiona Foley: Forbidden* (Sydney: Museum of Contemporary Art, 2009).

22 Anna Clark, *Private Lives, Public History* (Melbourne, Melbourne University Press, 2016).

23 An additional $200,000 was added to the cost of the commission to transport it from the site of its fabrication in New Zealand to Queensland.

24 Fiona Foley, "Fiona Foley for Creative Capital", in *Creative Capital* (Brisbane: Arts Queensland, 2011).

25 Ibid.

26 Statement made by Suhanya Raffel, Deputy Director, Curatorial and Collection Development Queensland Art Gallery while in attendance at the *Creative Capital Forum*, Brisbane, 14 December 2011.

27 Foley, "The Elephant in the Room", presented at *Creative Capital Forum*, Brisbane, Arts Queensland, 14 December 2011.

28 John Stafford, interview by the author, December 2013. In an email to the author dated 25 April 2021, Stafford clarified his meaning: "The trifecta to which my quote refers was the disappearance of a generous government-backed public art program which supported many Queensland artists for many years–right across the state in places like Bamaga, not just Brisbane. This demise was due to the politics of inept politicians who the people of Queensland tossed out unequivocally at their very first opportunity after just one term. However Queensland's public art program went down the gurgler with them. And Labor has never reinstated it since, even with successive majorities for three terms."

29 Michaela Boland, "South Bank World Turns Once More", *The Australian*, 1 April 2015.

30 ProppaNow, "About Us", https://proppanow.wordpress.com/about-us/.

31 Ibid.

32 When director Tony Ellwood broke a five-year contract with QAGOMA in 2012 to return to Melbourne, where he had been appointed new director of the National Gallery of Victoria, he took with him significant senior staff as GOMA was preparing to host the 7th Asia Pacific Triennial of Contemporary Art in December of that year.

33 Fiona recalls these comments made by Morrell, then a Queensland Art Gallery curator, during the Third Asia-Pacific Triennial conference held at the Brisbane Convention and Exhibition Centre, 1999. The conference papers record Fiona challenging Morrell who acknowledged that his paper contained "oversimplifications". He was comparing the Indigenous situation during colonisation in Australia to that in New Zealand, and indicated that Aboriginal people did not resist the incomers. Morrell's presentation and comments from Fiona Foley and other audience members are published in "Session 4: Regional Perspectives II", *Beyond the Future: Papers from the Third Asia Pacific Triennial of Contemporary Art, 10–12 September 1999*, eds. Caroline Turner and Morris Low (Brisbane: Queensland Art Gallery, 2000), 71—74.

EIGHT

POLITICS AND SPACE

The **2016 Adelaide Biennial Exhibition of Australian Art** cited art and its cultural power as a driver for change. The theme of art as a *Magic Object* related to the curiosity and wonderment that art inspires in its audiences. Then director of the Art Gallery of South Australia Nick Mitzevich wrote, "At *Magic Object*'s core is the optimistic belief in the power of art to transform people's perceptions about aspects of their world, to alter their thinking and feelings. This indeed is the magic of art."[1] Aboriginal artist and academic Danie Mellor was included in this exhibition with a new photographic series. One of the fourteen circular images titled *On a noncorreolationist thought I–XIV* (2016) focuses closely on a staghorn in his characteristic blue-grey tones. The detail of this plant is disorienting, with leaves appearing like bodily organs, the trunk of a tree to the right reading like a tilted ground plane, and long leaves reaching forward as though to embrace the viewer. This plant appears strange, other-worldly. Yet it is just a staghorn—although its epiphytic qualities (which see it grow from spores on the surface of another plant to feed on air, rain and water, and the debris that may land on it) do feel magical.

When Fiona began exhibiting in the mid-1980s, narratives from urban Aboriginal artists like Mellor were far from mainstream. Mundine sees this period of Aboriginal art as the fourth phase, during which, "under the influence of postcolonial writing, artists of the 1980s who attended Western art schools now use Western materials, concepts and references to some extent to tell their Aboriginal story".[2] Foley is also part of the fifth phase, with her involvement in the activities of Boomalli instrumental in taking control of the Aboriginal art movement. This drove Aboriginal and Torres Strait Islander involvement in writing about, curating and marketing Aboriginal work. It feels like progress. The Aboriginal story has increasing profile in the mainstream community. Yet Mundine refers to a sixth phase as, "the Empire strikes back", with some non-Aboriginal groups viewing gains in Aboriginal social and political areas as potentially threatening. He writes, "Although we are visible through our art, what is the place we have come to?"[3] On 26 October 2017, then prime minister Malcolm Turnbull rejected the proposed constitutional change put forward by the 2017 Uluru Statement from the Heart. Under these circumstances, a degree of progress toward recognition (let alone reconciliation) would appear to have been jammed into reverse.

In 2011 Fiona was in the French city of Lyon with a Radio National documentary crew in tow. An incredibly lifelike plaster cast of a Badtjala man named Boni (*Australien lançant le Boomerang*) has been in what is now the Muséum d'Histoire Naturelle de Lyon since 1883.

The precision with which his bodily imprint has been captured is astonishing. The cast records his face and beard, a broad nose and intense face. He has initiation scars across his chest, muscle in his shoulders, back and legs, all thick with detail of his presence. He is life-size, holding a boomerang above his head, with hair tightly curled around his scalp. Fiona told broadcaster Daniel Browning, in his programme "Cast Among Strangers" for Radio National, "It feels a little bit jarring and a little bit sad. I was thinking about how he would have travelled to Lyon and what his journey from K'gari would have been like. There are lots of questions and very few answers."[4]

The cast was made with Boni's consent; he would have had to stand very still while he was swathed with bandages and a cold setting solution; the imprint of goose bumps standing on his skin was captured during the process. Found in a storeroom in the Muséum d'Histoire Naturelle de Lyon, Boni's cast is evidence of the trade in live Aboriginals who were trafficked overseas, to perform for circuses, fighting, singing and boomerang throwing. Information is scant. Fiona had read a book by Roslyn Poignant called *Professional Savages: Captive Lives and Western Spectacle* (2004) which described this trade in humans, their display in the equivalent of a human zoo. There are a few lines about three people from K'gari who ended up in a human circus in Germany. A pen drawing from *Illustrirte Zeitung* (9 September 1883) includes an image of Jurono, Boni's countryman, and Aboriginal figures are shown performing with boomerangs in the Zoological Garden in Dresden. Two of the three died while they were in Germany; Boni survived them—for a while.

Many newspaper archives were lost to fire in Dresden during the Second World War, but Browning located a paragraph in a German newspaper that suggested that Boni, "an Australian Niger [*sic*]", was travelling with a Laplander Circus that ended up on the outskirts of Lyon, close to where the Muséum d'Histoire Naturelle was being built. Apart from the full-body cast are casts of his feet and hands, with the tag "Boni Australien" attached. In one of the photographs posted on the Radio National website, Fiona places her smaller hands over his, as though hand to hand she might reach him through history. She related:

> All I could rely on was my emotional response. I was overjoyed, amazed, but also incredibly sad because you come face to face with this man who is a forebear. There is a family resemblance to my brother Shawn. You don't know anything about his life, and it is all so second and third hand. So, you are surmising and just wondering, trying to piece it together. But you don't get any closer to the story.[5]

The pursuit of pseudo-scientific knowledge drove the practice of collecting Aboriginal remains and artefacts. In Queensland the "Protectors"—Walter Roth who was Northern Protector (later Chief Protector) and Archibald Meston who was Southern Protector—became an active part of the collecting network. It often caused disquiet to those who were asked to acquire these items; they felt it was desecration. These objects were purported to "prove" European racial superiority, but they also extended possession to encompass the bodies of Aboriginal people and their remains. Researcher Gemmia Burden notes, "By removing Aboriginal people and culture, the invaders were writing their own narratives of ownership over the land. As settler colonies were built on the dispossession of Indigenous people, the removal of cultural materials became part of the appropriation of land."[6]

Re-establishing an emotional and physical connection to land, however temporary, drove Fiona's vision of her 2014 ephemeral art exhibition at the University of Queensland, titled *Courting Blakness*. I first heard about it when Fiona phoned me on a Saturday afternoon, and began without preamble: "I've got a project for you." Fiona Foley had met Fiona Nicoll some twelve years earlier, at a conference Foley convened at Griffith University in 2005. *The Art of Politics/The Politics of Art* was organised under the auspices of Foley's Adjunct Professorship at Griffith University (2003–2009). In 2011, Nicoll was instrumental in facilitating Foley's appointment as an Adjunct Professor at the University of Queensland and described the beginnings of *Courting Blakness* as a recipe:

> Take Australia's leading public artist to curate an exhibition
> of eight Aboriginal artists and mix with an institution
> with a population of nearly 7,000 staff and close to
> 60,000 undergraduate and research higher degree students.
> Then stir. The results of this experiment were as rich as they
> were challenging for the sandstone university.[7]

Fiona Nicoll observed that, "Fiona has an amazing capacity to cut through to the core issue. She notes the links and divisions between Indigenous and non-Indigenous art. Through working with her,

I've learned how she works through that in her public art."[8] And it was public art that provided Nicoll's first introduction to Foley. She recalls:

> I was finishing my PhD, inner Melbourne was my milieu. I was walking past the town hall, and I had this sense of disorientation because there were these extra slabs in front of the building. There were sounds—bird noises, and different languages. I looked at what was written on the slabs, which read, "scissors, mirrors, beads, axes, etc.". I realised that this was referring to John Batman and his attempt at a treaty, his token attempt to negotiate with the people from the Kulin nations, in Victoria. So, that was my first encounter with [the work of] Fiona Foley.[9]

Courting Blakness culminated in two linked events, both produced during Fiona's period as Adjunct Professor at the University of Queensland (2011–2017). The initial idea, to occupy space in the Great Court, the University's heart, came from University of Queensland academic Morgan Briggs.[10] The curating of the exhibition dominated Fiona Foley's period at the university, a revolutionary installation of temporary public art that staked an Aboriginal land claim—for a few weeks—into both the symbolic real estate and the European cultural traditions of Queensland's oldest university. Around the Great Court are faculties that include law, history, philosophy, literature, science and engineering, all central to the function of Western democracy. *Courting Blakness* was designed to create space to think about structural change and the potential for Aboriginal artists to be at its forefront. The Honourable Linda Burney (MP, Parliament of Australia) said at the opening event:

To see a sandstone university, to see this place, absolutely
telling the story of identity is extremely powerful ... *Courting
Blakness* is about relationships between Aboriginal people
and the university; it's about reinterpreting space in the
Great Court of this university. It's about reshaping all of
our identities as Aboriginal and Australian people. It's
also about challenging our political thoughts; it's about
creating dialogue.[11]

Artworks politicise the spaces in which they are exhibited; Fiona took
over the central University of Queensland heritage-listed space and
politicised it with art. On this hallowed ground, a circle of buildings
made from Helidon sandstone channels the tradition of the European
university. Within this Great Court, glossy green stretches of manicured
lawn (more than six acres) are interrupted by a central pathway, jacaranda
and gum trees offering a little shade. Decorated with gargoyles and
sculpted imagery, they refer to academics from history, Australian flora
and fauna, and the crests of other (European) universities. There are
also Aboriginal peoples as noted by Louise Chiodo who writes, "Are the
people in these scenes the ancestors of the Jagera and Turrbal peoples
whose land the Great Court occupies? They appear frozen in time, in
the facade of this stylistically confused building that, architecturally
speaking, could be almost anywhere in the world."[12]

The sandstone buildings evoke their architectural antecedents,
education and culture and speak to the aspirations of the university as
one of the country's intellectual capitals. Fiona's selection of artists—
Ryan Presley, Archie Moore, Christian Thompson, Michael Cook,
Karla Dickens, Natalie Harkin, REA and Megan Cope—mediated

visually and conceptually on place and possession. Both remain unresolved hot spots in the contemporary Australian debate about historical acknowledgement and reconciliation with this country's First Peoples.

/

This project successfully unsettled the parameters of ownership. Yet its delivery was harrowing for both Fiona Foley and Fiona Nicoll as they negotiated logistics and funding. Their final disappointment was the revocation by Professor Peter Høj, Vice-Chancellor and President of the University of Queensland, of the initial approval to share the flagpoles on the central Forgan Smith Building in the Great Court with Aboriginal artist Archie Moore. Moore's flags were intrinsic to his *14 Nations* installation, which was to begin on the ground and ascend to the rooftop. Instead, his flags lined the path on the ground plane, the spine that divides the Great Court in two, and connected the Forgan Smith Building to its counterpart opposite. Louise Chiodo noted the dialogue between Moore's flags and the official flags that flew from the top of the building:

> Through *Courting Blakness*, the Great Court became a
> palimpsest on which new meanings had been re-inscribed,
> if only for a moment. The new art spoke not only to the
> complexities of belonging and identity in Australia, or the
> power and tension within this particular space, but also to the
> reality that no matter where we are in this nation we're always
> going to be standing on Indigenous Country.[13]

Moore's flags are fictions, although arguably no more so than "official" flags that may or may not represent individuals or groups in a way with which they identify. Flags can be flashpoints, the focus of nationalistic or group sentiments. Moore's installation was inspired by a map of Queensland, created in 1900, which divided the state into fourteen discrete (albeit incorrectly defined) Aboriginal nations. He writes:

> My masquerade as flags. They do not require the status of Australian National Flags nor are they required to follow existing protocols. They are false flags and, as such, do not hide their dualities. They are ambiguous and contradictory, raise questions of authenticity, and evoke my own fragmented personal identity.[14]

However, the exclusion of his flags from the pinnacle of the university rooftops, a casualty of the university's "flag-flying protocols", prove that a flag has an ability to "include or exclude", "like a skin" that confines and restricts contemporary identities. In 2018 these flags became an intrinsic part of a public artwork for Sydney International Airport, a highly satisfying outcome with a significant profile.

Ryan Presley's *Debt* (2014) was also a dominant sculpture in the Great Court. Letters papered with redrawn Australian currency spelt "X CHANGE". Partly embedded into the grass, their stature as insecure as the global economic system; they referred to the first work Presley had showed publicly—redrawn Australian currency—$10, $20, $50 and $100 notes. In his iterations, Aboriginal leaders replace the familiar (white) faces on our legal tender. Presley's work also suggests that a capitalist economy is a construct that corrodes country, environment, morality and ethics. This alternative reality was created within the sandstone courtyard of the Great Court in a way which symbolised the angst and exploitation of colonial times. *Courting Blakness* infiltrated this established space with Aboriginal history to argue for a different style of authority and relationship.

Fiona Foley and Fiona Nicoll remain disappointed that bureaucratic obstacles—political, personal and historical—prevented the flying of Moore's flags. Together they had endured a baptism of fire and difficulty and much was achieved, even if the final hurdle could not be cleared. Fiona Nicoll told me,

> *Courting Blakness* was about helping Fiona make something happen ... Incredibly creative solutions were required; we moved sideways and managed the event. Archie Moore's situation was the most painful. Fiona has a strong moral compass and says of herself, "Where people see shades of grey, I see black and white". *Courting Blakness* was really an act of generosity and solidarity. The provocation in what she does licenses people to push her beyond reasonable bounds ... She has learned and observed the push back.[15]

At the opening of the symposium on 5 September 2014 which launched *Courting Blakness*, Fiona stood centre stage in front of friends, fellow artists Ryan Presley, REA, Natalie Harkins and Karla Dickens, academics, colleagues, students and conference delegates, and spoke her truth. With artist Archie Moore at her side, she said, "A European system of protocols has won the day over an Aboriginal man who had an original concept. History does have a way of repeating itself."[16]

The project's achievements are evident in an ongoing website presence under the banner of the University of Queensland's BlackWords (this resource has indexed Aboriginal literature since 2006).[17] The book that contains a record of the conference papers, art and ideas that graced this "experiment in socially transformative education" makes a case for art as a way into the conversation.[18] The transformative force of a project like this one whittles away at the rebuttal of Australia's histories, creating a presence where erasure had been the norm.

Yet the project had some fallout; and discernible personal shifts for those involved. Fiona Nicoll subsequently left the University of Queensland for an academic role in Canada. Fiona Foley enrolled at the Queensland College of Art to undertake a doctorate and, six months behind, the exhibition and associated events, saw the tangible beginnings of this book.

In recent decades art in the urban realm has accelerated in Australia. For Fiona, public art offers a broader audience for her work, outside museums and galleries and into the mainstream. Andrew Baker, who has represented Fiona in Brisbane since 2002, told me that, "Fiona's public art is some of the best in the country, because she won't be stultified by bureaucrats".[19] Baker observed that Fiona's negotiation of her life and career has required her to "create a persona with which she met the world: the art world in particular. Her work deals with difficult issues; people often take criticism personally. People in the arts habitually can't separate the person from the issues involved. Anyone who raises difficult issues is often attacked personally." In his view, Fiona's generation has changed the thinking of the whole country in a short time. He noted, "They have had to take on very difficult concepts. When society disregards the truth for two hundred years, that takes a lot of unravelling. These artists have been prepared to take the heat in order for the general population to have a better understanding."[20] Fiona is not prepared to accept the status quo, and her raison d'être is to question historical untruths. She will not be silenced on the issues these histories raise. The fallout is, at times, difficult to bear.

Baker observed that, "In the arts, various things are left unsaid. This explains many of the problems—with the person, not the idea, attacked. The only way things will improve is to change that central problem."[21] He believes that "all of her work is part of one big, lifelong project. There is a dialogue in her oeuvre, with themes echoing from early in her career." Baker revels in her skill as an exhibiting artist. Fiona has made films, photographs, paintings and sculpture. He admires her use of language, the few words she needs to channel the essence of her message. "The blankets she made for *Stud Gins* use seven words, less than a haiku, that become chilling in their message."[22]

In 2006 Fiona was offered what was, at that stage, her most ambitious public art venture in the Queensland coastal city of Mackay. Robert Heather, Artspace Mackay's inaugural director, suggested that Architectus approach Fiona with the opportunity to develop one of Australia's most ambitious public art projects throughout Mackay's Bluewater Trail. The client, the Mackay Regional Council, had made a rare decision: to offer this large commission to a single artist, together with the scope to choose her sites. I have been to Mackay a few times since these works became part of the city's fabric. The Bluewater Trail is a long and discursive route around the city, which takes you from the urban centre, along the river, and around the city perimeter. Other significant public artworks around this territory now include Donna Marcus's vibrantly colourful *True North* (2009) installed close to Caneland Central shopping centre. In the broader landscape, it is Fiona's *Mangrove Cap*, with its long sight lines and size, that beckons. A forty-minute walk, into sea grass and open landscapes, through a nature-scape buffer to the industrial city, its tall, rust-coloured shape is magnetic. Finally, dwarfed by its iconic size, it offers a nurturing place to stand under and within.

The project began in earnest in 2006 when Fiona visited Mackay and the Pioneer River area that was to be redeveloped, to undertake research and consultation. In making art for the public realm, liaison with local communities—in this case the Aboriginal Yuiberra people and the Mackay-based South Sea Islander communities—was central. Public art may challenge the status quo, and Fiona was keen to create new pathways through hidden material, with acknowledgement of difficult histories in this forum requiring commitment from Mackay's population. She said, "At one point, I knew I had to think about sculpture like the artist Louise Bourgeois. Digesting the information and layering the sculptures with meaning is how I usually work." During a later public address she said:

> There was more to Mackay than met the eye. Not all history
> is visible or sits on the surface plane. Research involves the
> act of looking as well as the act of listening. Surveying the
> landscape to see who is written in and who is written out of
> the history of Mackay was revealing.[23]

Ideas within the visual language of public art are required to be succinct. In Mackay, Fiona began to pinpoint threads of information, to refine her language and find a way to communicate a message. About working with the local Aboriginal and South Sea Islander communities, she says, "What people want is a relationship. You have to make yourself available to talk to people and sometimes that discussion can be quite tricky. They may not accept you as an artist in their community, or your approach may be the wrong approach. I often need to start a different type of conversation, physically meet people and spend time with them." A turning point in the Mackay project came about through meeting an older South Sea Islander woman at the library:

> Rowena Trieve told me her grandmother's story. As a fifteen-year-old her grandmother had been brought to Mackay from the islands, to work on the sugar cane farms, and one day she escaped the farm. The farm owner tracked her down, hunted her on horseback. She was shackled too tightly around the ankles and had indentations on them for the rest of her life. When Rowena was a young girl, she saw the scarring and the story unfolded.

Fiona recalls Trieve's emotion, and her own, "I made a conscious decision in that library to tell the story about the South Sea Islander people. Their history and contribution to the sugar industry needed to be recalled in the centre of that town."

When they arrived on boats, South Sea Islander people were thumbprinted and auctioned to the highest bidder. Fiona's *Sugar Cubes* features 213 thumbprints of descendants from those early groups. The sculpture is not far from the Customs House on the banks of the Pioneer River, where human cargo would be taken from the boat at low tide and walked on the mud flats up to where they were auctioned under the Leichhardt Tree. It is marked by a small plaque, not easy to see, and when Fiona first visited with Robert Heather, the Leichhardt Tree had been vandalised; it was partly burnt and nearly dead. She told me,

> I think the recognition for me was getting all those thumbprints. They believed we could make a difference. It was difficult. Mackay Council didn't want all of the boats named to be human cargo trading boats. So I gave them seven of those, the others were all names of human cargo boats. The South Sea Islander people were on board, they got their recognition in the CBD, with more recognition on the outskirts of town.

Later she wrote: "We must never forget the forced 'black-birding' of South Sea Islander men, women and children from their islands to Queensland shores for indentured work on sugar cane plantations, sometimes labouring in shackles."[24]

Ultimately six works were created to populate the Bluewater Trail, with four works in the busy CBD area near the wharf and bridge, and two others, *Crows* located in a public pool/play area, and *Mangrove Cap* sensitively placed in the more remote landscape by the river, albeit visible, given its size at nine and a half metres tall, from all over the city. These works are united by a cohesive artistic vision relating local stories. A narrative unfolds throughout the nineteen-kilometre walking/cycling trail that circles the border of Mackay's CBD.

Within her process it was also crucial to meet with the traditional owners, Aboriginal representatives Melanie Kemp and Gary Mooney. Fiona researched the Yuiberra nation, also seeking out material culture from this area. Shield designs were permanently inscribed and the word "YUWI" stands proudly in red in a prominent position, visible from upriver and the CBD. Incorporation of important local narratives has brought light and recognition to them. Yet the Mackay project did not leave her unscathed. Some of the local art community (non-Indigenous) were disgruntled and critical.

Mangroves themselves, while comparatively tiny, are integral to the marine ecosystem. The health of rivers and environment is nurtured by the quality of mangrove stocks, and the size of Fiona's mangrove denotes its importance. One of the largest public artworks created in Australia, its aesthetic presence and integrity is in keeping with its scale. Creating this giant statement in corten steel, designed to further age in a salty environment, and using solar-powered lights to glow through and beneath the cap, with pricks of light visible after dark, Fiona offered the public imagination the phenomena of the mangrove. She said, "I am not a deeply religious person but when I first stood under the mangrove cap on the current site in Mackay, I felt like I was in church". The *Badtjala–English Word List* notes that Pir'ri means mangrove, but also hands and fingers, an immensely poetic understanding of the tree's root system. Fiona mused, "While living at Urangan as a child, and on and off at Booral in my early twenties, my extended family would go out on to the mud flats and hunt and gather oysters, periwinkles and mud crabs. For me it was a treasure trove—I'd collect flotsam and jetsam washed up from high tides. I'd bring home turtle bones, dugong bones and various parts of mangrove seed-pods."

In *Mangrove Cap*, Fiona's experiences, memories and country are unified with visible power.

//

Eight Notes

1 Nick Mitzevich, "Director's Message", *Articulate* (Autumn 2016): 3.

2 Mundine, "30 Years Ago Today".

3 Ibid.

4 Daniel Browning, "Cast Among Strangers", *AWAYE!*, Radio National, 2014.

5 Fiona Foley, interview by the author, 2016.

6 Gemmia Burden, "The Violent Collectors Who Gathered Indigenous Artefacts for the Queensland Museum", *The Conversation* (28 May 2018).

7 Fiona Foley, Fiona Nicoll and Louise Martin-Chew, eds, *Courting Blakness: Recalibrating Knowledge in the Sandstone University* (St Lucia: UQP, 2015), 3.

8 Fiona Nicoll, interview by the author, 2016.

9 Ibid.

10 Ibid.

11 Opening event for *Courting Blakness: Recalibrating Knowledge in the Sandstone University*, 4 September 2014.

12 Ibid., 41.

13 Ibid., 46.

14 Archie Moore in *Courting Blakness*, 122.

15 Fiona Nicoll, interview by the author, 2016.

16 Fiona Foley was disappointed that Richard Bell, who was asked to speak on the first day of the symposium, did not arrive to meet his commitments as a panelist.

17 University of Queensland, *Courting Blakness: Recalibrating Knowledge in the Sandstone University*, https://www.austlit.edu.au.

18 Fiona Nicoll, "Recalibrating Knowledge in the Sandstone University", in *Courting Blakness*, 10.

19 Andrew Baker, interview by the author, 19 August 2016.

20 Ibid.

21 Ibid.

22 Ibid.

23 Fiona Foley, "Public Art Laced with Memory", speech delivered in Mackay, 2010. Unpublished notes.

24 Fiona Foley, "I Speak to Cover the Mouth of Silence", *Art Monthly Australia*, 250 (2012): 56.

NINE

ON COUNTRY

Fiona Foley's historical narratives in photographs and film, paintings and sculpture, emerge from her experience of K'gari as a child. She recalls the simplicity of her childhood immersion in that place and the experience of untrammelled freedom.

> Your main concerns in life were collecting wood for the fire,
> water, keeping out of the wind and finding good shady spots
> to camp. Washing was done by hand down by the creek.
> Our family loved those experiences and the freedom they
> brought. We did so much on the island there was never a dull
> moment. The only communication we had from the outside
> world was a radio.

From this beginning she is comfortable all over the world, in every environment. She has made an installation in a derelict Irish church and created artwork based on a Buddhist word on a pond in rice-growing

Japan.[1] She has worked in Chile and the USA. She said, "I believe, we, as Indigenous peoples from many countries have similar experiences in life but our respective traditional way of life sets us apart as unique peoples in the world as custodians of particular tracts of land. A Navajo friend once said to me, 'we have had parallel lives but on opposite sides of the world.'"[2]

Fiona's most recent series of photographs, *Horror has a face* were first exhibited at Andrew Baker Art Dealer in 2017. In the photographs she stretches toward memories that are not hers but are drawn from research and her family background. They comprise places and spaces based in history but with her own imaginative essay built around their potential realities. As images they close the viewer into a confined world, with only one of the nineteen images having a clear view of the horizon. The others draw us into a claustrophobic historical fiction in which we are captured as effectively as their stage-managed subjects.

In these works, it is possible to see Foley's aesthetic within an Aboriginal compositional frame. I am reminded of Kim Mahood's words describing her own aesthetic disorientation as a white artist when assisting artists from Balgo in their desert paintings. Mahood writes that the horizon is "omnipresent, hovering in the space around the paintings".[3] She finds herself applying (in her own painting) an "emphatic horizontal" and relates that "the horizon is one of the perceptual faultiness that runs between white and Aboriginal ways of understanding country".[4]

In these terms Mahood acknowledges her outsider status with a sense of frustration. It is, as she notes later in the book, a cocktail of genes, emotion and heritage that exclude her. She notes, "If I were to join the dots, it would create a lattice of tracks linking people, place, memory and metaphor. This is my unfinished map, with all the stories not yet told, the stories that have not yet happened, the stories that aren't mine to tell."[5] I am, like Mahood, an outsider looking in, albeit without her life-long connections to Aboriginal people and place. The south-east Queensland bushland environment within which I live nonetheless imprints me with its sights, sounds and wildlife. Sitting outside, the cicadas chorus, their cyclical volume moving around me to create a seamless undercurrent in the summer afternoon, their rhythm nudging my consciousness.

While I see Fiona's arsenal of images in contrast to artists who live in remote areas of Australia, there are, from time to time, formal elements that evoke heritage in common. Her work is distinctively her own—Fiona shows us her realities, research interests and her cultural affinity with place, but perhaps most importantly, her power as an individual.

In *Horror has a face* (2017), I believe that Fiona draws the elements of her mature work together. It is an ambitious series which captures her filial, personal and historical memories. Set late in the 1800s and early 1900s, they conjure a time when opium was subject to legislation, a political pawn for the colonisers. While the colonial intentions may have been to rectify, in some way or another, the dysfunction, disease and death that the first one hundred years of invasion had brought, the effect was to exacerbate the existing damage and to create new craters of disconnection. The memories that Fiona writs large for us are not her own but are an imaginative conjuring up of the places and spaces her research has taken her.

The first of the nineteen images shows *Colonial Captor* sitting in front of a tent, a kangaroo-skin rug under his feet, musket in his hand. *Protector's Camp* widens the vista to show his campsite, a clearing of leaf litter surrounded by trees. His Aboriginal companions are dressed in period clothing and serve him; a fire underway, tea being made and an Aboriginal man wearing a breast plate marked "Badtjala Warrior", locating the camp itself in the bush of K'gari. This was the site of the first mission that brought Aboriginals together from all over Queensland to quarantine them from white society. The *Colonial Captor* is Archibald Meston, Southern Protector of Aboriginals (1898–1904), and in this second image his gun rests back on his right shoulder, a master of the benign domain in front of him.

This narrative unfolds over seventeen more images, with its storyline journeying through the pristine natural environment, the gently draped tent, glorying in the beauty of its Aboriginal subjects, their costumes and accoutrements. In *Watching and Waiting*, children look through telescopes to the sea, feet in the sand, relaxed. The next image shifts into the opium den, scenes opulent but also threatening with the introduction of the den master, who wears a whip around his neck and the sense of dominant white man stepped up a level. The girls are scantily clad, one bare-breasted, and they sit on the floor while both men (one Aboriginal, one white) sit above them. *Licenced Licentiousness* continues to develop this theme of structural inequality, then *Lucky Dip* offers a focused view of the opium snuff box and accessories, held in black hands, bare chest behind. *Night Rider, Ruby Joy* and *Sweet Pea* are images of a single Aboriginal beauty on a couch, peacock feathers, red and black surfaces holding them like pearls in a jewel box. In *Den Master* we glimpse the humanity of the controlling figure. *Silent Witnesses* show us older Aboriginal women and their concern.

Bogimbah's Bell-Ringer is the precursor to the final image, with Ernest Gribble presiding over the graves that were the sad outcome of Bogimbah Mission, mounds of sand decorated by bush flowers, and with the minister overseeing. In this series Fiona explores K'gari, its importance as the first site of the Bogimbah Creek Reserve mission, her family heritage in this place, the sadness and tragedies that unfolded here and the dysfunction caused, that builds and ricochets into the future. There is an emotional tenor in these works, a taut resonance that speaks to her ancestry, the power she holds as a mature Aboriginal woman, and an artist whose reputation is established. As is the case for any artist, this most recent body of work is financially, emotionally and psychologically invested. Its critical and commercial response (the validation of sales) may fall short of the toll that its creation has involved.

Fiona and her colleagues have paved the way for a new generation of artists such as Tony Albert, Robert Andrew, Eric Bridgeman, Elisa Jane Carmichael, Megan Cope, Dale Harding, Carol McGregor, Archie Moore, Ryan Presley and so many more. Moore and Presley were central to the *Courting Blakness* exhibition at the University of Queensland in 2014. These artists have continued a way of making art that brings together lost connections, keeps traditional stories alive, and overlays them with contemporary ways of being. Some of these artists are not much younger than Fiona, but the movement she was part of in the 1980s makes their working environment a different landscape. Their work is personal and individual but also understands and acknowledges the significance of what has gone before, to bring a gently respectful intelligence and individuality to their own work. I see their contribution as an offering from descendants of the age-old original custodians, an act of generosity that is priceless, compelling and electrifying.

Drusilla Modjeska writes: "Even the briefest acquaintance with psychoanalysis alerts us to the deep structures of subjectivity laid down from infancy, so that while we might all bleed, our sense of ourselves and our understanding of self in relation to others and society can differ radically."[6] Aboriginal cultural connection offers up longevity that is, for those of us of immigrant heritage, unfathomable and intriguing. Fiona tells me:

> I grew up as a teenager with my family exploring every place (every sand dune) on K'gari. We camped from the top of the island to the bottom of the island. From Sandy Cape where there is no water and we had to dig for it, to places near Ocean Lake, Waddy Point, Akuna Creek. We would camp for a month every year (me, my siblings, Mum and Dad) in those locations and fish every day. My Uncle Horrie was also part of those trips. At night both he and Mum would tell stories around the fire. Listening to Mum and Uncle Horrie talk about the old times, the old *giviids* was something we all could visualise. Then we would find stone axes on our walks, old campsites and even skeletal remains once at

Indian Head. We were the only Aboriginal family going to K'gari at that time because Mum and Dad had a four-wheel-drive vehicle.

Every Aboriginal artist I have had contact with has a direct and instinctive political thread in their work. In Aboriginal communities—in a way also different to artists of non-Aboriginal heritage—artists lead. Creative work embeds, expresses and shares their connection to the land. Equally, the disputed ownership of Australia, usage by others and status, is aired in this forum. Raymond Walker describes his connection to Quandamooka and Minjerribah with dance, a physical connection of stamping, singing, calling up ancestors present and past. Craig Tapp overwrites his stories on the beach, offering up their tidal transience with his own relatively brief sojourn on the ancient earth. Delvene Cockatoo-Collins uses photographs of her ancestors to claim kinship and sovereignty. Elisa Jane Carmichael returns to Quandamooka country to find family, inspiration and subject.[7] I have less personal interaction with Aboriginal writers, but a similarly political drive is evident in the work of Larissa Behrendt, Wesley Enoch, Anita Heiss, Melissa Lucashenko, Kim Scott and Alexis Wright.

Before I moved into the bush on Brisbane's suburban fringe, I had never lived anywhere for long. My childhood was transient, regular interstate stints of anything from six months to two years duration; the nine primary schools I attended were in four different Australian states. I lived in the same house for the five years of high school but, between then and now, my reality has been share-houses and flats, in and around Sydney and Brisbane. This is common enough but, as a result of the transience in my past, if there is a place that I might belong it is here, in the hard Sclerophyll forest and rocky soil—stable, stoic and suitable only for vegetation that has the requisite toughness. This part of south-east Queensland, where I have lived for over twenty years, is where I tentatively extend roots.

HERVEY BAY, NOVEMBER 2018

My trip to see Fiona in Hervey Bay is important. Her little house nestles on a long and narrow half-acre block, a modern and airy studio between the house and the quiet street. There are views to K'gari, and in the morning, bird song is all around me. I open my eyes and, through the window, see a branch move. I look more closely and the blurry shape on the branch becomes three frogmouth birds packed together like one, on the branch of the paperbark, the largest on the outside, a medium-sized bird in the middle and a tiny fluffy baby frogmouth between the mother and the trunk of the tree.

The evening of 9 November 2018, Fiona launched the new edition of her mother's dictionary at Torquay's Mary Ryan's Books, banners on The Esplanade outside proclaiming the 50th anniversary of the launch of *The Legends of Moonie Jarl.* In front of her Wondunna clan, family and friends, Fiona expressed herself "incredibly proud of Shirley's research" and signed each of the forty-five copies sold. The event was a triumph for the Wondunna Aboriginal Corporation; Fiona's pride also evident in her sister Mellissa's endeavours which have driven the reprint and organisation for the launch. Afterwards, we went to the pub with Fiona's friends and family. An Annual General Meeting the next day had high stakes—control of the Badtjala Aboriginal Corporation and the ability to direct the limited resources that Native Title has granted.

The next evening, I was home in Brisbane when Fiona texted, "Lost the vote by two. Mellissa back on the board."

What stays with me most strongly is the nature around the land that surrounds Fiona's home, and her two loved and faithful companions. Her German Shepherd Pir'ri (mangrove) tilts his large head when she speaks, tuning in to every nuance. Her re-homed Cocker Spaniel-cross is named Narangi (little), and his antics make her laugh. She walks them every day and there are regular games on the grass out the back. She throws Pir'ri's ball for a while, and then relaxes on the veranda where Narangi jumps his front paws into her lap, his dark-rimmed eyes seeking hers. It will not be long though before Fiona lifts her gaze to the island, her future, her past and her present. Her next project is an ambitious re-imagining of the Badtjala song, the poetic words from 1770 recast to music, with her unique vision of this history recreated in film.[8]

//

Nine Notes

1 Djon Mundine, "I'm Not Sure That I Exist (After Borges)", *Artlink* 35, 2 (2015).

2 Ibid.

3 Mahood, *Position Doubtful*, 35.

4 Ibid.

5 Ibid., 299–300.

6 Drusilla Modjeska, "The Informed Imagination," *Meanjin* 74, 2 (2015): 61.

7 Louise Martin-Chew, "Art of place: Interviews with artists from Australia," (2015). Unpublished.

8 This film, titled *Out of the Sea Like Cloud* was released in 2019.

PROVOCATEUR

It is hard to assess the ripple effect from where someone drops in and changes the algorithm of history. Fiona's fresh approach has viewed and appreciated the politics of talk, activism, academia and as a creative artist. There are so many different limbs to her tree, it would be a profound understatement to say that she has changed the landscape of Australian art. It has been history in the making; the last thirty years have influenced change at so many levels that it is hard to see what that catchment is. She has global recognition and plenty more to achieve. She will keep creating and her line and ascendancy will keep going. I wish her thirty more good years and nothing but an ascending moment. She has a revered place in our hearts. People that love her love her. When we need each other we talk, and relying on and loving each other after all these years is pretty cool thing.

—**Bronwyn Bancroft, founding member, Boomalli**[1]

From very early in her career, Fiona Foley has been prepared to say what she thinks no matter the consequences. This outspoken leadership might have been less confronting if she was male. Alec Doomadgee, a descendent of Waanyi, Garawa and Gangalidda tribes from the Aboriginal community of Doomadgee in the Gulf of Carpentaria in Queensland, produced the documentary *Zach's Ceremony* (2016) about the coming to age of his son Zach, and spoke at the Brisbane Writer's Festival at the State Library of Queensland in 2017 (under Fiona's *Black Opium* sculpture built into the building's ceiling). He claimed that artists "are not afraid to say shit. White people can't take ownership of black stories. Culture is everything—our creator is Mother Earth: no land no purpose no culture no existence."[2] Fiona's diminutive female frame is defied by her instinct to speak. Within her family her mother modelled strength matched by toughness that is echoed in Fiona's life and work.

Fiona is defined by her Aboriginality, as it defines her in the wider world. She learnt to be an artist and her work has become a vehicle with which she explores her world view and conveys the injustices that continue to plague Aboriginal people. She also invests in her community, and looks for opportunities to boost outcomes, particularly for Badtjala youth:

> I remember being different as a child when I first went to
> Urangan Primary School. I also remember the love of being a
> part of an extended Aboriginal family growing up in Hervey
> Bay. I remember encountering many forms of racism from a
> very early age and having to fight against boys, both verbally
> and physically, boys my own age and sometimes older than
> me. That was an everyday occurrence to and from school in
> Hervey Bay and in Hornsby, north of Sydney.

At every step of your life from childhood to adulthood you're being defined and judged by others because of your race. Having to prove "who you are"—emotionally that takes a toll. I am very glad I was born into a family who encouraged education and I am also glad I had an enquiring mind to seek out answers for myself and start to analyse Australian society. Australians are deeply scared by their history and what they continue to do to Aboriginal people is a generational continuum. In turn they have traumatised a race of people.

/

Since Fiona completed her doctorate in late 2017, her segue as an artist-academic has been seamless. She was offered a prestigious two year post-doctoral fellowship at Queensland College Art in Brisbane in 2018 (till 2020), which transitioned into her current position as Lecturer at the same institution. She was selected as feature artist at the Ballarat International Foto Biennale and a new survey exhibition of thirty years of her work, *Who are these strangers and where are they going?* was curated by Djon Mundine in 2019 and travelled to the National Art School, Sydney in 2020. A new film, *Out of the Sea Like Cloud* about the Badtjala view of Cook's *Endeavour* was launched at the Gallery of Modern Art Cinematheque on 14 December 2019. Her academic book, *Biting the Clouds: A Badtjala perspective on the Aboriginals Protection and Restriction of the Sale of Opium Act, 1897* was published by UQP in 2020. Other awards, grants and accolades have followed, with a compelling vindication of her decision to spread her educative influence beyond art.

/

Fiona's journey, as Bancroft suggests above, has been driven by and accompanied a ground-breaking shift in understanding of art and Aboriginality. My collaboration with Fiona places the words outside the quotes as mine; but the story and the art which inspired them is hers. I acknowledge and thank Fiona for her contribution, not only to this text but for the power of her art.

When I asked Fiona how it felt to be working with a non-Aboriginal woman on this biography, she said,

> It doesn't feel like intellectual colonisation because we have a friendship and I feel comfortable. Like Fiona Nicoll, there are a few people you have in your life where you admire and respect one another. That is how Fiona and I could jointly do *Courting Blakness*. She understood the hierarchy of the university structure, she manoeuvred that project through that system. She knew how to do that, and I brought other things that she didn't have. I had social capital and had to push back on the academics. I was not afraid to threaten going to the press or [barrister] Andrew Boe. You need a sense of courage to push through the obstacles that presented themselves. I know there are few people of that calibre. We go on, forever in transition into other versions of ourselves as women in our lives, but a friendship is always there. That is how I see it.

The twin babies who were not born when I first met Fiona are teenagers, young adults moving independently into their lives. This dramatic transformation is similar to the imprinting of this biography on my relationship with Fiona. The coming together and crystallisation of this narrative in recent years has transformed our relationship.

I believe in Fiona, the power of her work, her spirit and remain awed by her courage. Her father Barry Foley told me that her career was so immense he was unable to really comprehend its trajectory. So often we extend our experience beyond our parents' generational horizons. Fiona's brother Rowan notes his sister's talent and determination, and tells me, "I could see from very early that as an artist she was the next cut above. She has a star quality in her work."[3] Amidst swirling misconceptions, the strenuous and political nature of her art and her ability to deliver uncomfortable truths, Fiona's fierceness is often amplified. Yet there is no question that she is a flashpoint, as I witnessed when I saw two men, both senior arts professionals, stand over her at a public event, their anger palpable, a physical threat in the air. She stood her ground, powered by her identity as a Badtjala woman, who leans into community, into art, into heritage and history, to find her way. As part of her *Horror has a face* body of work, she exhibited breast plates like those forced on Aboriginal people in colonial times, which define the wearer—*WHITE WOMAN, PROTECTOR OF ABORIGINES, BLACK VELVET*. The most beautifully detailed of these reads *BADTJALA WARRIOR* and it is this one which I believe Fiona represents.

//

Conclusion Notes

1   Bronwyn Bancroft, interview by the author, 23 March 2017.

2   Address to the Brisbane Writers Festival, 2017.

3   Rowan Foley, interview by the author (telephone), 3 January 2019.

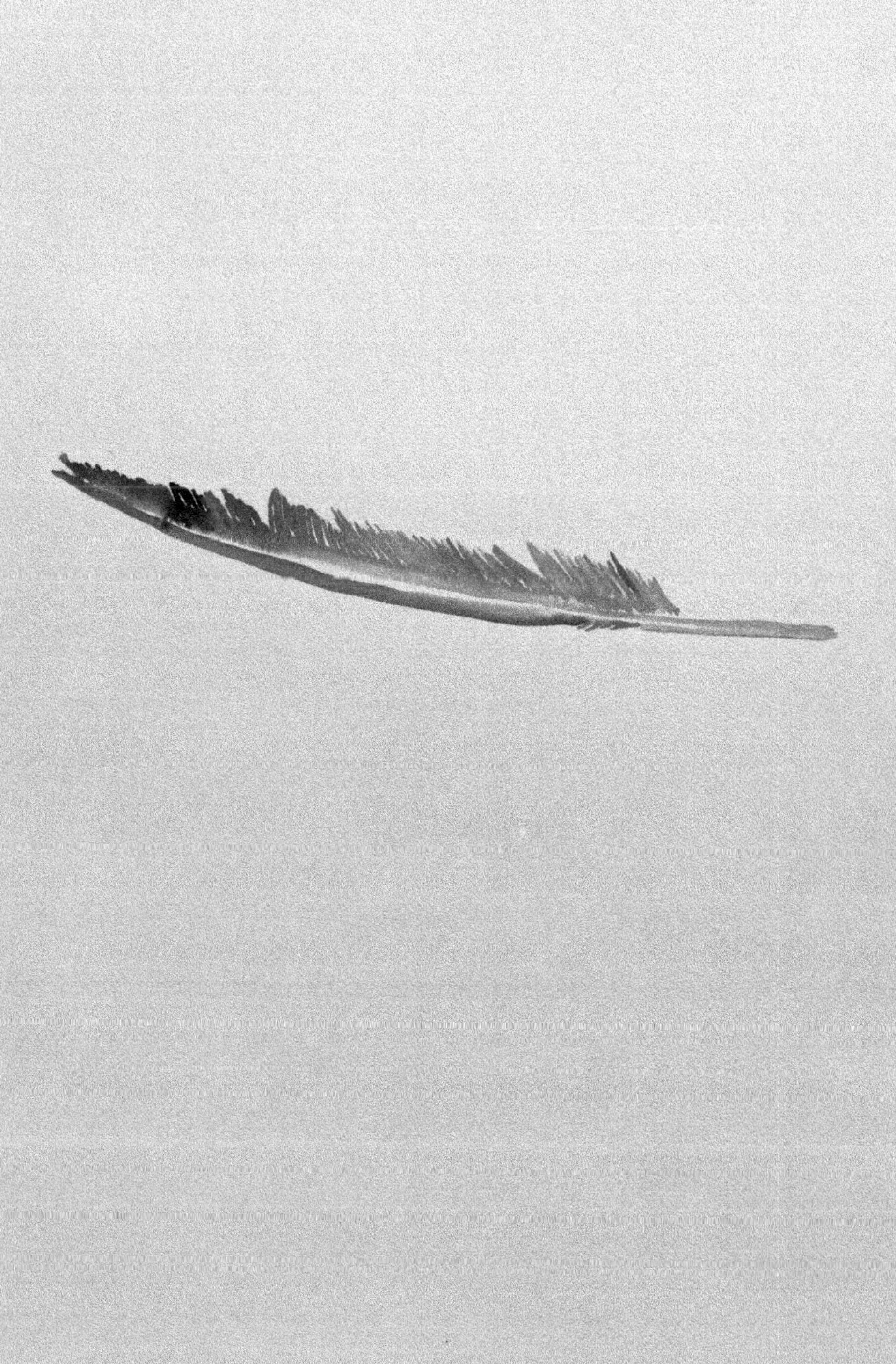

NB: *Only major solo exhibitions and selected group exhibitions are included in this listing. For more detail www.fionafoley.com.au*

1964	Born in Maryborough, Queensland
	The Legends of Moonie Jarl by Wilf Reeves and Olga Miller is published by Jacaranda Press, Brisbane
1969	Starts school at Urangan Primary, Hervey Bay
	During her childhood, the family moves include to Beenleigh, Hervey Bay (twice), Mount Isa and Sydney. However every year the family spent several weeks camping on K'gari
1977–1981	Attends Asquith Girls High School, Asquith, Sydney. Lived in Hornsby, Sydney
1983	Certificate of Arts, East Sydney Technical College
1984–1986	Bachelor of Visual Arts, Sydney College of the Arts
1984	*Koori Art 84*, Artspace, Sydney (group exhibition)
	Fiona Foley travels to Ireland, the first of her immediate family to return to the country of her grandfather's birth

1985   Travels to Ramingining and Miningimbi, Northern Territory, using funds from her first Australia Council grant. In 1987 she will spend seven months there, and will visit regularly until 1993

1986   *Urban Koories*, Willoughby Workshop Arts Centre, Sydney (group exhibition)

While still a student, the National Museum of Australia in Canberra purchases Fiona Foley's *The Annihilation of the Blacks*, her first institutional acquisition

1987   Co-founds Boomalli Aboriginal Artists Co-Operative, Sydney

Boomalli Au-Go-Go, Boomalli Aboriginal Arts Co-Operative, Sydney (group exhibition)

Diploma of Education, Sydney Institute of Education, University of Sydney

1988   On 26 January the bicentennial celebrations in Australia, marking 200 years of European colonisation, are the focus of protests across the country

Fiona has her first commercial exhibition, at Roslyn Oxley9 Gallery, Sydney, from which the Art Gallery of New South Wales acquires *Men's Business* (1987)

My Fishing Line is Still in the Ocean (solo exhibition), Central Theatres Gallery, Griffith University, Brisbane

Artist in Residence, Griffith Artworks, Griffith University, Nathan Campus

1989   Shirley Foley establishes Thoorgine Education and Culture Centre to host visitors to K'gari

Fiona is included in *Australian Perspecta*, Art Gallery of New South Wales

A Three Legged Dog Day, Maningrida Arts and Craft, Northern Territory; Roslyn Oxley9 Gallery, Sydney

1990	Thoorgine Educational and Culture Centre Aboriginal Corporation receives a special lease for a six-hectare site on K'gari/Fraser Island (20 years from 1 January 1990)
1991	With Djon Mundine, Fiona curates *Tyerabarrbowaryaou: I shall never become a white man* for the 5th Havana Biennial, Cuba
	By Land and Sea I Leave Ephemeral Spirit, Roslyn Oxley9 Gallery, Sydney (solo exhibition)
1992	*Tyerabarrbowaryaou II: I shall never become a white man*, Museum of Contemporary Art, Sydney (group exhibition)
1993	Contributes to the Australia Post Stamp Issue celebrating the International Year of Indigenous People
	9th Biennale of Sydney, Boomalli Aboriginal Artists Co-Operative at the Performance Space, Sydney and tour (group exhibition)
	Fiona resigns from Boomalli Aboriginal Arts Co-Operative
	Lick My Black Art, Australian Centre for Contemporary Art, Melbourne (solo exhibition)
1994	Contributes a poster design, Adelaide Festival of the Arts
	The Badtjala People: A Cultural and Environmental Interpretation of Fraser Island is published by the Thoorgine Educational and Cultural Centre Aboriginal Corporation
	Fiona Foley and Olu Oguibe, Roslyn Oxley9 Gallery, Sydney
1995	*Edge of the Trees*, public artwork with Janet Laurence, Museum of Sydney (Historic Houses Trust of NSW)
	Australian Perspecta 1995, Art Gallery of New South Wales, Sydney
	Exotica Under the Microscope, Institute of Modern Art, Brisbane (solo exhibition)

Land Deal—Velvet Waters, Savode Gallery, Brisbane
(solo exhibition)

Fiona leaves Sydney to live in Hervey Bay, Queensland

1996   Museo de Arte Contemporaneo, Santiago de Chile, Banco BHN,
La Paz, Bolivia (group exhibition)

Wun'Duman, Roslyn Oxley9 Gallery, Sydney (solo exhibition)

Designs the sets for the Australian Ballet's *Alchemy* (set design),
Sydney Opera House and Victorian Arts Centre, Melbourne

Shirley Foley completes a dictionary of Badtjala–English words,
which is published by the Wondunna Aboriginal Corporation

1997   *The Lie of the Land*, public artwork Melbourne Town Hall (City
of Melbourne)

Dulingbara—People of the Nautilus Shell, Hervey Bay Regional
Gallery; Savode Gallery, Brisbane (solo exhibition)

1998   *Living with the Wind*, Roslyn Oxley9 Gallery, Sydney
(solo exhibition)

2000   VALE Shirley Foley née Wondunna (1938–2000)

Aboriginal Art in Modern Worlds, Hermitage Museum, Saint
Petersburg, Russia; National Gallery of Australia, Canberra
(group exhibition)

Invisible Voices, Bundaberg Arts Centre, Queensland; Yarrabah
Museum, Queensland; The Tanks, Cairns, Queensland (2000–
2002) (solo exhibition)

2001   *River of Corn*, Contemporary Art Museum, University of South
Florida, Tampa, United States (solo exhibition)

Fiona Foley: Solitaire by Benjamin Genocchio is published by
Piper Press

Pir'ri—Mangrove, Queensland Art Gallery, Brisbane
(solo exhibition)

Falling Tide—Kung Dhu'marami, Redback Art Gallery, Brisbane
(solo exhibition)

Fiona Foley, Niagara Galleries, Melbourne

Winged Harvest, public artwork, Centre for Cross-Cultural
Research, Australian National University, Canberra

Tribute to A'vang, public artwork, Joint House Department,
Parliament House, Canberra

2002   Fiona moves to Brisbane from Hervey Bay

              Fiona is appointed to the board of the Institute of Modern Art,
              Brisbane (until 2006)

              Wild Times Call, Roslyn Oxley9 Gallery, Sydney (solo exhibition)

              Them There Bones, New Land Gallery, Adelaide (solo exhibition)

2003–2009   Adjunct Professor, Queensland College of Art, Griffith
              University, Brisbane

              Samsara, Andrew Baker Art Dealer, Brisbane (solo exhibition)

              Red Ochre Me, Queensland College of Art Gallery, Griffith
              University, Brisbane (solo exhibition)

2004   Convenor, Bachelor of Visual Arts, Contemporary Australian
              Indigenous Arts, Queensland College of Art, Brisbane

              Bring It On (a.k.a. HHH), International Studio Curatorial
              Program, Brooklyn, New York, United States (solo exhibition)

              Beyond the Sea, Presentation Convent, Carlow,
              Ireland (solo exhibition)

              Wandering, Niagara Galleries, Melbourne (solo exhibition)

Fiona Foley, Karen Brown Gallery, Darwin

Witnessing to Silence, public artwork, for Department of Justice and Attorney-General, Queensland Government, Brisbane Magistrates Court

2005   Residency, University of East Anglia, Norwich United Kingdom

No Shades of White, Andrew Baker Art Dealer, Brisbane; Niagara Galleries, Melbourne; Roslyn Oxley9, Sydney; Kluge-Ruhe Aboriginal Art Collection, University of Virginia, Charlottesville, United States (2005–2007) (solo exhibition)

2006   *Black Opium*, public artwork, State Library of Queensland, Brisbane

Travels to Auckland and London

Strange Fruit, October Gallery, London (solo exhibition)

Black Friday, Andrew Baker Art Dealer, Brisbane (solo exhibition)

Red Ochre Me, survey, Casula Powerhouse Arts Centre, Sydney (solo exhibition)

2007   *No Shades of White*, Kluge-Ruhe Aboriginal Art Collection, The University of Virginia, Charlottesville, United States (solo exhibition)

Travels to New York, Denmark and Ireland

2008   Public art for Redfern Park, Sydney (City of Sydney)

Sea of Love, photographic series, Andrew Baker Art Dealer, Brisbane (solo exhibition)

2009   Six major public artworks for the Bluewater Trail, Mackay (Mackay Regional Council)

Nulla 4 Eva, photographic series, Niagara Galleries, Melbourne (solo exhibition)

2009–2010	*Fiona Foley: Forbidden*, Museum of Contemporary Art, Sydney and The University of Queensland Art Museum, Brisbane
2010	*Bearing Witness* (2009) photographic series, 17th Biennale of Sydney, 2010
	Circumspect Circumstances, Andrew Baker Art Dealer, Brisbane (solo exhibition)
2011	Travels to France with *AWAYE!* Radio National documentary team to view a plaster cast of Badtjala man, Boni, in the Muséum d'Histoire Naturelle de Lyon. "Cast Among Strangers" is broadcast on 5 November 2011
2012	*Flotsam and Jetsam*, watercolours, Andrew Baker Art Dealer, Brisbane (solo exhibition)
	The Oyster Fishermen, Niagara Galleries, Melbourne (solo exhibition)
2013	*Fiona Foley: Portrait of the Artist* series, State Library of Queensland
	Retro-active: A 25 year retrospective, Andrew Baker Art Dealer, Brisbane (solo exhibition)
2011–2017	Adjunct Professor, University of Queensland, Brisbane
2014	Convenor, *Courting Blakness: Recalibrating Knowledge in the Sandstone University*, Conference and Outdoor Exhibition, University of Queensland, Brisbane
	Fiona is awarded the Australia Council Visual Arts Award
	On 24 October Native Title is granted as the Butchulla People #2 Fraser Island Claim reaches Consent Determination
	Vexed, film, Northern Centre for Contemporary Art, Darwin
2015	Fiona moves from Brisbane to Hervey Bay to assist with the developments from the successful Butchulla Native Title claim

2016   Fiona moves from Hervey Bay to Lismore, New South Wales
            where she completes study toward her PhD

            A Quintessential Act, film, Andrew Baker Art Dealer, Brisbane

2017   VALE Barry Patrick Foley (1935–2017)

            Appointed Fellow, National Art School, Sydney

            Horror has a face, photographic series, Andrew Baker Art Dealer,
            Brisbane (solo exhibition)

2018   In August Fiona leaves Lismore to return to live in Hervey Bay

            Because of Her We Can, Lifetime Achievement, Fraser Coast
            NAIDOC Award

            Badtjala–English, English–Badtjala Word List is republished
            (third edition) by the Wondunna Aboriginal Corporation,
            launched Hervey Bay, Queensland

2018–2020   Postdoctoral Fellow, Queensland College of Art, Griffith
            University, Brisbane

2019   *Who are those strangers and where are they going?*, 30-year survey
            exhibition, Ballarat International Foto Biennial, Victoria. Toured
            to National Art School, Sydney in 2020

2020   Cherish Fund grant, Australia Council (new photographic series,
            Badtjala country)

            Inaugural Monica Clare Research Fellow, State Library of
            Queensland, Brisbane

            Capstone Editing Early Career Academic Research Grant for
            Women

            *Biting the Clouds: A Badtjala Perspective on the Aboriginals
            Protection and Restriction of the Sale of Opium Act, 1897* is
            published by University of Queensland Press

Louise Martin-Chew

Winner, Best Art Writing by an Indigenous Australian, awarded
by the Art Association of Australia & New Zealand, 2020

Lecturer, Griffith University, Queensland College of Art,
Brisbane

Queensland College of Art Executive

2021   *Fiona Foley: Veiled Paradise*, QUT Art Museum, Brisbane

Works Cited

Ah Kit, Shantel. "Mount Isa." In "A History of the Wondunna Clan." Hervey Bay: Wondunna Aboriginal Corporation, 2000 [Unpublished].

Alhabash, Saleem, Kayla Hales, Jong-hwan Baek and Hyun Jung Oh. "Effects of Race, Visual Anonymity, and Social Category Salience on Online Dating Outcomes." *Computers in Human Behavior* 35 (2014): 22–32.

Australian Government: Australian Law Reform Commission. "Recognition of Aboriginal Customary Laws." *ALRC Report* 31, 1986.

Behrendt, Larissa. *Finding Eliza: Power and Colonial Storytelling.* Brisbane: UQP, 2016.

Behrendt, Larissa and Fiona Foley. *K'gari: The Real Story of a True Fake.* SBS with support from NITV, 2017.

Bell, Richard. "Gordon Bennett: Richard Bell's Tribute to the Passing of an Australian Art Great." *The Guardian*, 14 June 2014.

Bird Rose, Deborah. "Dingo Kinship." *Wildlife Australia* 50, 2 (2013): 33–35.

Blake, Thom. *A Dumping Ground: A History of the Cherbourg Settlement.* St Lucia: UQP, 2001.

Boland, Michaela. "South Bank World Turns Once More." *The Australian*, 1 April 2015.

Browning, Daniel. "Cast Among Strangers." *AWAYE!* Radio National, 2014.

———. "Djon Mundine on 21 Years of Aboriginal Art." *AWAYE!* Radio National, 2013.

Burden, Gemmia. "The Violent Collectors Who Gathered Indigenous Artefacts for the Queensland Museum." *The Conversation*, 28 May 2018.

Came, Heather and Derek Griffith. "Tacking Racism as a 'Wicked' Public Health Problem: Enabling Allies in Anti-Racism Praxis." *Social Science & Medicine* 199 (2018): 181–188.

Carroli, Linda. "Fiona Foley—No Shades of White." Roslyn Oxley9 Gallery, 31 March 2005.

Clark, Anna. *Private Lives, Public History*. Melbourne: Melbourne University Press, 2016.

Cosic, Miriam. "Francesco Clemente's Encampment at Carriageworks." *The Saturday Paper*, 30 July–5 August 2016, 18–19.

Cowie, Jefferson. "The Great White Nope." *Foreign Affairs* 95, 6 (2016): 147–152.

Croft, Brenda L. "Up in the Sky, Behind the Clouds." In *Michael Riley: Sights Unseen*. Canberra: National Gallery of Australia, 2006.

DeSatge, Bronwyn. "Mount Isa." In "A History of the Wondunna Clan", 33. Hervey Bay: Wondunna Aboriginal Corporation, 2000 [Unpublished].

Donne, John. "The Ecstasy." In *Love Poems*. London: Phoenix, 1996.

Ellinghaus, Katherine. *Taking Assimilation to Heart: Marriages of White Women and Indigenous Men in the United States and Australia, 1887–1937*. Lincoln: University of Nebraska Press, 2006.

Foley, Fiona. "A Touch of the Tar Brush." In *The Art of Politics/The Politics of Art: The Place of Indigenous Contemporary Art*. Edited by Fiona Foley, 24–27. Brisbane: Keeaira Press, 2006.

———. "An Act of Largesse." *Race, Whiteness and Indigeneity: An International Conference*. Gold Coast, 6–8 June 2017.

———. "A Blast from the Past." *Periphery* 31 (May 1997): 165–168.

———. "Biting the Clouds: *The Aboriginals Protection and Restriction of the Sale of Opium Act,* 1897." Exegesis, Queensland College of Art, 2017.

———. "The Elephant in the Room." Presented at *Creative Capital Forum,* Arts Queensland, 14 December 2011.

———. "Fiona Foley for Creative Capital." In *Creative Capital*. State Library of Queensland, Brisbane: Arts Queensland, 2011.

———. "I Speak to Cover the Mouth of Silence." *Art Monthly, Australia* 250 (2012): 55–57.

———. *Fiona Foley: Invisible Voices*. Bundaberg: Bundaberg Arts Centre, 2000.

———. "Just Little Bits of History Re-Repeating." *MCA Collection*, 24–29. Sydney: Museum of Contemporary Art, 2012.

———. "Letter from Fiona Foley to Luca Belgiorno-Nettis, Chairman, Board of Biennale of Sydney." 25 May 2010 [From the artist's collection].

———. "Public Art Laced with Memory." Speech delivered in Mackay, 2010 [Unpublished notes].

———. "Speech: Fraser Island." 2014.

———. "The Spectacle of Aboriginal Frontier War Memorial Research." *Arts Hub Australia*, 6 July 2018.

———. *Fiona Foley: Forbidden*. Sydney: Museum of Contemporary Art, 2009.

Fiona Foley, Fiona Nicoll and Louise Martin-Chew (eds). *Courting Blakness: Recalibrating Knowledge in the Sandstone University*. St Lucia, Queensland: UQP, 2015.

Foley, Fiona and Julie Ewington. *Fiona Foley: Pir'ri – Mangrove*. Brisbane: Queensland Art Gallery, 2001.

Foley, Rowan. "Eulogy for Barry Foley." 2017. [Unpublished].

———. "How a Market for Ethical Carbon Revealed an Indigenous to Indigenous Model." TedX Talk, Brisbane, 18 December 2018.

Foley, Shawn. *The Badtjala People: A Cultural and Environmental Interpretation of Fraser Island, a Unique Land and Seascape to which We Belong*. Hervey Bay: Thoorgine Educational and Culture Centre Aboriginal Corporation Inc, 1994.

Foley, Shirley. "Oral History Transcript." Hilary Boscott (transcriber), 1993.

———. "Hervey Bay." In "A History of the Wondunna Clan", 48–49. Hervey Bay: Wondunna Aboriginal Corporation, 2000 [Unpublished].

FORM. *Kurlkayima Ngatha–Remember Me*. Perth, February 2016.

Fuller, Reverend E. "The Fraser Island Aboriginal Mission." *The Brisbane Courier*, 7 September 1872.

Geczy, Adam. "The Air-Conditioned Desert: Curating Aboriginal Art." *Art Monthly Australia*, 250 (2012): 44–46.

Genocchio, Ben. "Lick My Black Art." In *Fiona Foley: Invisible Voices*, edited by Bundaberg Arts Centre, 4–6. Bundaberg: 2000.

Genocchio, Benjamin and Djon Mundine. *Fiona Foley: Solitaire.* Annandale, NSW: Piper Press, 2001.

Gelder, Ken and Jane Jacobs. *Uncanny Australia: Sacredness and Identity in a Postcolonial Nation.* Melbourne: Melbourne University Press, 1998.

Greer, Germaine. *On Rage.* Melbourne University Press, 2008.

Haebich, Anna. "Red Ochre Me." Sydney: Casula Powerhouse, 2006.

Halse, Christine. *A Terribly Wild Man.* Crows Nest, NSW: Allen & Unwin, 2002.

Hoy, W. E., P. Kincaid-Smith, M. D. Hughson et al. "CKD in Aboriginal Australians." *American Journal of Kidney Diseases* 56, 5 (2010): 983–993.

Hutak, Michael. "On the Couch: Roslyn Oxley." *Art Collector* (April–June 2017).

Isenberg, Nancy. *White Trash: The 400-Year Untold History of Class in America.* New York: Penguin Books, 2017.

Kidd, Rosalind. *The Way We Civilise.* Brisbane: UQP, 1997.

Killer, Rachel. "Mount Isa." In "A History of the Wondunna Clan", 42. Hervey Bay: Wondunna Aboriginal Corporation, 2000. [Unpublished].

Kubler, Alison. "Fiona Foley and Her Fearful Symmetry." In *Black Opium: Fiona Foley*, edited by Ian Were, 31–33. Brisbane: State Library of Queensland, 2010.

Laurence, Janet. "Edge of the Trees." *JanetLaurence.com.* http://www.janetlaurence.com/edge-of-the-trees/.

Mahood, Kim. *Position Doubtful: Mapping Landscapes and Memories.* Melbourne: Scribe, 2016.

Marmot, Michael. "Social Determinants and the Health of Indigenous Australians", *Medical Journal of Australia* 194, 10 (2011): 512.

Marr, David. *The Henson Case.* Melbourne: Text Publishing, 2008.

Martin-Chew, Louise. "Art of Place: Interviews with Artists from Australia." 2015. [Unpublished].

———. "Fiona Foley Courage." Redcliffe: Moreton Bay Regional Council, 2014.

———. "Integrating Culture and Community: Global Arts Link (Ipswich) and Fire-Works Gallery (Brisbane)." *Art and Australia* 37, 3 (2000): 422.

Michaels, Eric. *Bad Aboriginal Art: Tradition, Media, and Technological Horizons.* Minneapolis: University of Minnesota Press, 1994.

Miller, Wilf Reeves and Olga. *The Legends of Moonie Jarl.* 50th Anniversary edition. Ultimo: The Indigenous Literacy Foundation, [1964] 2014.

Mitzevich, Nick. "Director's Message." *Articulate* (2016): 2–3.

Modjeska, Drusilla. "The Informed Imagination." *Meanjin* 74, 2 (2015): 50–63.

Morrell, Tim. "Collector's Dossier: Fiona Foley." *Art Collector* 50 (October–December 2009): 196–203.

Moreton-Robinson, Aileen. *The White Possessive: Property, Power and Indigenous Sovereignty.* Minneapolis, London: University of Minnesota Press, 2015.

Mundine, Djon. "30 Years Ago Today: 1980–2013." *Sturgeon*, 6 (2013): 44–51

———. "I'm Not Sure That I Exist (After Borges)." *Artlink* 35, 2 (2015): 17–21.

———. "In Praise of Shadows and Otherness." In *Tracey Moffatt My Horizon*, edited by Natalie King, 18–21. Australia: Australia Council for the Arts and Thames & Hudson, 2017.

———. "Introduction." *Michael Riley* Albury: Murray Art Museum Albury, 2018: 2–8.

———. "Seeing Black: Degrees of Invisibility: Djon Mundine: Fiona Foley." *RealTime* 95 (2009): 52.

National Constitutional Convention. Uluru Statement from the Heart. Uluru, 2017.

National Library of Australia. "Fingleton, Di (1947–)," Trove, 2008, https://nla.gov.au/nla.party-579027.

O'Conor, Juliet. "The Legends of Moonie Jarl: Our First Indigenous Children's Book." *The LaTrobe Journal* 79 (2007): 66–81.

Ogulbe, Olu. "Medium and Memory in the Art of Fiona Foley." *Third Text* 9, 33 (1995): 51–60.

Oodgeroo, Noonuccal. "Son of Mine" (1990), accessed Australian Poetry Library.

Pascoe, Bruce. *Dark Emu*. Broome: Magabala Books, 2014.

Pollock, Zoe. "Boomalli Aboriginal Artists' Cooperative." *Dictionary of Sydney*. http://dictionaryofsydney.org/entry/boomalli_aboriginal_artists_cooperative.

Pose, Melanie. "Indigenous Protest, Australian Bicentenary, 1988." *Museum Victoria Collections*. https://collections.museumvictoria.com.au/articles/2835.

ProppaNow. "About Us." https://proppanow.wordpress.com/about-us/.

Riley Michael and Paul Humfress. *Boomalli: Five Koorie Artists. Ethnographic Video Online* 3. Acton, ACT: National Film and Sound Archive of Australia, 1988.

Rittel, Horst W. J. and Melvin M. Webber. "Dilemmas in a General Theory of Planning." *Policy Sciences* 4 (1973): 155–169.

Save Fraser Island Dingoes Inc. "The Fraser Island Dingo." http://savefraserislanddingoes.com.

Seeto, Aaron. "Ground Cover: Fiona Foley + Reuben Paterson: Indigenous Strategies for Public Art." *Public Art Review* 21, 2 (2010): 32–35.

Simkins, Russ. "Townsville." In "A History of the Wondunna Clan", 15. Hervey Bay: Wondunna Aboriginal Corporation, 2000 [Unpublished].

Skinner, Graeme. "The Invention of Australian Music." *Musicology Australia* 37, 2 (2015): 289–306.

Turner, Caroline and Morris Low, eds. *Beyond the Future: Papers from the Conference of the Third Asia-Pacific Triennial of Contemporary Art, 10–12 September 1999* (Brisbane: Queensland Art Gallery, 2000).

University of Queensland. *Courting Blakness: Recalibrating Knowledge in the Sandstone University*. https://www.austlit.edu.au/austlit/page/10043258.

Urist, Jacoba. "Why Can't Great Artists Be Mothers?" *New York Times*, 21 May 2015.

Van Tiggelen, John. "Once Were Emus." *Good Weekend Magazine, Sydney Morning Herald*, 9 February 2002: 14–18.

Winter, Joan G. "Against Their Will: A Post Contact Badtjala Heritage." In *Fiona Foley Invisible Voices*, edited by Bundaberg Arts Centre, 7–8. Bundaberg: Bundaberg Art Centre, 2000.

Wickes, Judi "'Never Really Heard of It': The Certificate of Exemption and Lost Identity." *Indigenous Biography and Autobiography*. http://press-files.anu.edu.au/downloads/press/p119111/mobile/ch06.html.

Wilson, Jacqueline Zara "Invisible Racism: The Language and Ontology of 'White Trash'." *Critique of Anthropology* 22, 4 (2002): 387–401.

Wondunna Aboriginal Corporation. "A History of the Wondunna Clan." Hervey Bay: Wondunna Aboriginal Corporation, 2000 [Unpublished].

———. *Badtjala–English/English–Badtjala Word List*. Hervey Bay: Wondunna Aboriginal Corporation, 2019.

Cover image

Cover image (detail) Fiona Foley, *The Oyster Fishermen #10*, 2011, inkjet print on Hahnemühle paper, edition 15, 60 × 80 cm. Courtesy the artist and Andrew Baker Art Dealer.

Inside front cover

Dingo prints on K'gari, Photograph Jo-Anne Driessens, 2021.

Page viii

Fiona Foley, *Flotsam and Jetsam #13*, 2011, gouache and graphite on Arches paper, 31 × 41 cm. Courtesy the artist and Andrew Baker Art Dealer. Photograph Mick Richards.

Page xiv

Fiona Foley, *Badtjala Warrior II*, 2017, brass and enamel paint, 15 × 25 cm. Courtesy the artist and Andrew Baker Art Dealer. Photograph Mick Richards.

Plates – Page 1

Shirley Foley and Fiona Foley at Roslyn Oxley Gallery9, Sydney, 1988. Courtesy Fiona Foley Archive.

Olga Miller (Wandi) and Wilf Reeves, 1964, authors of *The Legends of Moonie Jarl*, Fryer Library Pictorial Collection, UQFL477, PIC835, https://espace.library.uq.edu.au/view/UQ:218893.

Fred Wondunna, Kirra Beach, c. 1934. Courtesy John Oxley Library, State Library of Queensland.

Plates – Page 2

Front cover, Wilf Reeves and Olga Miller, *The Legends of Moonie Jarl*, Indigenous Literacy Foundation, 2014 (first published by Jacaranda, 1964).

Plates – Page 3

Fiona Foley, *Dog Howling*, c. 1991, oil on canvas, 30 × 23 cm. Courtesy the artist and Andrew Baker Art Dealer. Photograph Mick Richards.

Plates – Page 4

Fiona Foley, Perspecta protest, 1985, artist performance on the steps of the Art Gallery of New South Wales, Sydney. Photograph courtesy of the artist and Roslyn Oxley9 Gallery, Sydney.

Fiona Foley, *The Annihilation of the Blacks*, 1986, wood, paint, plant fibre, hair and feathers, 267 × 204.5 × 85.7 cm. Collection National Museum of Australia, Canberra.

Plates – Page 5

Founding members of Boomalli, 1987: Michael Riley, Fernanda Martens, Euphemia Bostock, Arone Meeks, Fiona Foley, Brenda Croft, Jeffrey Samuels, Tracey Moffatt, Avril Quail and Bronwyn Bancroft. Margaret Olah Photography.

Plates – Page 6

Fiona Foley, *Badtjala Shield*, 2010, oil on linen, 137 × 92 cm. Courtesy the artist and Andrew Baker Art Dealer. Photograph Mick Richards.

Plates – Page 7

Fiona Foley, *Native Blood*, 1994, type C photograph, edition 15, 40 × 50 cm. Courtesy the artist.

Fiona Foley, *Black Velvet II*, 1996, cotton fabric with cotton appliqué, nine bags: 99 × 20 cm (with handle, each), 180 × 200 cm (installed, variable).

Purchased 2001, Queensland Art Gallery Foundation Grant. Collection: Queensland Art Gallery. © The artist. Photograph courtesy Northern Centre for Contemporary Art, Darwin.

Plates – Page 8

Fiona Foley, *Red Ochre Me* (exhibition), 2003, Queensland College of Art Gallery, Brisbane. In the foreground *Massacre Site,* 2003. On the wall, *Stud Gins*, 2003, six of seven blankets, each 190 × 148 cm (irregular). Photograph courtesy QCA Galleries, Griffith University.

Fiona Foley, *HHH #1*, 2004, ultrachrome print on paper, edition 15, 76 × 101 cm. Courtesy the artist and Andrew Baker Art Dealer.

Plates – Page 9

Fiona Foley, *Witnessing to Silence*, 2004, installation view, Brisbane Magistrates Court, Brisbane, lotus stems: cast bronze, etched pavers, diameter: 180 × 140 cm diameter; water feature: stainless steel, laminated glass, five pillars, 210/350 × 25 × 25 × 25 cm. Photographs courtesy the artist and UAP, Brisbane.

Plates – Page 10

Fiona Foley, *Signpost II*, 2005, Epson UltraChrome K3™ inks on Ilford white film, edition 15, 100 × 100 cm. QUT Art Collection. Purchased through the Betty Quelhurst Fund, 2006. Courtesy the artist and Andrew Baker Art Dealer.

Fiona Foley, *Signpost I*, 2005, Epson UltraChrome K3 inks on Ilford white film, edition 15, 100 × 100 cm. QUT Art Collection. Purchased through the Betty Quelhurst Fund, 2006. Courtesy the artist and Andrew Baker Art Dealer.

Plates – Page 11

Fiona Foley, *Black Opium*, 2006, installation view, State Library of Queensland, Brisbane. 777 cast aluminium poppies, 394 × 155 cm. Photograph courtesy the artist and UAP, Brisbane.

Fiona Foley, detail *Mood Room (Gold)*, *Black Opium,* 2006, State Library of Queensland. Photograph courtesy the artist and UAP, Brisbane.

Plates – Page 12

Fiona Foley, *Nulla 4 Eva #3*, 2008, photograph rag bright white 310 gsm paper, 80 × 120 cm. Courtesy the artist and Andrew Baker Art Dealer.

Fiona Foley, *Mangrove Cap,* 2009, weathered steel, 9.5 m high, Bluewater Trail, Mackay. Photograph courtesy the artist and UAP, Brisbane.

Plates – Page 13

Fiona Foley, *Bearing Witness* IV, 2009, inkjet print on Hahnemühle paper, edition 15 , 150 × 100 cm. Courtesy the artist and Andrew Baker Art Dealer.

Plates – Page 14

Fiona Foley, *The Oyster Fishermen* #11, 2011, inkjet print on Hahnemühle paper, edition 15, 60 × 80 cm. Courtesy the artist and Andrew Baker Art Dealer.

Fiona Foley, *The Oyster Fishermen* #16, 2011, inkjet print on Hahnemühle paper, edition 15, 60 × 80 cm. Courtesy the artist and Andrew Baker Art Dealer.

Plates – Page 15

Fiona Foley, *Black Velvet*, 2015, timber, aluminium, enamel and acrylic paints, 120 × 850 ×80 cm (length variable). Courtesy the artist and Andrew Baker Art Dealer. Photograph Mick Richards.

Plates – Page 16

Fiona Foley, *Horror has a face #17 Missionary zeal,* 2017, Fujiflex digital print, edition 15, 45 × 80 cm. Courtesy the artist and Andrew Baker Art Dealer.

Fiona Foley, *Horror has a face #09 Opiate of opulence*, 2017, Fujiflex digital print, edition 15, 45 × 80 cm. Courtesy the artist and Andrew Baker Art Dealer.

Page 203

Fiona Foley, *Flotsam and Jetsam* #15, 2011, gouache and graphite on Arches paper, 31 × 41 cm. Courtesy the artist and Andrew Baker Art Dealer. Photograph Mick Richards.

From its first moment as a kernel of an idea, this project has had such momentum. First I thank Fiona Foley for her generosity and interest in sharing (and I acknowledge the intense scrutiny that accompanies being a living biographical subject). Fiona Nicoll assisted me in taking the project to the University of Queensland as a PhD topic and I thank Stuart Glover for opening the door at the School of Communication and Arts. Jessica White and Gillian Whitlock assisted my negotiation of the academic landscape and kindly accommodated my inexperience with its strictures. I thank Fiona's friends, family and colleagues who contributed their time and insights through the interview process, especially Barry Foley, Rowan Foley, Melissa Foley and Shawn Wondunna-Foley. And those who were part of this developing journey at the university, especially my informal reading group: Jill Barker, Jill Brown, Kathryn Brimblecombe-Fox and Matthew Wengert. Those precious days of reading, talking and feedback were crucial.

I am thrilled that QUT Art Museum have published this book as part of their interest in broadening the conversation about art and artists, and express heartfelt thanks to the Australia Council of the Arts for their funding of this project during the highly competitive Covid-19-impacted year of 2020.

Editor Bronwyn Mahoney was an unerring guide of this text and I'm grateful to Miriam Prystupa for the index, and the assistance of Felix Cehak. I thank QUT's Vanessa Van Ooyen and Sarah Werkmeister for their interest in every aspect of its delivery. Sandy Cull's design expresses with elegance the intent of the book.

Finally and always thanks to my family: Jim Baker, Tallis Martin Baker, Lian Baker, Jasper Baker, Linda Martin-Chew, Dion Martin and my father Lance Chewe. Each has taken an interest and been involved at some level (and often involuntarily) in the telling of this story. Fiona's backdrop no matter where she is encompasses her Country on K'gari, a unique and changeable landscape almost twelve hundred kilometres north of here. My place, in the bush south-east of Brisbane, holds a space for my work and I thank its Quandamooka custodians for their care into the endless past. I also acknowledge Fiona's Badtjala people who fought so hard for their connections, and the family lineage of courage and leadership so evident in her life.

INDEX

Dr Fiona Foley is an Aboriginal artist, Badtjala woman and provocateur, part of a highly influential generation of urban Indigenous artists. Over a career now spanning thirty years she has consistently asked questions about hidden histories, the Frontier Wars waged against Aboriginal peoples, and brought the massacres and dispossession into galleries, public spaces and to a broader, society-wide debate. In recent years her exploration of the familial threads that join her Aboriginal heritage to the family of white missionaries who came to K'gari/Fraser Island in 1897 emerges as a tour de force.

Foley has had exhibitions all over the world. Retrospective exhibitions include *Fiona Foley: Veiled Paradise* at QUT Art Museum in 2021, *Who are these strangers and where are they going?* in Ballarat and Sydney in 2019–2020, and *Fiona Foley: Forbidden* at the Museum of Contemporary Art, Sydney and University of Queensland Art Museum, Brisbane in 2009. Her work is in every major institutional collection in Australia, many private collections, and occupies public spaces all over Australia, including in the State Library of Queensland.

At the heart of this book is friendship. It details Foley's meeting with art writer Louise Martin-Chew, the progression of their collegiate relationship, and crucial developments in Foley's art life until her most recent segue into academia. This book was shaped as a biography given the relevance of Foley's life to the work that she makes, and her emotional and historical investment in the disenfranchisement of her Badtjala people—as for all Aboriginal people—as subject matter for her art.

Louise Martin-Chew has written about the visual arts for thirty years. She has contributed regularly to national newspapers, art magazines, exhibition catalogues and books. This biographical project was part of a PhD at the University of Queensland (awarded 2019).

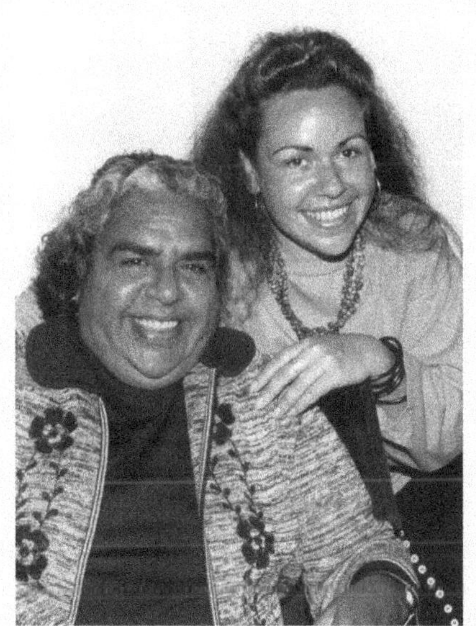

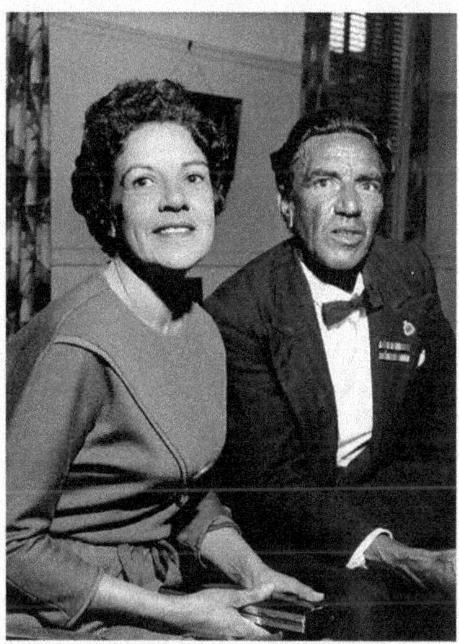

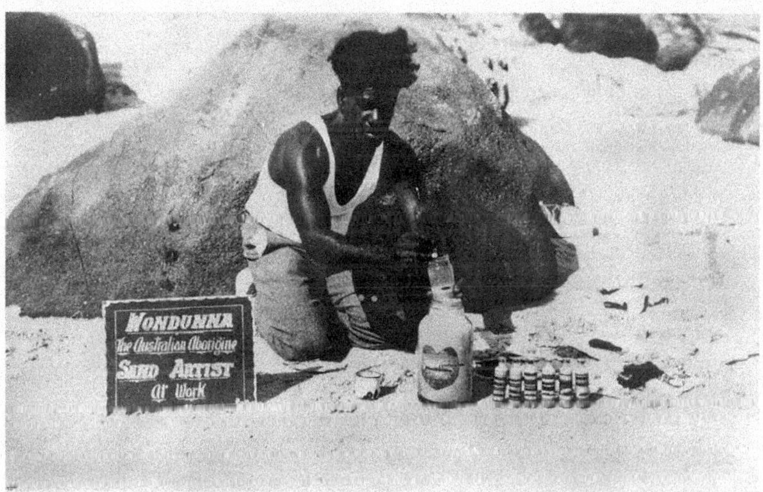

ABOVE LEFT Shirley Foley and Fiona Foley at Roslyn Oxley Gallery9, Sydney, 1988
ABOVE RIGHT Olga Miller (Wandi) and Wilf Reeves, 1964, authors of *The Legends of Moonie Jarl*
BOTTOM Fred Wondunna, Kirra Beach, c. 1934

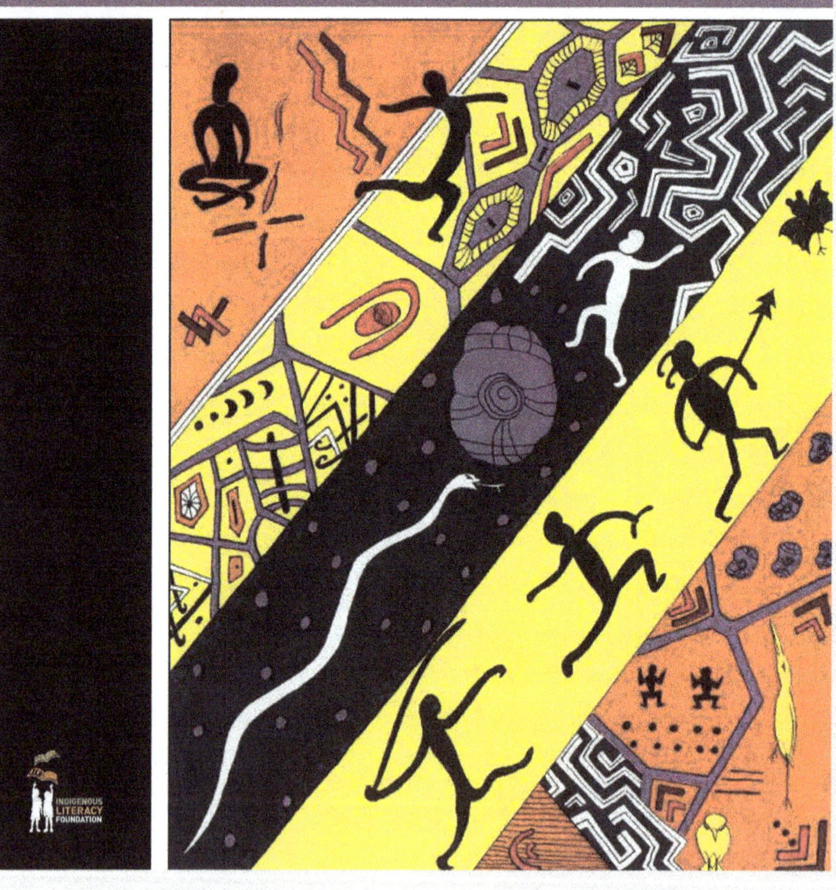

Front cover, *The Legends of Moonie Jarl*, Indigenous Literacy Foundation, 2014

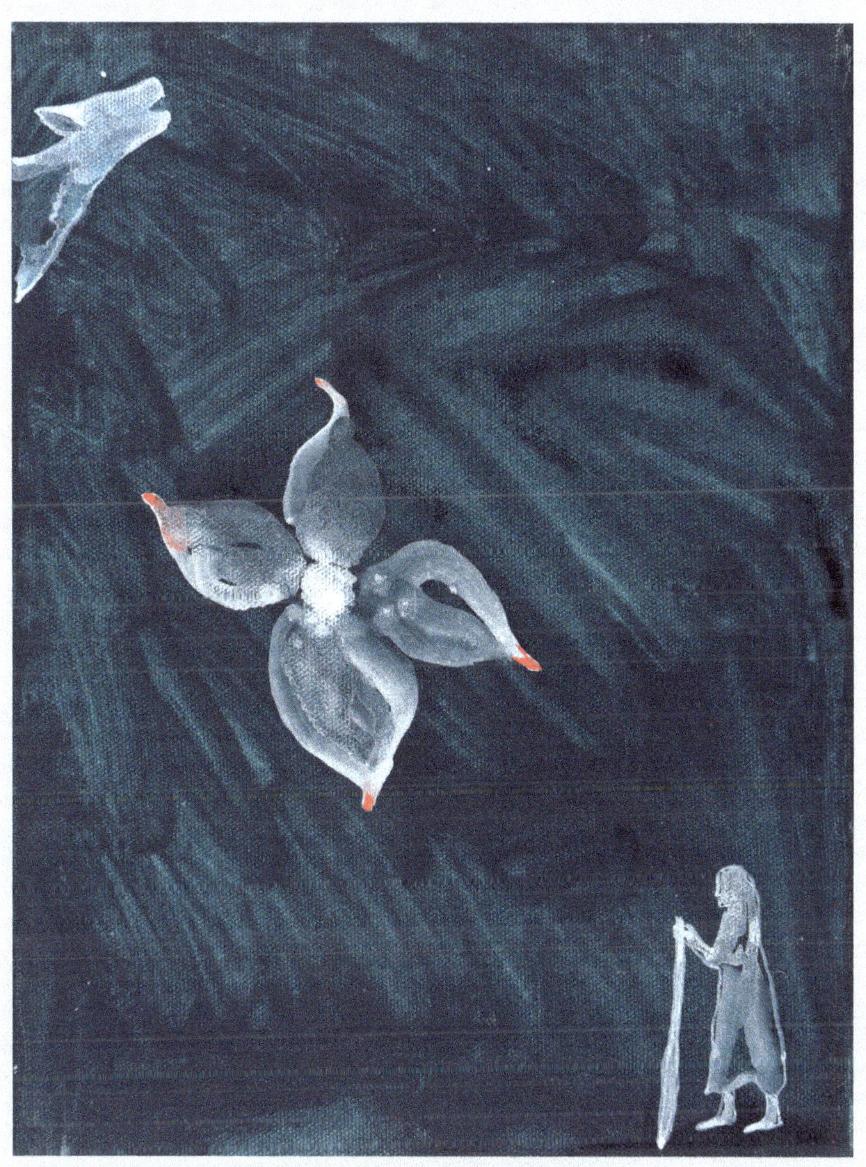

Fiona Foley, *Dog Howling*, c. 1991

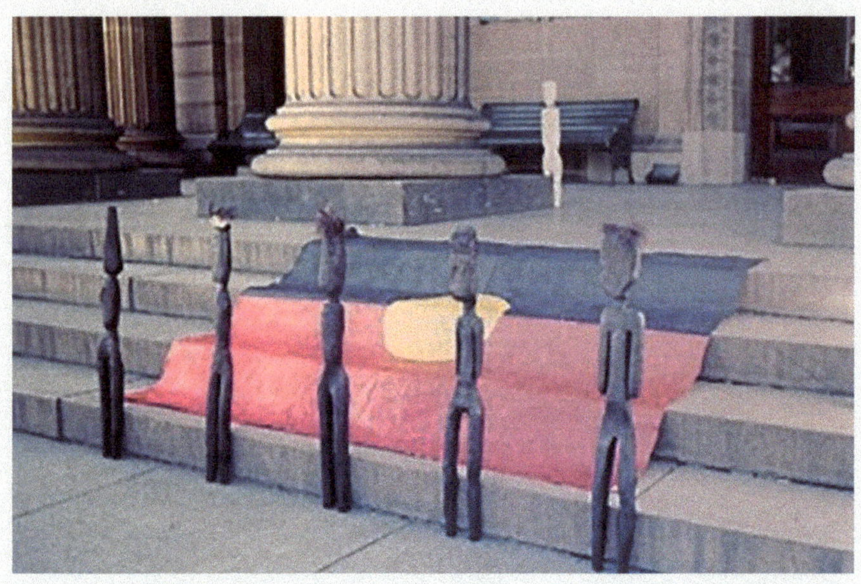

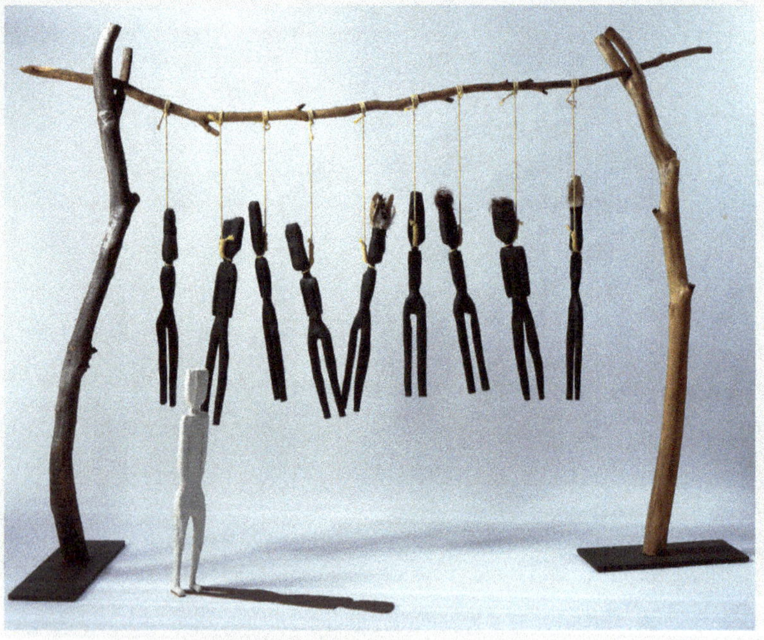

TOP *Perspecta* protest on steps of the Art Gallery of New South Wales, 1985
BOTTOM Fiona Foley, *The Annihilation of the Blacks*, 1986

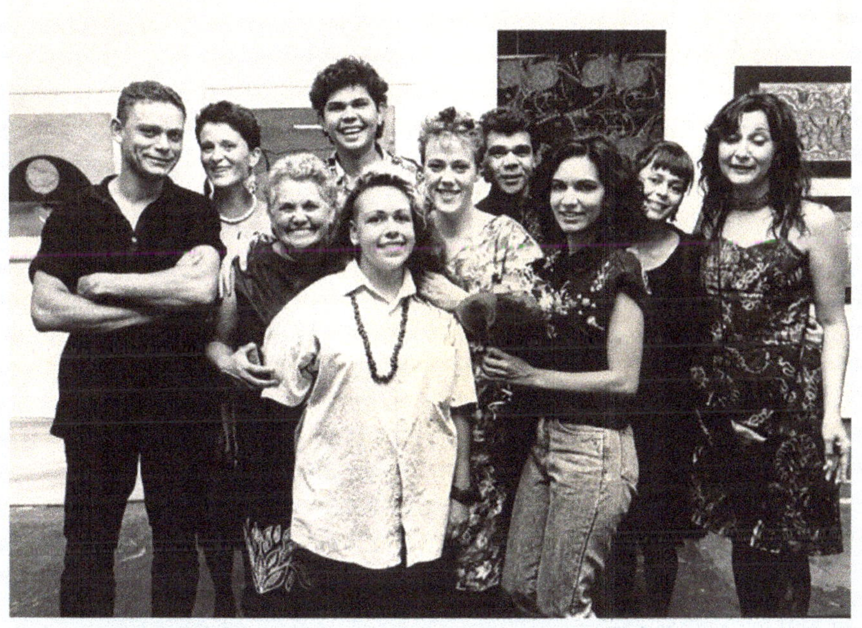

Founding members of Boomalli: Michael Riley, Fernanda Martens, Euphemia Bostock, Arone Meeks, Fiona Foley, Brenda Croft, Jeffrey Samuels, Tracey Moffatt, Avril Quaill and Bronwyn Bancroft, 1987

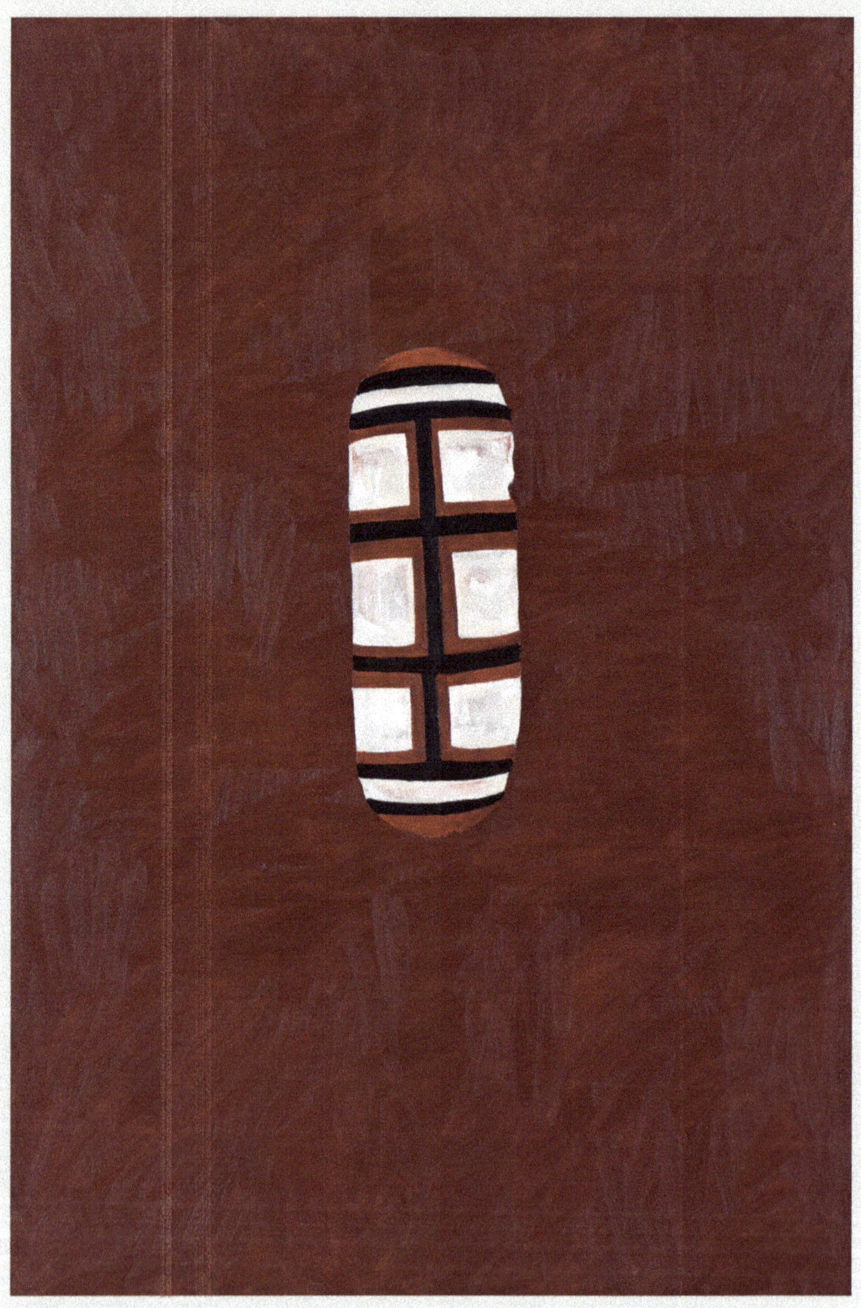

Fiona Foley, *Badtjala Shield*, 2010

———

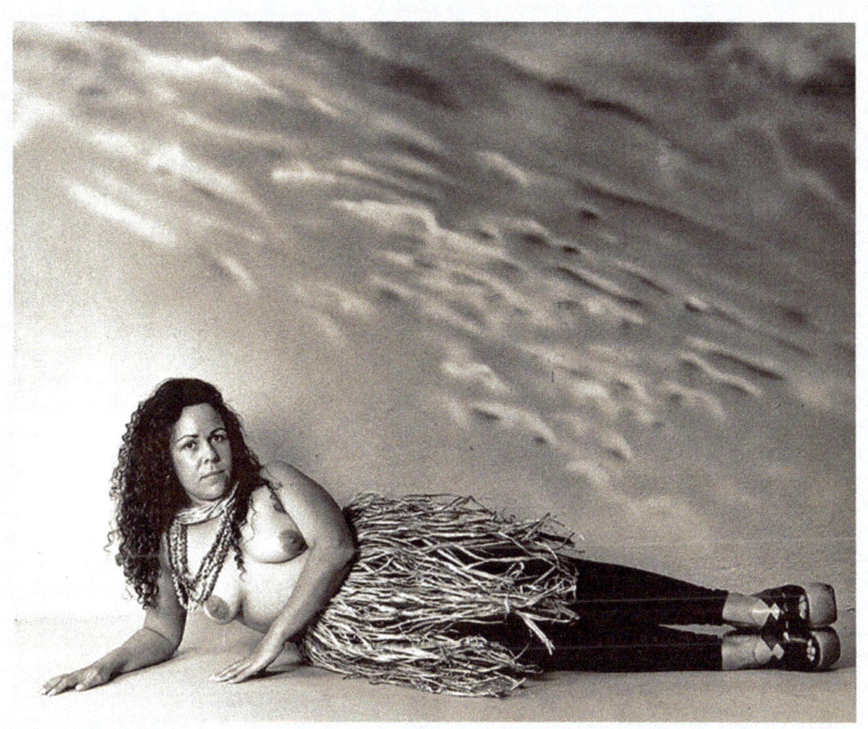

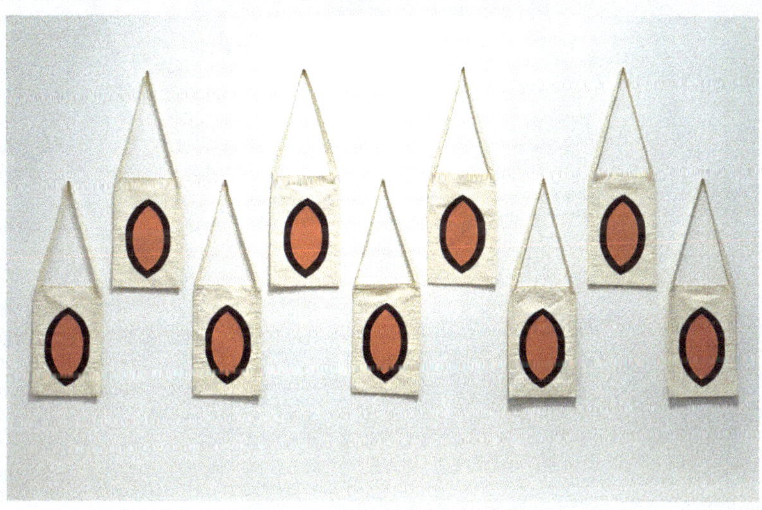

TOP Fiona Foley, *Native Blood*, 1994
BOTTOM Fiona Foley, *Black Velvet II*, 1996

—

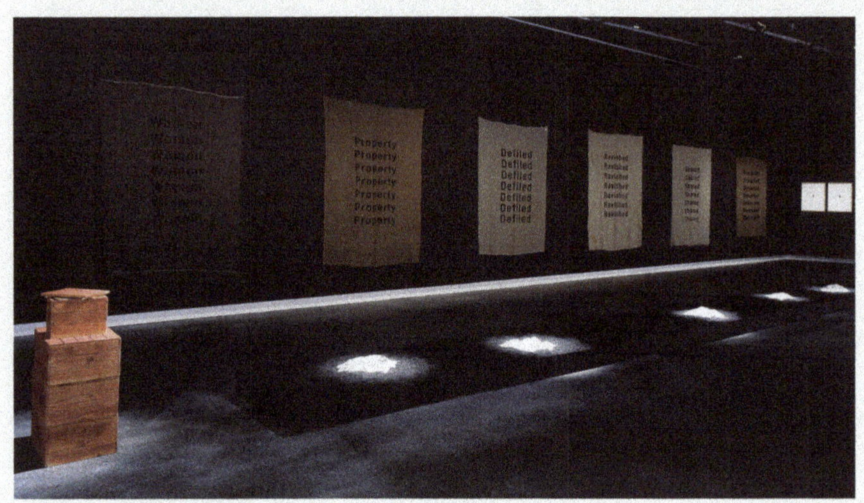

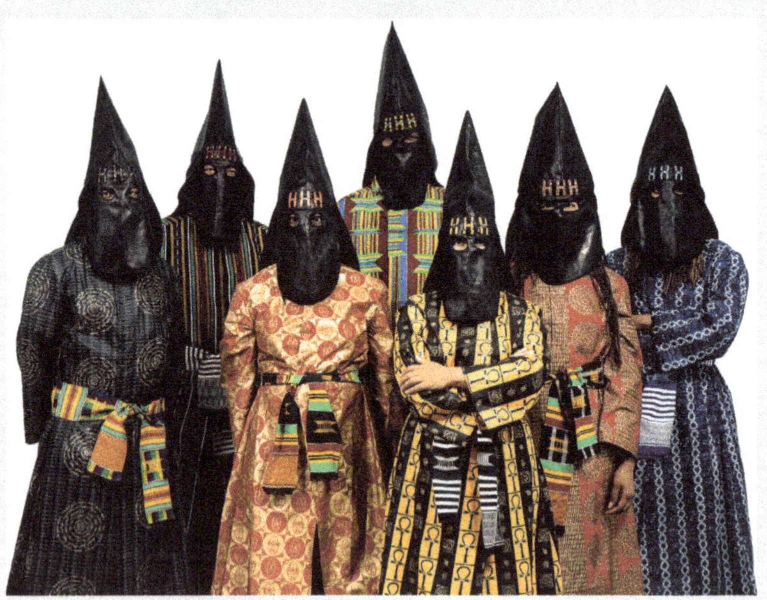

TOP Fiona Foley, *Red Ochre Me*, 2003
BOTTOM Fiona Foley, *HHH #1*, 2004

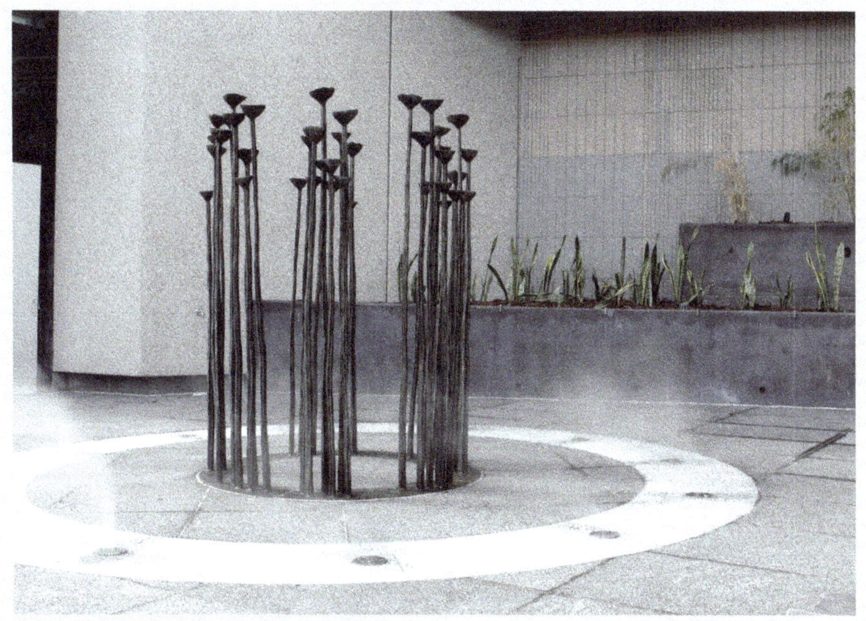

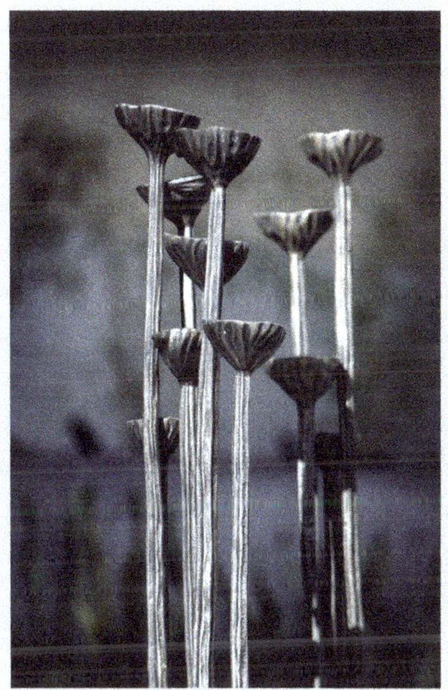

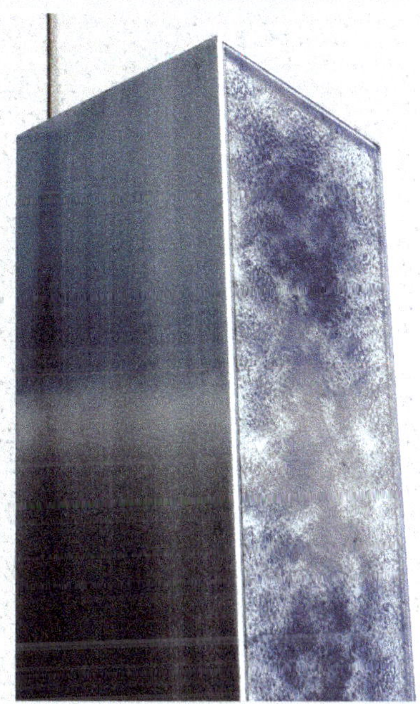

Fiona Foley, *Witnessing to Silence* for Brisbane Magistrates Court, 2004

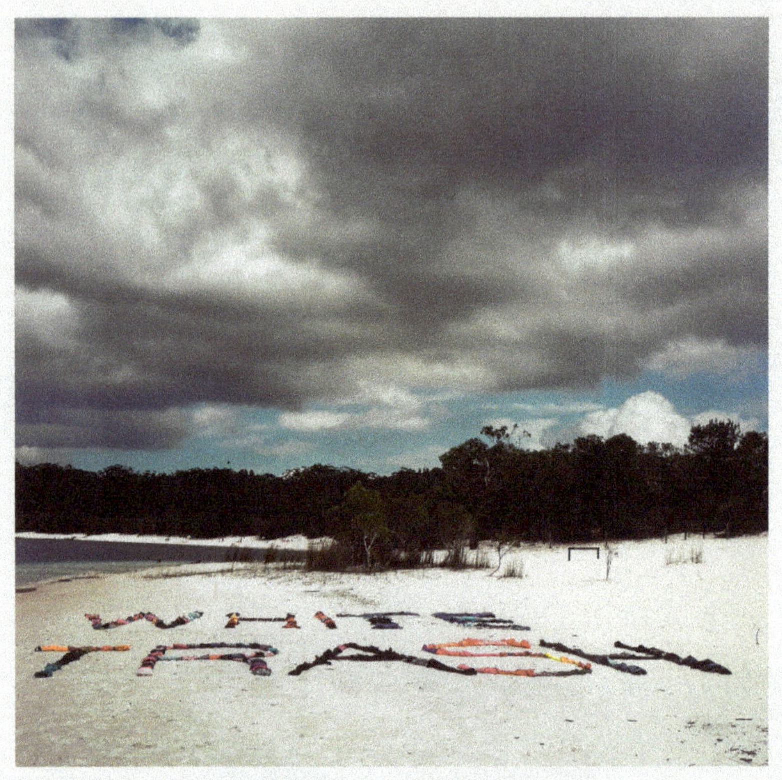

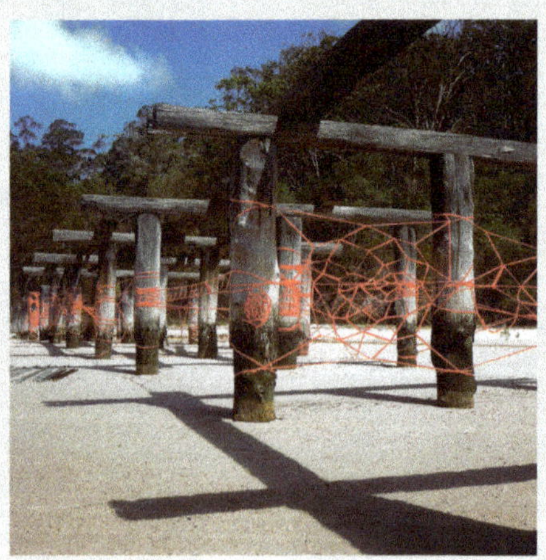

TOP Fiona Foley, *Signpost II*, 2006
BOTTOM Fiona Foley, *Signpost I*, 2006

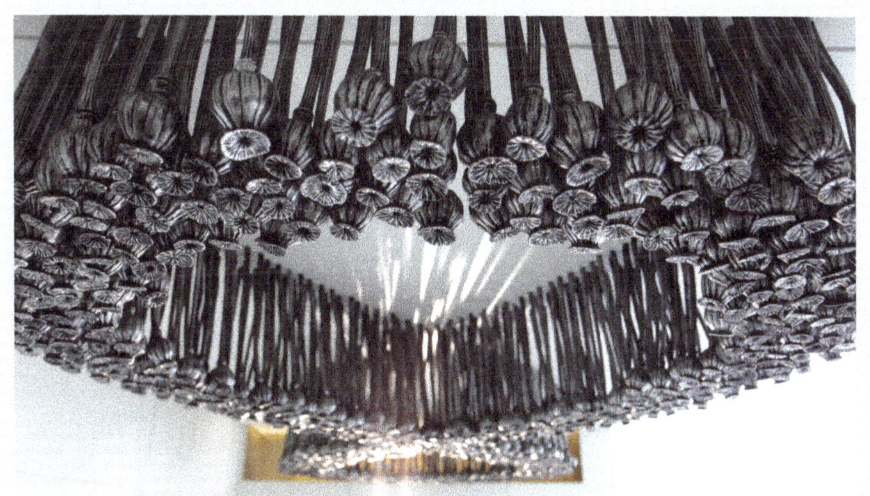

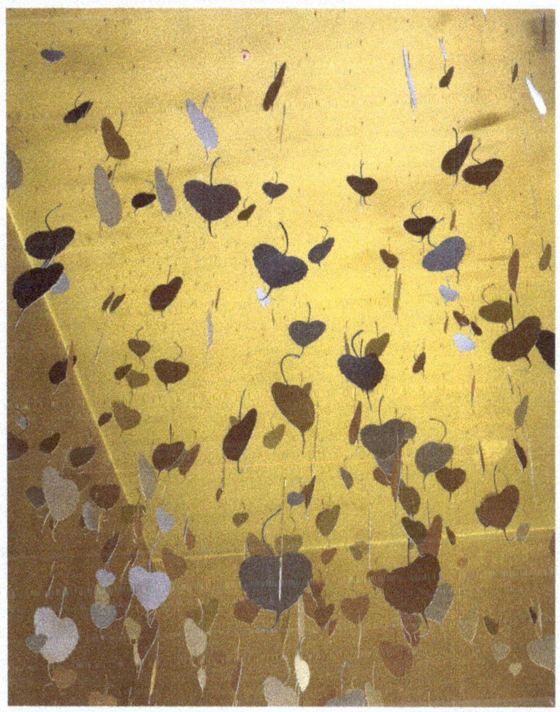

TOP Fiona Foley, *Black Opium*, State Library of Queensland, 2006
BOTTOM detail *Mood Room* (Gold), part of *Black Opium*, 2006

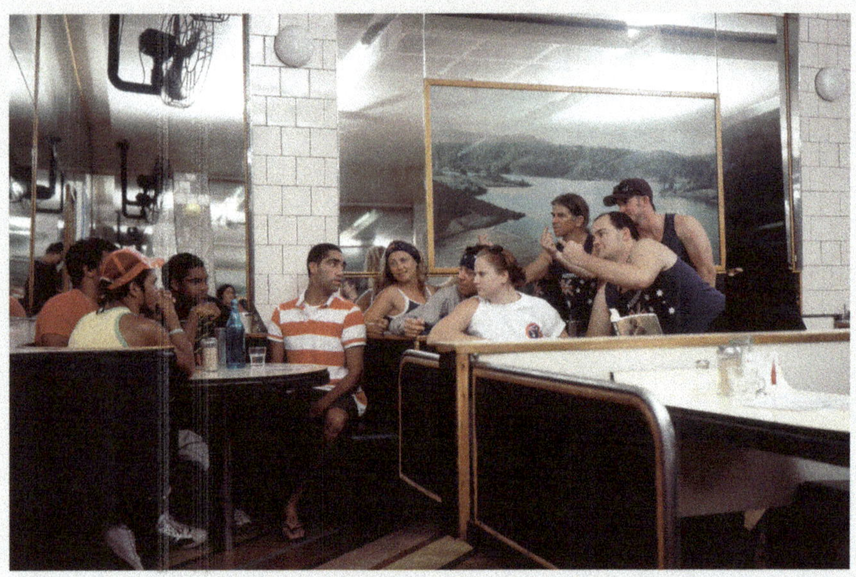

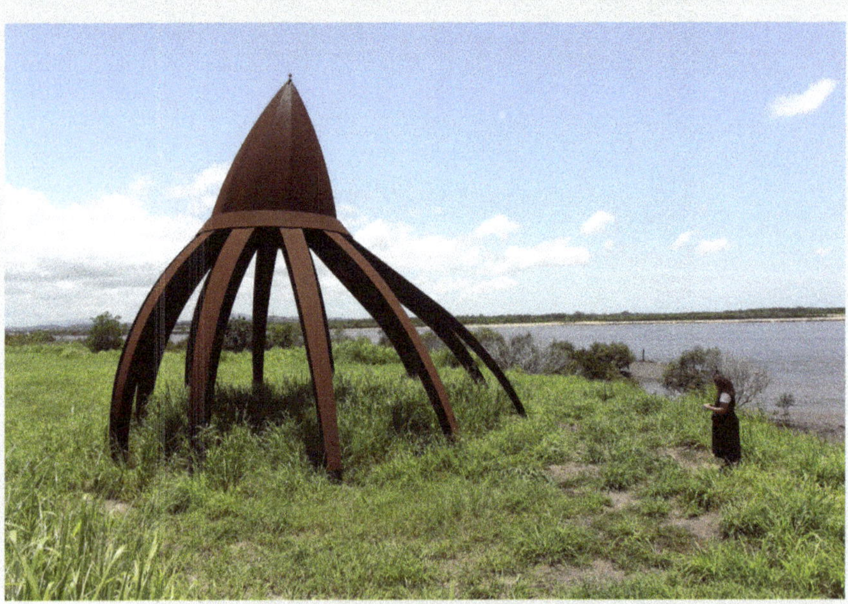

TOP Fiona Foley, *Nulla 4 Eva #3*, 2008
BOTTOM Fiona Foley, *Mangrove Cap*, 2009

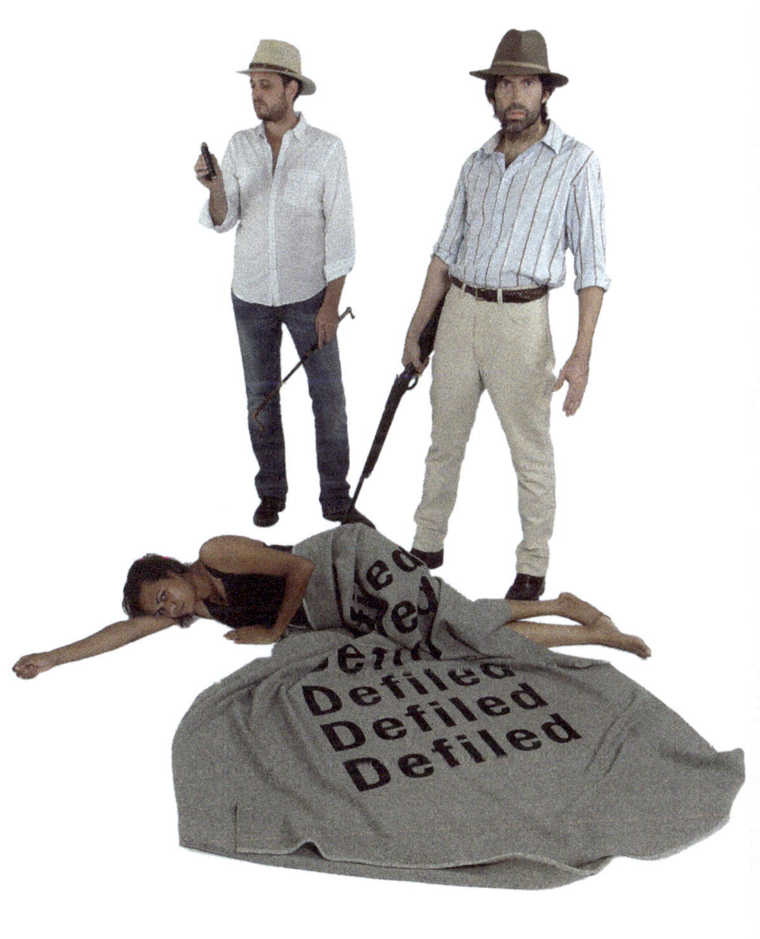

Fiona Foley, *Bearing Witness IV*, 2009

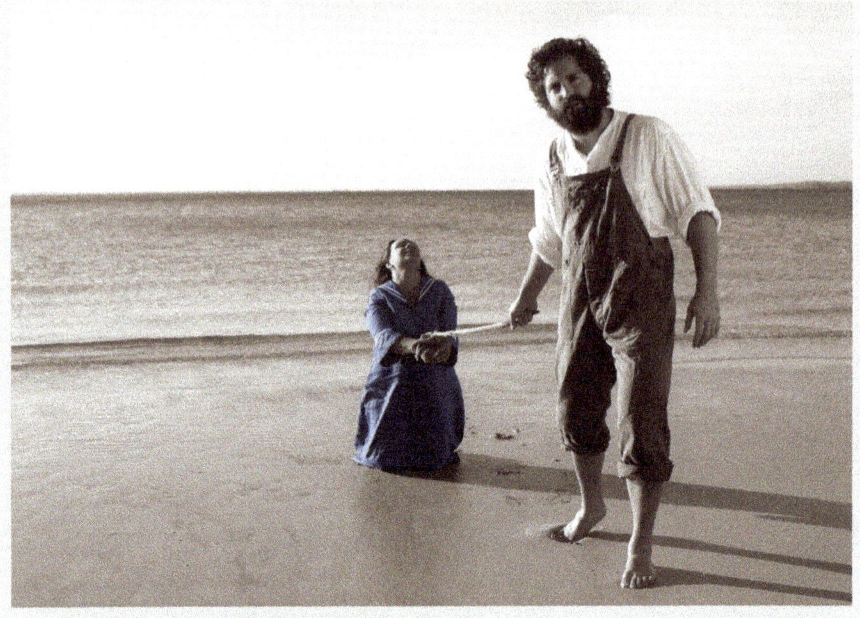

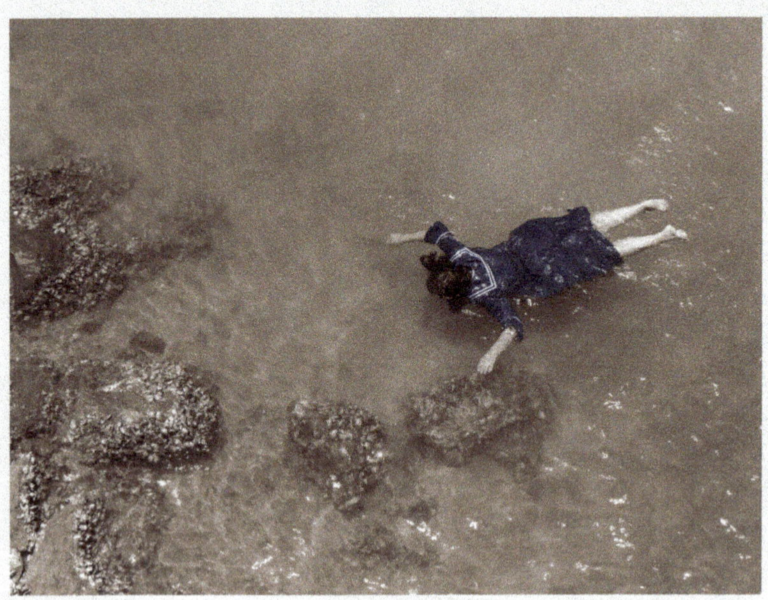

TOP Fiona Foley, *The Oyster Fishermen #11*, 2011
BOTTOM Fiona Foley, *The Oyster Fishermen #16*, 2011

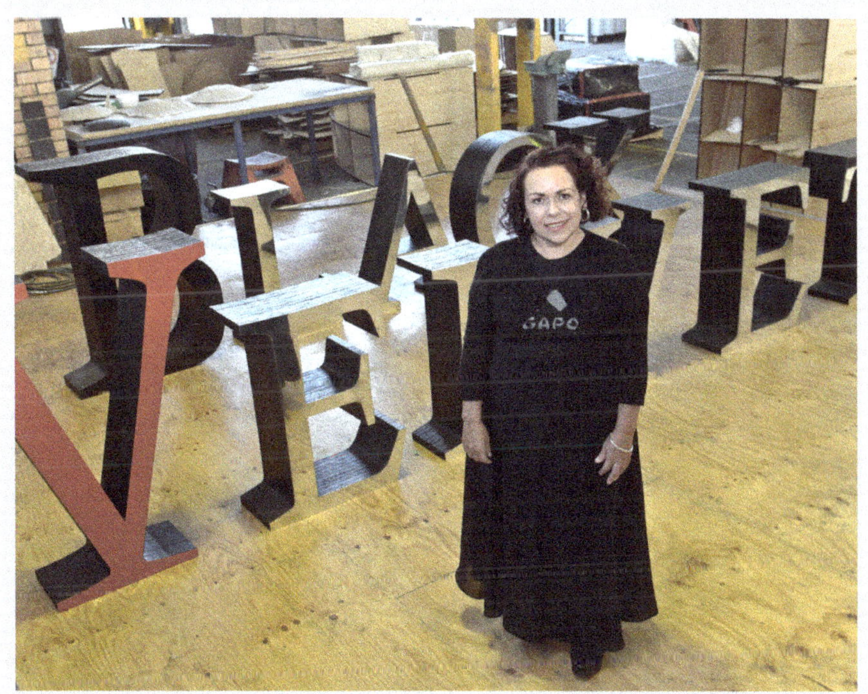

Fiona Foley with *Black Velvet*, 2014

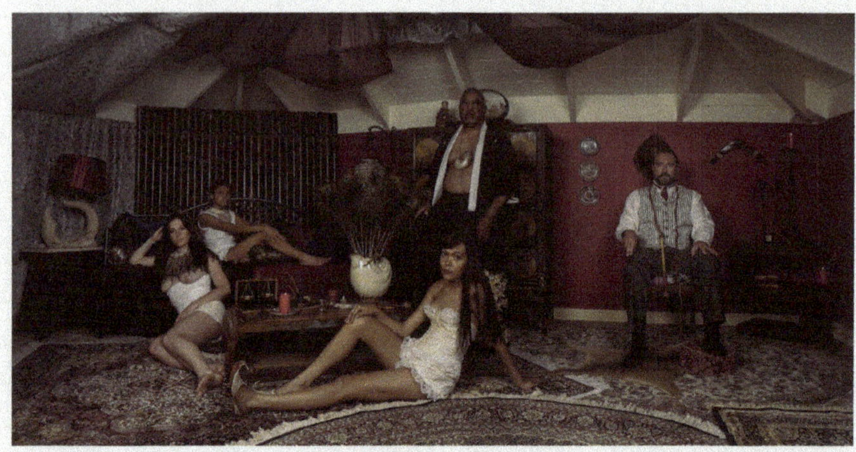

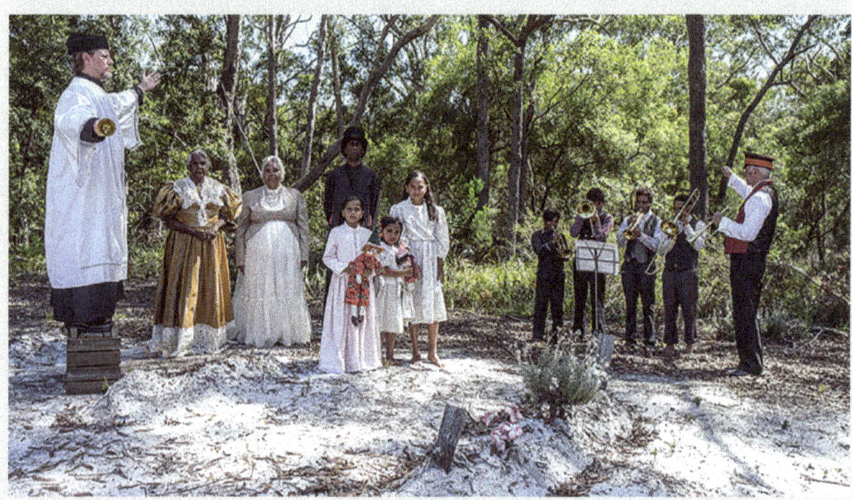

TOP Fiona Foley, *Horror has a face #09 Opiate of opulence*, 2017
BOTTOM Fiona Foley, *Horror has a face #17 Missionary zeal*, 2017